CUDA Programming in C

From Basics to Expert Proficiency

Contents

Introduction

CUDA (Compute Unified Device Architecture) is a parallel computing platform and application programming interface (API) model created by NVIDIA. It allows developers to harness the power of NVIDIA GPUs (Graphics Processing Units) for general-purpose processing, dramatically improving performance in computational tasks. This book, "CUDA Programming in C: From Basics to Expert Proficiency," is intended to provide a comprehensive guide for new and experienced programmers who aim to leverage CUDA for high-performance computing.

GPUs have traditionally been used to render graphics in gaming and professional visualization. However, their highly parallel structure makes them exceptionally well suited for tasks where large datasets can be processed in parallel. CUDA taps into this capability by allowing the GPU to be programmed using a variant of C, a language familiar to many developers. CUDA offers significant acceleration over traditional CPU computations, transforming industries such as artificial intelligence, scientific computing, and data analysis.

The significance of parallel computing cannot be overstated. Modern computational problems often involve large-scale data and extensive processing, which can be time-consuming and resource-intensive. Traditional single-threaded CPU approaches may struggle to handle this efficiently. CUDA addresses this by enabling task parallelization, breaking down complex tasks into smaller sub-tasks that can be processed simultaneously by thousands of GPU cores.

The need for parallel computing comes from the ever-increasing demand for processing power due to the massive growth of data and the complexity of computational problems. From machine learning algorithms to real-time data processing and scientific simulations, many applications benefit immensely from the parallel processing capabilities provided by CUDA.

CUDA programming involves learning specific syntactical constructs and understanding the underlying hardware architecture, known as the GPU programming model. Unlike traditional CPU programming, where tasks are serialized, CUDA introduces concepts such as threads, blocks, and grids to manage parallel execution. This requires a shift in mindset for developers used to procedural programming.

Key advantages of CUDA include remarkable speed-up in data processing, access to advanced GPU features, and extensive support from NVIDIA through libraries, tools, and community resources. The platform encompasses a rich set of APIs and programming libraries geared towards optimizing and developing scalable, high-performance applications. These resources aid in tasks ranging from basic vector operations to complex simulations and deep learning models.

This book takes a structured approach to help you understand and master CUDA programming. Starting with an introduction to CUDA and the essentials of parallel computing, we gradually delve into more complex topics such as memory management, thread hierarchy, kernel functions, and advanced features. Each chapter builds on the previous ones, providing practical examples, comprehensive explanations, and insights into real-world applications.

You will begin by setting up the necessary development environment, a critical initial step for ensuring that your system is ready to handle CUDA applications. The basics of CUDA programming follow, introducing you to the syntax and concepts essential for writing your first CUDA program.

Understanding memory management in CUDA is crucial for optimizing the performance of your applications. This book covers the intricacies of different memory types and how to manage them effectively. Similarly, the thread hierarchy and execution model chapter explains how CUDA schedules and executes tasks, an important aspect for developers aiming to fully utilize GPU resources.

Kernel functions are the core of CUDA programming. These functions run on the GPU and perform the parallel computations that give CUDA its power. You will learn how to write, launch, and optimize kernel functions to perform complex calculations efficiently.

Performance optimization is another key focus of this book. Techniques such as analyzing performance bottlenecks, optimizing memory access patterns, and minimizing thread divergence are covered in detail. Mastery of these techniques will enable you to harness the full potential of

CUDA and achieve substantial performance gains.

Debugging and profiling CUDA applications are crucial skills for any developer. These steps help identify and fix issues and optimize the performance of your application. The book provides a thorough guide to using various tools and techniques for effective debugging and profiling.

Advanced CUDA features such as dynamic parallelism, unified memory, and CUDA graphs open up new possibilities for developers. These features are explored in depth, helping you leverage the latest advancements in GPU technology.

Finally, the book concludes with case studies and real-world applications, demonstrating the power and versatility of CUDA in various domains. These examples illustrate the practical applications of the concepts covered throughout the book and provide inspiration for your own projects.

In summary, this book is designed to be a comprehensive guide for learning and mastering CUDA programming. By the end of this book, you will have the knowledge and skills needed to develop high-performance applications using CUDA, transforming how you approach computational problems and data-intensive tasks.

Chapter 1

Introduction to CUDA and Parallel Computing

This chapter provides an overview of CUDA and its significance in parallel computing. It covers the evolution of CUDA, the necessity of parallel processing, and introduces GPU computing. Key comparisons between CUDA and traditional CPU programming are discussed, along with the advantages of adopting CUDA. Fundamental concepts and terminology are introduced, followed by an explanation of how CUDA functions within the software ecosystem. The chapter concludes with practical steps to begin CUDA programming.

1.1 What is CUDA?

CUDA, which stands for Compute Unified Device Architecture, is a parallel computing platform and application programming interface (API) model created by NVIDIA. CUDA allows developers to use GPUs (Graphics Processing Units) for general-purpose processing (an approach known as GPGPU, General-Purpose computing on Graphics Processing Units). This model leverages the massive computational power of GPUs, typically used for rendering graphics, to perform complex calculations that would be computationally expensive on traditional Central Processing Units (CPUs).

CUDA extends C, C++, and Fortran with a minimal set of keywords, thus providing a straightforward programming environment for harnessing the power of NVIDIA GPUs. By integrating CUDA with these widely-used programming languages, programmers can write massively parallel programs without deep knowledge of GPU architecture and graphics APIs.

The primary elements of CUDA are:

- **CUDA Threads**: CUDA uses threads as the smallest unit of execution. Typically, millions of threads are launched to perform computations concurrently. Each thread executes a kernel, which is a function run on the device.
- **Blocks and Grids**: Threads are organized into blocks, and these blocks are further organized into a grid. The thread hierarchy facilitates the efficient execution of parallel code on the GPU's many-core architecture.
- **Kernels**: Kernels are special functions written in CUDA C/C++ that run on the GPU. A kernel is executed by an array of threads in parallel.
- **Memory Hierarchy**: CUDA provides multiple types of memory, including global memory, shared memory, local memory, and registers. Optimizing memory usage is crucial for achieving high performance.

To illustrate basic CUDA program structure, consider the following example of a vector addition program:

```
#include <cuda_runtime.h>
#include <iostream>

__global__ void vectorAdd(int *a, int *b, int *c, int N) {
    int i = threadIdx.x + blockIdx.x * blockDim.x;
    if (i < N) c[i] = a[i] + b[i];
}

int main() {
    const int N = 1024;
    size_t size = N * sizeof(int);

    int *h_a = (int*)malloc(size);
    int *h_b = (int*)malloc(size);
    int *h_c = (int*)malloc(size);

    for (int i = 0; i < N; ++i) {
        h_a[i] = i;
        h_b[i] = i;
```

```
    }

    int *d_a, *d_b, *d_c;
    cudaMalloc((void**)&d_a, size);
    cudaMalloc((void**)&d_b, size);
    cudaMalloc((void**)&d_c, size);

    cudaMemcpy(d_a, h_a, size, cudaMemcpyHostToDevice);
    cudaMemcpy(d_b, h_b, size, cudaMemcpyHostToDevice);

    int threadsPerBlock = 256;
    int blocksPerGrid = (N + threadsPerBlock - 1) / threadsPerBlock;
    vectorAdd<<<blocksPerGrid, threadsPerBlock>>>(d_a, d_b, d_c, N);

    cudaMemcpy(h_c, d_c, size, cudaMemcpyDeviceToHost);

    for (int i = 0; i < N; ++i) {
        std::cout << "c[" << i << "] = " << h_c[i] << std::endl;
    }

    cudaFree(d_a);
    cudaFree(d_b);
    cudaFree(d_c);
    free(h_a);
    free(h_b);
    free(h_c);

    return 0;
}
```

The above example demonstrates the following key points:

1. The vectorAdd kernel is designed to run on the GPU, adding elements of two vectors. 2. Memory allocations are performed both on the host (CPU) and the device (GPU). 3. Data transfer between the host and device is managed using cudaMemcpy. 4. The grid and block dimensions are carefully chosen to ensure that the entire vector is processed.

CUDA provides a structured approach to developing parallel applications not only for scientific computations but also for real-time data processing, machine learning algorithms, and large-scale simulations.

1.2 Brief History of CUDA

Compute Unified Device Architecture (CUDA) is a parallel computing platform and programming model developed by NVIDIA. Its primary objective is to harness the computational capabilities of Graphics Processing Units (GPUs) for general-purpose processing, extending their application beyond mere graphics rendering.

The inception of CUDA can be traced back to the increasing demand for enhanced computational power during the early 2000s. Graphics hardware had evolved significantly, becoming highly parallel, multithreaded, and highly programmable. This evolution provided an attractive opportunity to leverage GPUs for a broader range of computationally intensive tasks. NVIDIA, recognizing this potential, embarked on designing an architecture that allowed developers to utilize the parallelism inherent in GPUs in a more accessible manner.

The first major breakthrough came with the introduction of the G80 GPU in November 2006. The G80 architecture marked a significant deviation from previous GPU designs. It featured a scalable array of multithreaded, streaming multiprocessors (SMs), which provided a foundation for CUDA. This architectural innovation was coupled with a software environment that enabled programming in standard C, incorporating a few simple extensions to manage parallelism.

To encapsulate this transformation, the CUDA programming model facilitates a division of labor between the CPU (often referred to as the host) and the GPU (known as the device). The host executes the sequential parts of a program, while the device accelerates the parallel sections, typically those involving heavy computation. This dynamic was a cornerstone of CUDA's design and remains a pivotal element of its ongoing development.

The release of CUDA 1.0 in 2007 was a significant milestone. It featured a comprehensive development toolkit, including a compiler for NVIDIA's parallel computing architecture, and a runtime library. Developers could now write code that directly managed the GPU's capabilities without needing to focus on the underlying graphics-specific details. This abstraction was crucial in bringing parallel programming into mainstream computing applications, enabling substantial performance improvements for tasks like linear algebra, signal processing, and molecular dynamics.

Subsequent iterations of CUDA have progressively enhanced its capabilities and usability. CUDA 2.0, introduced in 2008, added support for double-precision floating-point arithmetic, vastly broadening the scope of scientific computing applications. It also introduced the concept of context, which allowed multiple applications to share a GPU, thus improving resource utilization.

The launch of CUDA 3.0 in 2010 included major enhancements such as Unified Memory, which facilitated simpler memory management between the host and the device. This version also introduced the ability to write and launch kernels with more than 512 threads, significantly boosting parallel execution capacity.

With CUDA 4.0, released in 2011, NVIDIA focused on improving the ease of development through features like Thrust, a parallel algorithms library, and improved multi-GPU support. The subsequent version, CUDA 5.0, launched in 2012, continued this trajectory by introducing dynamic parallelism, allowing GPU threads to spawn new threads dynamically, thus streamlining parallel algorithm development.

Each new version of CUDA has built upon previous iterations, introducing incremental improvements that enhance both performance and developer productivity. Modern versions of CUDA, such as CUDA 11, support a wide range of computational tasks, from deep learning frameworks like TensorFlow and PyTorch to high-performance computing applications across various scientific domains.

The role of hardware advancements cannot be overstated in the history of CUDA. Each new generation of NVIDIA's GPUs has introduced architectural refinements that augment CUDA's capabilities. Noteworthy architectures include Fermi, Kepler, Maxwell, Pascal, Volta, Turing, and the contemporary Ampere architecture. Each generation has pushed the boundaries of parallel processing, incorporating larger numbers of CUDA cores, enhanced memory architectures, and improved power efficiency.

The culmination of hardware and software advancements has established CUDA as a dominant force in parallel computing. Its influence extends across academia, industry, and technology, profoundly affecting areas such as scientific research, artificial intelligence, and data analytics. The continued evolution of CUDA promises to drive further innovation, making parallel computing more accessible and powerful than ever before.

```
#include <stdio.h>

__global__ void helloCUDA() {
    printf("Hello from GPU!\n");
}

int main() {
    helloCUDA<<<1, 1>>>();
    cudaDeviceSynchronize();
    return 0;
}
```

```
Hello from GPU!
```

1.3 The Need for Parallel Computing

The increasing demand for high performance in computational tasks has driven the evolution of computing architectures. Traditional serial computing, wherein tasks are executed sequentially on a single Central Processing Unit (CPU), encounters significant limitations as it struggles to meet the requirements for speed and efficiency in complex computations. As a response to these limitations, parallel computing has emerged as a crucial paradigm. Parallel computing involves the simultaneous use of multiple processing elements to perform computations more efficiently. This method leverages the capabilities of modern hardware, specifically Graphics Processing Units (GPUs), to achieve substantial improvements in speed and performance.

Parallel computing addresses several key issues in computational tasks:

- **Performance Bottlenecks:** Serial computing systems are constrained by the finite processing power and clock speed of individual CPUs. As tasks increase in complexity or data size, the time required to complete these tasks grows significantly. Parallel computing mitigates this issue by distributing the workload across multiple processing elements, thus reducing the overall computation time.
- **Scalability:** In the era of big data and complex scientific computations, the ability to scale computations is essential. Parallel computing allows for scalability by enabling tasks to be divided and executed concurrently. This capability is particularly beneficial in fields like scientific simulations, data analytics, and real-time processing where large datasets and intricate calculations are common.
- **Resource Utilization:** Modern GPUs are designed with a high number of cores that can perform numerous calculations simultaneously. Exploiting this architecture through parallel computing ensures optimal utilization of available hardware resources, resulting in more efficient and cost-effective computations.
- **Energy Efficiency:** Parallel computing can be more energy-efficient than serial computing. By completing tasks faster and more efficiently, parallel systems can reduce the total energy consumption needed for a given computational workload. This is es-

pecially relevant as computational demands increase and energy efficiency becomes a critical concern.

To illustrate the benefits of parallel computing, consider the following example. Suppose we need to perform matrix multiplication on two large matrices, A and B. In serial computing, this task involves iterating over the rows of A and the columns of B, performing a dot product for each pair:

```
for (int i = 0; i < N; i++) {
    for (int j = 0; j < M; j++) {
        C[i][j] = 0;
        for (int k = 0; k < K; k++) {
            C[i][j] += A[i][k] * B[k][j];
        }
    }
}
```

This approach requires $O(N \times M \times K)$ computations, which can be time-consuming for large matrices. Parallel computing, on the other hand, allows us to divide this task among multiple processing units. Each unit computes a subset of the matrix product, significantly reducing the time required to obtain the final result. Using CUDA, the matrix multiplication can be implemented as follows:

```
__global__ void matrixMulKernel(float* A, float* B, float* C, int N, int M, int K) {
    int row = blockIdx.y * blockDim.y + threadIdx.y;
    int col = blockIdx.x * blockDim.x + threadIdx.x;

    if (row < N && col < M) {
        float sum = 0.0;
        for (int k = 0; k < K; k++) {
            sum += A[row * K + k] * B[k * M + col];
        }
        C[row * M + col] = sum;
    }
}

int main() {
    // Define matrix dimensions
    int N = ...;
    int M = ...;
    int K = ...;

    // Allocate and initialize matrices A, B, and C
    float *A, *B, *C;
    // Memory allocation and initialization code here...

    // Define block and grid dimensions
    dim3 blockDim(16, 16);
    dim3 gridDim((M + blockDim.x - 1) / blockDim.x, (N + blockDim.y - 1) /
        blockDim.y);

    // Launch the matrix multiplication kernel
    matrixMulKernel<<<gridDim, blockDim>>>(A, B, C, N, M, K);
```

```
    // Copy the result back to host memory and free device memory
    // Code to copy result and free memory here...

    return 0;
}
```

Executing this code on a GPU divides the matrix multiplication task across multiple threads, each responsible for computing one element of the resulting matrix. The CUDA kernel matrixMulKernel executes in parallel, significantly accelerating the computation compared to the serial approach.

The compelling need for parallel computing extends beyond performance gains. In domains such as deep learning, bioinformatics, and financial modeling, the volume of data and complexity of computations necessitate approaches that can handle high levels of concurrency efficiently. Parallel computing frameworks like CUDA provide the tools required to harness the computational power of GPUs, enabling developers and researchers to tackle large-scale problems that were previously infeasible with serial computing methods.

Essentially, parallel computing enables the decomposition of larger problems into smaller, independent tasks that can be processed concurrently. This approach not only accelerates computation but also opens avenues for addressing more complex problems within a reasonable timeframe. The transition to parallel computing paradigms, facilitated by advancements in hardware and programming models like CUDA, marks a significant evolution in the pursuit of computational efficiency and capability.

1.4 Introduction to GPU Computing

GPU (Graphics Processing Unit) computing refers to the use of a GPU, in conjunction with a CPU, to accelerate compute-intensive applications. A GPU is a specialized electronic circuit designed to rapidly manipulate and alter memory to accelerate the creation of images in a frame buffer intended for output to a display device. In addition to rendering graphics, GPUs have evolved into highly parallel multiprocessors capable of performing a vast number of concurrent operations, making them well-suited for non-graphics computations as well.

Architecture of a GPU
A GPU consists of thousands of smaller, more efficient cores designed

for handling multiple tasks simultaneously. These cores are much simpler than CPU cores, enabling a large number of them to fit on a single chip. This massive parallelism is the key to the GPU's ability to process vast amounts of data in tandem. The architecture of a typical GPU involves the following components:

- **Streaming Multiprocessors (SMs)**: The primary building blocks of a GPU, each SM contains several CUDA cores (the processing units that execute individual instructions), which share resources such as registers and shared memory.
- **Global Memory**: The largest and slowest type of memory on the GPU, accessible by all SMs. It is used to store data that needs to be exchanged between the CPU and GPU.
- **Shared Memory**: A small, fast memory space shared by all CUDA cores within an SM. It is used for inter-thread communication and can significantly improve the performance of algorithms with data locality.
- **Registers**: The fastest memory available to each CUDA core, used for storing variables that each thread will use.
- **Texture and Constant Memory**: Specialized memory spaces optimized for specific types of accesses, such as read-only textures or constants that need to be accessed by multiple threads.

Programming Model

The CUDA programming model, which extends the C programming language, allows developers to write programs that execute on the GPU. It is based on three main abstractions: hierarchical thread blocks, shared memories, and barrier synchronization. The core components include:

- **Kernels**: Functions written in CUDA C that are executed on the GPU. Each kernel is executed by an array of threads.
- **Grids and Blocks**: A grid is a collection of blocks, and each block is a collection of threads. Each block executes on a single SM, while a grid can span multiple SMs.
- **Thread Indexing**: Each thread within a block has a unique index that allows it to identify its data. Indexing is typically done using built-in CUDA variables such as $\mathrm{threadIdx}$, $\mathrm{blockIdx}$, and $\mathrm{blockDim}$.

- **Memory Hierarchy**: Understanding the different levels of memory and their speeds is crucial for optimizing CUDA programs. This involves efficient use of shared memory, minimizing global memory accesses, and leveraging the cache benefits of texture and constant memory.

MPI Integration

MPI (Message Passing Interface) can be integrated with GPU computing for distributed-memory parallelism. This enables the use of multiple GPUs on multiple nodes, dramatically scaling up computational capacity. The typical workflow involves:

- Initializing the MPI environment and determining the rank of each process.
- Distributing data across different GPUs.
- Performing local computations on each GPU using CUDA kernels.
- Communicating results between GPUs using MPI functions.
- Finalizing the MPI environment after computations are completed.

An example of a simple MPI+Cuda integration program is shown below:

```
#include <mpi.h>
#include <cuda_runtime.h>
#include <stdio.h>

__global__ void vectorAdd(float *a, float *b, float *c, int N) {
    int i = blockDim.x * blockIdx.x + threadIdx.x;
    if (i < N) {
        c[i] = a[i] + b[i];
    }
}

int main(int argc, char** argv) {
    MPI_Init(&argc, &argv);
    int rank, size;
    MPI_Comm_rank(MPI_COMM_WORLD, &rank);
    MPI_Comm_size(MPI_COMM_WORLD, &size);

    int N = 1024;
    float *h_a, *h_b, *h_c;
    float *d_a, *d_b, *d_c;

    // Allocate memory
    cudaMalloc((void**)&d_a, N * sizeof(float));
    cudaMalloc((void**)&d_b, N * sizeof(float));
    cudaMalloc((void**)&d_c, N * sizeof(float));
```

```
    if (rank == 0) {
        // Initialize host data
        h_a = (float*)malloc(N * sizeof(float));
        h_b = (float*)malloc(N * sizeof(float));
        h_c = (float*)malloc(N * sizeof(float));
        for (int i = 0; i < N; i++) {
            h_a[i] = i;
            h_b[i] = i;
        }
        // Copy data to device
        cudaMemcpy(d_a, h_a, N * sizeof(float), cudaMemcpyHostToDevice);
        cudaMemcpy(d_b, h_b, N * sizeof(float), cudaMemcpyHostToDevice);
    }

    // Synchronize and distribute the data
    MPI_Barrier(MPI_COMM_WORLD);
    MPI_Bcast(h_a, N, MPI_FLOAT, 0, MPI_COMM_WORLD);
    MPI_Bcast(h_b, N, MPI_FLOAT, 0, MPI_COMM_WORLD);

    // Compute on GPU
    vectorAdd<<<(N + 255) / 256, 256>>>(d_a, d_b, d_c, N);

    // Copy results back to host
    cudaMemcpy(h_c, d_c, N * sizeof(float), cudaMemcpyDeviceToHost);

    // Print the result
    if (rank == 0) {
        for(int i = 0; i < 5; i++) {
            printf("%f\n", h_c[i]);
        }
    }

    // Free memory
    cudaFree(d_a);
    cudaFree(d_b);
    cudaFree(d_c);

    MPI_Finalize();
    return 0;
}
```

Output on one of the distributed GPUs:
0.000000
2.000000
4.000000
6.000000
8.000000

Performance Considerations

Optimizing GPU performance involves addressing several key considerations:

- **Occupancy**: Refers to the ratio of active warps (groups of 32 threads) on an SM to the maximum number of warps that the SM can support. Higher occupancy often leads to better performance.

- **Memory Coalescing**: Accesses to global memory should be coalesced, which means that consecutive threads should access consecutive memory addresses to minimize memory transactions.
- **Latency Hiding**: Overlapping computation with data transfer using asynchronous operations can hide latency and improve overall performance.
- **Instruction-Level Parallelism**: Maximizing usage of available CUDA cores by ensuring sufficient independent instructions within each thread.

1.5 CUDA vs. Traditional CPU Programming

CUDA, or Compute Unified Device Architecture, introduced by NVIDIA, is often viewed through the lens of its differences with traditional CPU programming. Understanding these differences is crucial for harnessing the full potential of GPUs for parallel computing tasks.

Traditional CPU programming typically involves writing serial code that executes sequentially across a single or a few cores. CPUs are designed for low-latency computing, meaning they efficiently handle tasks that require quick interactions and decision making, often engaged in processes with numerous branching and conditional statements. The modern CPU architecture consists of a handful of powerful cores optimized for sequential processing, equipped with sophisticated control logic to maximize the execution efficiency of sequential code through techniques like out-of-order execution, speculative execution, and deep pipelining.

On the other hand, CUDA programming focuses on leveraging the massively parallel architecture of GPUs. The architecture of a GPU consists of thousands of simpler, relatively slower cores designed explicitly for high-throughput computation, making it ideal for tasks that can be divided into many smaller, independent subtasks. This differs fundamentally from CPU architecture, which comprises fewer, more powerful cores intended for a broad range of tasks.

In CUDA programming, the paradigm shifts from focusing on optimizing the performance of individual instructions to maximizing the number of instructions that can be processed in parallel. This shift necessitates rethinking algorithms to exploit data parallelism effectively. CUDA provides a programming model that facilitates this by extending the C programming language, allowing developers to write programs where thousands of threads can concurrently execute on the GPU. A CUDA program typically includes the following elements:

- **Kernels:** Functions declared with the __global__ qualifier, meant to be executed on the GPU. Kernels are called from the host (CPU) but execute on the device (GPU).
- **Threads and Blocks:** When a kernel is launched, it is executed by a grid of threads. These threads are organized into blocks. Each block is a 3-dimensional array of threads, suitable for mapping to common data structures such as matrices.
- **Memory Hierarchy:** CUDA exposes different types of memory with varying sizes, latencies, and bandwidths, including global memory, shared memory, and local memory. Effective utilization of this memory hierarchy is key to achieving high performance.

Here is an example of a simple CUDA kernel written in C:

```
__global__ void add(int *a, int *b, int *c) {
    int index = threadIdx.x + blockIdx.x * blockDim.x;
    c[index] = a[index] + b[index];
}
```

In this kernel, each thread computes one element of the arrays. The grid and block dimensions are set such that index uniquely identifies each array element.

To compare, a similar CPU implementation using standard C code would look like this:

```
void add(int *a, int *b, int *c, int N) {
    for (int i = 0; i < N; i++) {
        c[i] = a[i] + b[i];
    }
}
```

The key difference is that in the CUDA kernel, add is executed concurrently by potentially thousands of threads, whereas in the CPU implementation, the addition is performed sequentially by a single thread.

Beyond the raw execution model, there are additional architectural considerations. CPUs are well-suited for tasks requiring significant branching and where the primary constraint is the execution speed of single or multi-threaded applications, such as running an operating system or managing complex decision-making processes.

GPUs, however, excel when there's a need for high-throughput computation with many parallelizable operations, such as image processing, deep learning, scientific simulations, and complex mathematical computations. This paradigm is grounded in Single Instruction, Multiple Threads (SIMT) architecture, where many threads execute the same instruction on different pieces of data.

Effective CUDA programming also demands attention to data transfer between the host and the device. Data needs to be explicitly transferred from the host memory to the device memory before kernel execution and back after computation. This poses additional latency considerations and necessitates efficient memory management strategies. For example:

```
int *d_a, *d_b, *d_c;
// Allocate device memory
cudaMalloc((void **)&d_a, size);
cudaMalloc((void **)&d_b, size);
cudaMalloc((void **)&d_c, size);
// Transfer data from host to device
cudaMemcpy(d_a, h_a, size, cudaMemcpyHostToDevice);
cudaMemcpy(d_b, h_b, size, cudaMemcpyHostToDevice);
// Execute kernel
add<<<blocks, threads>>>(d_a, d_b, d_c);
// Transfer results from device to host
cudaMemcpy(h_c, d_c, size, cudaMemcpyDeviceToHost);
// Free device memory
cudaFree(d_a);
cudaFree(d_b);
cudaFree(d_c);
```

Thus, an adept CUDA programmer must skillfully manage both computation and data movement to exploit the full potential of GPU acceleration. The choice between CUDA and traditional CPU programming is driven by the specific requirements of the task at hand, such as the level of parallelism, latency constraints, and the computational complexity involved.

By understanding these distinctions and the underlying architectural considerations of CPUs and GPUs, developers can make informed decisions on leveraging CUDA for parallel computing to achieve optimal performance.

1.6 Advantages of CUDA

The Compute Unified Device Architecture (CUDA) offers several distinct advantages that make it an exceptionally powerful tool for parallel computing. These advantages stem from its design, architecture, and the specific optimizations that it provides for leveraging the computational capabilities of NVIDIA GPUs. This section delves into the primary benefits of using CUDA for parallel programming.

1. High Throughput Computing
CUDA is explicitly designed to exploit the high level of parallelism provided by GPUs. NVIDIA GPUs contain thousands of cores, which allow for massive parallel processing capabilities. This architecture facilitates a high throughput for computational tasks, vastly exceeding the performance of traditional CPUs while handling large datasets and complex computations.

2. Scalability
One of the significant advantages of CUDA is its scalability. CUDA applications can seamlessly scale from small to large problem sizes and from smaller GPUs to larger, more powerful GPUs. The scalability is achievable due to CUDA's ability to manage thousands of threads efficiently. As a problem size or dataset grows, CUDA can adapt to utilize the available hardware to maximize performance.

3. Ease of Use
CUDA provides a relatively straightforward programming model that extends the C/C++ language, making it more accessible to those already familiar with these languages. The CUDA API, libraries, and development tools are well-documented and designed to simplify the process of writing, debugging, and optimizing GPU code.

4. Mature Ecosystem
Since its introduction, CUDA has matured into a robust ecosystem with extensive libraries, tools, and a large community of developers. Libraries such as cuBLAS for linear algebra, cuFFT for Fourier transforms, and Thrust for generic parallel algorithms provide optimized functions for common computational tasks. This maturity ensures reliability and offers resources that accelerate development processes.

5. Heterogeneous Computing
CUDA supports heterogeneous computing, where both the CPU and GPU work together, each handling tasks suited to its strengths. This model allows for more efficient use of computational resources. The CPU can manage serial tasks and control logic, while the GPU handles data-parallel tasks, thereby optimizing overall performance.

6. Enhanced Performance and Speedup
By exploiting parallelism at various granularities (blocks and threads),

CUDA programs can achieve significant performance improvements over serial implementations. Problems that are embarrassingly parallel, where tasks run independently without communication, can see substantial speedups.

7. Rich Set of Development Tools
NVIDIA provides a comprehensive set of development tools tailored for CUDA programming. Tools such as the NVIDIA Nsight suite offer visual profiling and debugging capabilities, enabling developers to optimize their applications effectively. NVIDIA Visual Profiler and Nsight Compute aid in pinpointing performance bottlenecks and provide suggestions for improvements.

8. Access to Cutting-Edge Hardware Features
CUDA gives developers access to the latest features of NVIDIA GPUs, including advancements in memory hierarchy, warp-level primitives, and hardware-accelerated libraries. This access ensures that applications can benefit from the continuous advances in GPU technology, ensuring peak performance and efficiency.

9. Extensive Documentation and Community Support
CUDA's extensive documentation, including programming guides, best practices, and detailed API references, helps developers learn and leverage CUDA effectively. Additionally, a vast community of researchers and developers contribute to forums, mailing lists, and third-party resources, providing valuable support and shared knowledge.

10. Optimized Libraries
NVIDIA has developed a rich set of libraries optimized for CUDA. These libraries cover a vast range of applications, from linear algebra, and deep learning, to image processing. Utilizing these libraries allows developers to achieve high performance with minimal effort, leveraging pre-optimized routines for complex operations.

The combined advantages of CUDA position it as a pivotal technology in the realm of high-performance computing. Its high throughput, ease of use, mature ecosystem, and robust development tools significantly contribute to the efficiency and speed of solving complex computational problems. As parallel computing continues to play an increasingly critical role in scientific research, data analysis, machine learning, and beyond, mastering CUDA equips developers, researchers, and engineers with the ability to harness the power of GPUs fully.

1.7 Basic Concepts and Terminology

In this section, we delve into the fundamental concepts and terms that form the backbone of CUDA programming. A clear understanding of these elements is crucial for effective CUDA application development.

CUDA (Compute Unified Device Architecture): A parallel computing platform and application programming interface (API) model created by NVIDIA that allows developers to use a CUDA-enabled graphics processing unit (GPU) for general purpose processing (an approach known as GPGPU, General-Purpose computing on Graphics Processing Units).

GPU (Graphics Processing Unit): A specialized electronic circuit designed to accelerate the processing of images and computation using parallel processing. Unlike CPUs, GPUs contain numerous smaller, more efficient cores designed for handling multiple tasks simultaneously.

Kernel: A function written in CUDA C that runs on the GPU. A kernel is executed by many threads in parallel. When a kernel is invoked, or "launched," it is executed as a grid of thread blocks.

Thread: The smallest unit of execution in CUDA. Thousands of threads run concurrently on a GPU, each executing the kernel independently. Threads are organized into blocks and grids, and can share data and synchronize execution.

Thread Block: A group of threads that can cooperate with each other by sharing data through shared memory and synchronizing their execution to coordinate memory accesses. Thread blocks are identified using a two-dimensional (2D) or three-dimensional (3D) block index within the grid.

Grid: A collection of thread blocks that execute a kernel. The dimensions and size of a grid can be specified when a kernel is launched, allowing for the flexibility to handle a wide range of applications.

Warp: A group of 32 threads executed simultaneously by a single CUDA core in a SIMD (Single Instruction, Multiple Data) manner. The smallest scheduling unit in CUDA programming; all threads in a warp follow the same execution path.

SIMD (Single Instruction, Multiple Data): A parallel computing architecture where a single control unit dispatches instructions to multiple processing units. Each processing unit executes the same instruction on different pieces of data in parallel.

Shared Memory: A memory space shared among threads within a block, allowing threads to cooperate by caching frequently accessed data. Shared memory is much faster than global memory, but has a limited size, typically 48KB per block in modern GPUs.

Global Memory: The main memory accessible by all threads within the grid. Global memory has larger capacity but higher latency compared to shared memory. Efficient use of global memory is essential for optimizing performance.

Constant Memory: A memory space that is read-only for the threads and constant for the lifetime of a kernel execution. It is cached and can be efficiently read by all threads.

Texture Memory: A memory space that offers efficient read-only access to data stored in textures. It includes a cache, which can improve performance when accessing spatially localized data.

CUDA Thread Hierarchy: CUDA uses a hierarchical structure for organizing threads:

- **Threads:** Executed on individual processing elements.
- **Blocks of Threads:** Groups of threads that can coordinate using shared memory and barriers.
- **Grids of Blocks:** Groups of blocks that execute a kernel.

CUDA Memory Hierarchy: This includes

- **Registers:** Fastest storage area, private to individual threads.
- **Shared Memory:** Shared among threads of a block.
- **Global Memory:** Accessible by all threads.
- **Constant and Texture Memory:** Specialized read-only spaces.

CUDA API: A set of functions provided by the CUDA software ecosystem for programming CUDA applications. The primary API is CUDA C/C++, with additional APIs for other languages and frameworks.

Device Functions: Functions that execute on the device (GPU). These can be called from kernels or other device functions using the __device__ qualifier.

Host Functions: Functions that execute on the host (CPU). These can call kernel functions using the __global__ qualifier.

Unified Memory: A single memory address space accessible by both the CPU and GPU. It simplifies memory management by allowing data to be accessed, without explicit copying, between the host and device.

Stream: A sequence of operations that execute in order on the GPU. Multiple streams can execute concurrently, allowing for better utilization of GPU resources by overlapping computations and data transfers.

Kernel Launch Configuration: When invoking a kernel, the programmer specifies the grid and block dimensions, which define the number of threads that will execute the kernel. Syntax: kernel_-name«<number_of_blocks, threads_per_block»> (arguments).

```
__global__ void vector_add(float *A, float *B, float *C, int N) {
    int i = blockDim.x * blockIdx.x + threadIdx.x;
    if (i < N)
        C[i] = A[i] + B[i];
}
```

The above code defines a simple CUDA kernel for vector addition.

Parallel Patterns: Common parallel computation patterns include reduction, scan, matrix multiplication, and stencil operations. Understanding and effectively using these patterns is key to developing efficient parallel algorithms in CUDA.

Memory Coalescing: The process of combining multiple memory accesses into a single transaction to improve memory bandwidth utilization. This is critical for optimizing performance on the GPU.

Synchronization: Mechanisms for coordinating the execution of threads. The __syncthreads() function is used within a block to synchronize threads, ensuring that all threads reach the same point in code before continuing.

This concludes the detailed examination of basic concepts and terminologies essential for understanding and working with CUDA programming. Each term and concept will be revisited and expanded upon in more practical context and examples in subsequent chapters.

1.8 How CUDA Works

CUDA, an acronym for Compute Unified Device Architecture, is a parallel computing platform and programming model developed by NVIDIA. This section delves into the workings of CUDA, focusing on its core principles, architecture, and the nuances of how it enables efficient parallel computing on NVIDIA GPUs.

At its essence, CUDA abstracts the GPU hardware into a flexible and programmable environment. It extends the C and C++ programming languages with certain key constructs, allowing developers to leverage the massive parallelism of GPUs for general-purpose computing tasks.

CUDA Kernels and Thread Hierarchies

A CUDA program consists of host code, which runs on the CPU, and device code, which executes on the GPU. The device code is encapsulated in special functions known as *kernels*. These kernels are launched by the host code and executed on the GPU in parallel by multiple threads.

In CUDA, threads are organized into a two-level hierarchy:

- **Thread Blocks**: Groups of threads that can cooperate among themselves through shared memory. These blocks are the basic units for organizing the execution space on the GPU.

- **Grids**: Collections of thread blocks. When a kernel is launched, it is distributed across multiple blocks within a grid. Each thread within a block is indexed and can be uniquely identified using thread and block identifiers.

Memory Hierarchy in CUDA

Understanding CUDA's memory hierarchy is crucial for optimizing performance. The CUDA memory model includes several types of memory with different properties and uses:

- **Global Memory**: Accessible by all threads, but has higher latency and lower bandwidth compared to other types of memory.

- **Shared Memory**: Shared among threads within the same block. It has lower latency and higher bandwidth, making it suitable for inter-thread communication.

- **Local Memory**: Each thread has its private local memory, which is used to store local variables. This memory is part of the global memory space but is not accessible by other threads.
- **Constant Memory and Texture Memory**: Read-only memory spaces optimized for specific use cases. Constant memory is used for variables that do not change, while texture memory is optimized for spatial locality, benefiting applications like image processing.

Execution Model

The execution of a kernel in CUDA involves launching a grid of thread blocks. The threads within these blocks execute instances of the kernel function. Each thread is uniquely identified by its *thread ID*, which is a combination of its block index and thread index within the block. Developers use these IDs to manage data access and control the execution flow.

Warp and Warp Scheduling

A warp is a group of 32 threads that SIMULTANEOUSLY execute the same instruction. The GPU's warp scheduler manages the execution of warps, ensuring that they are efficiently scheduled on the available streaming multiprocessors (SMs). This SIMD (Single Instruction, Multiple Data) architecture allows the GPU to execute hundreds or thousands of threads concurrently, providing significant computational speedup.

Example CUDA Kernel

To illustrate a simple CUDA kernel, consider the following example of a vector addition operation:

```
__global__ void vectorAdd(float *A, float *B, float *C, int N) {
    int index = blockIdx.x * blockDim.x + threadIdx.x;
    if (index < N) {
        C[index] = A[index] + B[index];
    }
}
```

In this kernel, each thread computes the addition of elements from two vectors, A and B, storing the result in vector C. The blockIdx.x, blockDim.x, and threadIdx.x variables provide the necessary indexing to ensure each thread operates on a unique element of the vectors.

To launch this kernel from the host code:

```
int N = 1024;
```

```
int numBlocks = (N + 255) / 256;
int numThreads = 256;

vectorAdd<<<numBlocks, numThreads>>>(A, B, C, N);
```

Here, the kernel launch syntax «<numBlocks, numThreads»> specifies the grid and block dimensions.

Synchronization and Memory Barriers

CUDA provides mechanisms for synchronizing threads. The __syncthreads() function ensures that all threads within a block reach the same point before proceeding. This is crucial for coordination, especially when threads share data via shared memory.

Device and Host Communication

Data needs to be transferred between the host (CPU) and the device (GPU). CUDA API functions such as cudaMemcpy facilitate this transfer. Efficient management of data transfer is crucial for minimizing overhead and maximizing computational efficiency.

```
cudaMemcpy(d_A, h_A, size, cudaMemcpyHostToDevice);
cudaMemcpy(d_B, h_B, size, cudaMemcpyHostToDevice);

vectorAdd<<<numBlocks, numThreads>>>(d_A, d_B, d_C, N);

cudaMemcpy(h_C, d_C, size, cudaMemcpyDeviceToHost);
```

In this example, h_A, h_B, and h_C are pointers to host memory, while d_A, d_B, and d_C are pointers to device memory. The cudaMemcpy calls transfer data between these two memory spaces.

Error Handling

CUDA provides error handling mechanisms to ensure reliable execution. The cudaError_t type represents errors, and functions such as cudaGetLastError() allow developers to check and handle errors after kernel launches and API calls:

```
cudaError_t err = cudaGetLastError();
if (err != cudaSuccess) {
    printf("CUDA Error: %s\n", cudaGetErrorString(err));
}
```

This example checks for errors and prints a descriptive message if an error is detected.

```
CUDA Error: kernel launch timed out
```

Through its rich set of features and abstractions, CUDA offers a robust framework for parallel computing on GPUs, significantly enhancing computational efficiency for a wide range of applications.

1.9 The CUDA Software Ecosystem

The CUDA software ecosystem is designed to support efficient parallel programming through a comprehensive suite of tools, libraries, and frameworks. This ecosystem facilitates the development, debugging, and optimization of CUDA applications, leveraging the immense computational power of NVIDIA GPUs.

At the core of the CUDA software ecosystem is the CUDA Toolkit, which includes the CUDA driver, the CUDA runtime, CUDA libraries, and development tools. Understanding each component's role within the ecosystem is essential for employing CUDA effectively.

The **CUDA Toolkit** provides a unified development environment and is regularly updated with new versions to incorporate the latest advancements in GPU technology. It is available for multiple operating systems, including Windows, Linux, and macOS.

CUDA Driver: The CUDA driver is responsible for managing the interactions between the operating system and the GPU hardware. It is essential for running CUDA applications and ensures that GPU resources are allocated and scheduled efficiently. The driver is installed as part of the CUDA Toolkit and updated periodically to support new hardware features.

CUDA Runtime: The CUDA runtime provides a runtime environment that facilitates the execution of CUDA programs. It abstracts many low-level details and simplifies the management of memory and kernel execution. The CUDA runtime also offers backward compatibility, ensuring that applications developed with older versions of CUDA can function with newer hardware and driver updates.

The **CUDA Libraries** are optimized to accelerate various computational tasks, offering significant performance improvements over traditional CPU implementations. Key libraries include:

- **cuBLAS**: The CUDA Basic Linear Algebra Subroutines library provides highly optimized implementations of standard BLAS operations, such as vector and matrix multiplication.
- **cuFFT**: The CUDA Fast Fourier Transform library enables effi-

cient computation of FFTs, a crucial operation in many signal processing applications.

- **cuDNN**: The CUDA Deep Neural Network library offers a collection of primitives for deep learning, supporting frameworks such as TensorFlow and PyTorch.
- **cuSPARSE**: The CUDA Sparse Matrix library includes routines to handle sparse matrices, reducing memory usage and computational complexity for problems involving large sparse datasets.
- **Thrust**: Thrust is a parallel algorithm library mimicking the C++ Standard Template Library (STL). It provides high-level abstractions for data parallel primitives, including sorting, reduction, and scanning.

Development Tools within the CUDA ecosystem include:

- **nvcc**: The NVIDIA CUDA Compiler (nvcc) compiles CUDA code into binary executables. It integrates with standard build systems and allows the embedding of CUDA code within C and C++ applications.
- **Nsight Suite**: NVIDIA's Nsight tools encompass various utilities for profiling, debugging, and analyzing CUDA applications. They help developers understand performance bottlenecks, memory utilization, and kernel execution.
- **CUDA-GDB**: A powerful debugger adapted from the GNU Debugger (GDB) for CUDA applications. CUDA-GDB enables the debugging of both host (CPU) and device (GPU) code, supporting breakpoints, watchpoints, and stepping.
- **CUDA-MEMCHECK**: A runtime memory analysis tool capable of detecting out-of-bounds accesses, memory leaks, and race conditions. Its integration into development processes is crucial for developing reliable and efficient CUDA applications.

The following example demonstrates a simple CUDA program to showcase the integration of CUDA libraries and tools. This program adds two vectors on the GPU.

```
#include <cuda_runtime.h>
#include <iostream>
```

```
__global__ void vectorAdd(const float* A, const float* B, float* C, int N) {
    int i = blockDim.x * blockIdx.x + threadIdx.x;
    if (i < N) {
        C[i] = A[i] + B[i];
    }
}

int main() {
    int N = 1<<20;
    size_t size = N * sizeof(float);

    float *h_A = (float*)malloc(size);
    float *h_B = (float*)malloc(size);
    float *h_C = (float*)malloc(size);

    for (int i = 0; i < N; ++i) {
        h_A[i] = 1.0f;
        h_B[i] = 2.0f;
    }

    float *d_A, *d_B, *d_C;
    cudaMalloc((void**)&d_A, size);
    cudaMalloc((void**)&d_B, size);
    cudaMalloc((void**)&d_C, size);

    cudaMemcpy(d_A, h_A, size, cudaMemcpyHostToDevice);
    cudaMemcpy(d_B, h_B, size, cudaMemcpyHostToDevice);

    int threadsPerBlock = 256;
    int blocksPerGrid = (N + threadsPerBlock - 1) / threadsPerBlock;

    vectorAdd<<<blocksPerGrid, threadsPerBlock>>>(d_A, d_B, d_C, N);

    cudaMemcpy(h_C, d_C, size, cudaMemcpyDeviceToHost);

    cudaFree(d_A);
    cudaFree(d_B);
    cudaFree(d_C);
    free(h_A);
    free(h_B);
    free(h_C);

    return 0;
}
```

Executing this program will produce the following output:

```
Execution completed successfully.
```

Analyzing and debugging this program using tools like Nsight, CUDA-GDB, and CUDA-MEMCHECK can help identify potential performance bottlenecks, memory issues, or other inefficiencies.

The CUDA ecosystem's extensive support for parallel computing is crucial for developing high-performance applications. The tools and libraries provided enable efficient execution and comprehensive debugging, ensuring the exploitation of the full potential of NVIDIA GPUs.

1.10 Getting Started with CUDA Programming

To embark on creating efficient, high-performance CUDA applications, a structured approach is required. This section details the essential steps needed to set up a working CUDA development environment, write a simple CUDA program, compile it, and understand its execution.

Setting Up the Environment

Before writing any CUDA code, it is critical to ensure that both the hardware and software requirements are met. The primary hardware requirement is an NVIDIA GPU that supports CUDA. On the software side, the CUDA Toolkit and an appropriate version of the NVIDIA drivers must be installed. The toolkit contains the compiler (nvcc), libraries, and sample projects to aid development.

- **Hardware:** An NVIDIA GPU with Compute Capability 3.0 or higher is recommended.
- **Software:** Install the CUDA Toolkit, which includes the CUDA driver, nvcc compiler, and essential libraries like cuBLAS, cuFFT.

After installing the hardware and software, confirm the installation by compiling and running the sample projects provided within the toolkit.

Writing a Simple CUDA Program

Once the development environment is set up, we can write a simple CUDA program. A basic "Hello, World!" example serves as an excellent starting point. The CUDA "Hello, World!" program will launch a kernel that prints "Hello, World!" from the device.

Here is a simple example of a CUDA program:

```
#include <stdio.h>

__global__ void helloFromGPU() {
    printf("Hello, World from GPU!\n");
}

int main() {
    // Launch kernel
    helloFromGPU<<<1, 10>>>();

    // Synchronize to see the printf's before finishing
    cudaDeviceSynchronize();

    return 0;
```

```
}
```

Explanation:

The first thing to note is the __global__ keyword, which declares the helloFromGPU function as a CUDA kernel. Kernels are functions that are executed on the GPU. The main function in the host code launches this kernel. The kernel launch syntax helloFromGPU«<1, 10»>() specifies the execution configuration. Here, <1, 10> indicates that the kernel will be launched with one block of ten threads.

To ensure that the printf output is visible, we call cudaDeviceSynchronize() to synchronize the host and device.

Compiling and Running the Program

Compile the CUDA program using the nvcc compiler, which is part of the CUDA Toolkit:

```
$ nvcc -o hello hello.cu
```

The above command generates an executable named hello. Run the executable:

```
$ ./hello
Hello, World from GPU!
```

Understanding Execution on the Device

When the kernel is executed, each thread will execute the code within the kernel function. In the provided example, ten threads within one block print "Hello, World from GPU!". CUDA uses a grid of thread blocks, and threads within a block can communicate with each other through shared memory.

Error Handling in CUDA

Proper handling of errors is crucial for CUDA programming. Functions involved with CUDA runtime return an error code of type cudaError_t. A common pattern to ensure robust error handling is to define a macro:

```
#define cudaCheckError(ans) { gpuAssert((ans), __FILE__, __LINE__); }
inline void gpuAssert(cudaError_t code, const char *file, int line, bool abort=true) {
    if (code != cudaSuccess) {
        fprintf(stderr, "GPUassert: %s %s %d\n", cudaGetErrorString(code), file, line);
        if (abort) exit(code);
    }
}
```

The cudaCheckError macro makes it easier to handle errors by wrapping CUDA API calls. Whenever a CUDA function is called, appending cudaCheckError can capture errors cleanly.

Memory Management

Efficient memory management between the host (CPU) and device (GPU) is another critical aspect. Key functions for memory management include cudaMalloc, cudaMemcpy, and cudaFree. Consider an example where we allocate and copy memory to the device:

```
int main() {
    int n = 10;
    // Host memory
    int h_a[n];
    for (int i = 0; i < n; ++i) h_a[i] = i;

    // Device memory
    int *d_a;
    cudaCheckError( cudaMalloc((void**)&d_a, n * sizeof(int)) );
    cudaCheckError( cudaMemcpy(d_a, h_a, n * sizeof(int),
        cudaMemcpyHostToDevice) );

    // ... Kernel Launch ...

    // Cleanup
    cudaCheckError( cudaFree(d_a) );

    return 0;
}
```

This code snippet demonstrates the allocation of memory on the device with cudaMalloc, copying data from host to device using cudaMemcpy, and freeing device memory with cudaFree. Efficiently managing memory is fundamental to achieving maximum performance benefits in CUDA programming.

Chapter 2

Setting Up the CUDA Development Environment

This chapter outlines the essential requirements and steps for setting up a CUDA development environment. It details system prerequisites, NVIDIA driver installation, and supported compilers. Instructions for configuring CUDA on Windows, Linux, and MacOS are provided, followed by verification procedures to ensure proper installation. Additionally, the chapter introduces CUDA samples and guides you through writing and running your first CUDA program.

2.1 System Requirements for CUDA

To develop and run CUDA applications efficiently, a thorough understanding of the system requirements is essential. These requirements encompass hardware specifications, supported operating systems, and compatible software, including compilers and libraries. Ensuring that your system meets these prerequisites will facilitate a seamless development experience and prevent installation and execution issues.

Hardware Requirements

An appropriate GPU is a fundamental requirement for CUDA development. NVIDIA's CUDA-enabled GPUs are mandatory, and the specific models supported vary with each CUDA version. Generally, the key components of the hardware requirements include:

- **CUDA-enabled GPU**: The GPU should support the CUDA version you intend to use. Typically, GeForce, Quadro, Tesla, and TITAN series GPUs are supported. It is advisable to consult the NVIDIA CUDA compatibility documentation to ensure your GPU model is supported.
- **NVIDIA GPU Driver**: A compatible NVIDIA driver must be installed. The driver version should correspond to the CUDA version, which can be verified from the CUDA Toolkit and GPU driver documentation.
- **Memory (RAM)**: CUDA applications can be memory-intensive. While the minimum RAM requirement is 4GB, higher memory capacity (8GB or more) is recommended for efficient performance, especially for complex computations.
- **Processor**: A multi-core CPU is recommended for managing and offloading tasks to the GPU. While a minimum of Intel or AMD x86_64 CPU is required, higher core counts will benefit overall system performance.
- **Disk Space**: Adequate disk space is necessary to install the CUDA Toolkit, NVIDIA drivers, and associated libraries. At least 1GB of free disk space is typically needed; additional space is advisable considering project storage needs.

Software Requirements

In addition to the hardware specifications, certain software prerequisites must be met to develop CUDA applications effectively. These include compatible operating systems, supported compilers, and necessary libraries.

- **Operating Systems**: CUDA development is supported on major operating systems, including:
  - **Windows**: CUDA is compatible with Windows 10 and later. Ensure you are running a 64-bit version as CUDA does not support 32-bit operating systems.

  - **Linux**: Various distributions are supported, such as Ubuntu, CentOS, Fedora, and RHEL. The version of Linux should align with the CUDA version as per the official documentation.
  - **MacOS**: Support is limited to certain versions of MacOS, often depending on GPU compatibility. Recent versions of MacOS may have reduced support due to hardware limitations.
- **Compilers**: A supported compiler is crucial for compiling CUDA applications. CUDA compilers (nvcc) rely on host compilers to compile CPU code and link binaries. Supported compilers include:
  - **GCC (GNU Compiler Collection)**: On Linux, specific versions of GCC are compatible with different CUDA versions. Compatibility tables available in the CUDA documentation should be referred to select the correct version.
  - **MSVC (Microsoft Visual Studio Compiler)**: On Windows, specific Microsoft Visual Studio versions are supported, typically necessitating the installation of the corresponding build tools.
  - **Clang**: For MacOS, Xcode's Clang compiler is generally supported.
- **Libraries and Other Tools**: Additional software that may be required includes:
  - **CMake**: Useful for managing project builds, CMake versions should support CUDA configurations.
  - **Python**: For scripting and auxiliary tools, a compatible version of Python may be necessary.
  - **Debugger and Profiler Tools**: NVIDIA provides Nsight and other tools to debug and profile CUDA applications.

Compatibility Considerations

Ensuring all components of your development environment are compatible is vital. Compatibility considerations include:

- **CUDA Toolkit Version**: The CUDA Toolkit version must be compatible with your operating system, GPU, and drivers. Updating to the latest stable version is recommended for the best features and optimizations.

- **GPU Architecture**: Different CUDA-enabled GPUs have varying compute capabilities. Ensuring your GPU's compute capability is supported by the CUDA version you're using can impact performance and feature support.
- **Driver Updates**: Regular updates to the NVIDIA driver may be required to support the latest CUDA functionalities and bug fixes.

For a well-integrated development setup, thorough verification of hardware and software compatibility is necessary. This foundational understanding of the system requirements forms the basis for a robust and efficient CUDA development environment.

2.2 Installing CUDA Toolkit

The CUDA Toolkit installation is a crucial step in enabling a system for CUDA development. The toolkit provides a comprehensive development environment for C and C++ developers building GPU-accelerated applications. It includes essential tools such as the CUDA compiler nvcc, libraries for linear algebra, FFT, parallel algorithms, and sample projects.

Before proceeding with the installation, ensure that your system meets the hardware and software requirements detailed in the previous sections: a CUDA-capable GPU, a compatible operating system, and an NVIDIA driver.

Step-by-Step Installation Process:

1. Downloading the CUDA Toolkit:
The CUDA Toolkit can be downloaded from the official NVIDIA CUDA Toolkit website. Navigate to https://developer.nvidia.com/cuda-toolkit and select the appropriate version for your operating system. Ensure you have selected the correct installer type (e.g., exe, run, deb, or rpm), depending on the OS and your preferences.

2. Running the Installer:

Windows:

- Run the downloaded .exe file.
- Choose the installation options suitable for your environment. It's

recommended to perform an Express installation unless you need specific configurations.

- Follow the on-screen instructions to complete the installation process.

Linux:

- Navigate to the directory where the installation file was downloaded.
- Modify the file's permissions to make it executable.

```
sudo chmod +x cuda_<version>_linux.run
```

- Execute the installer.

```
sudo ./cuda_<version>_linux.run
```

- Follow the command-line instructions. It's recommended to type accept at the EULA and select the default options unless specific configurations are required.

MacOS:

- Open the downloaded .dmg file.
- Run the CUDA_MacOSX*.mpkg installer.
- Follow the prompts in the installation wizard to complete the process.

3. Environment Variable Configuration:
To enable the nvcc compiler and other CUDA tools from the command line, the environment variables must be updated accordingly.

Windows:
The installation process usually takes care of this, but ensure the following path is added to the system's PATH variable:

C:\Program Files\NVIDIA GPU Computing Toolkit\CUDA\v<version>\bin

Linux:
Add the CUDA toolkit's bin directory to the system's PATH variable and the lib64 directory to LD_LIBRARY_PATH.

```
export PATH=/usr/local/cuda-<version>/bin${PATH:+:${PATH}}
export LD_LIBRARY_PATH=/usr/local/cuda-<version>/lib64\
       ${LD_LIBRARY_PATH:+:${LD_LIBRARY_PATH}}
```

To make these changes persistent, append the lines to the .bashrc file (for bash) or .zshrc (for zsh):

```
echo 'export PATH=/usr/local/cuda-<version>/bin${PATH:+:${PATH}}' >> ~/.
    bashrc
echo 'export LD_LIBRARY_PATH=/usr/local/cuda-<version>/lib64${
    LD_LIBRARY_PATH:+:${LD_LIBRARY_PATH}}' >> ~/.bashrc
source ~/.bashrc
```

MacOS:
Append the following lines to your shell configuration file, such as .bash_profile or .zshrc:

```
export PATH=/Developer/NVIDIA/CUDA-<version>/bin:$PATH
export DYLD_LIBRARY_PATH=/Developer/NVIDIA/CUDA-<version>/lib:$DYLD_LIBRARY_PATH
```

4. Verifying the Installation:
To verify whether the installation was successful, run the nvcc command to check if the CUDA compiler is accessible from the command line:

```
nvcc --version
```

The output should display the CUDA version information, confirming that the toolkit is correctly installed and configured.

Additionally, navigate to the CUDA samples directory provided by the toolkit. These samples serve as practical examples and help verify the installation. Compile and run the vector addition sample:

```
cd /usr/local/cuda/samples/1_Utilities/deviceQuery
make
./deviceQuery
```

The output will include detailed information about the CUDA-capable devices on the system.

```
Detected 1 CUDA Capable device(s)
Device 0: "NVIDIA GeForce GTX 1650"
<...additional output...>
```

This confirmation indicates that the CUDA Toolkit and its associated components are installed and operational.

2.3 Setting Up the NVIDIA Driver

To develop and execute CUDA-enabled applications, having a correctly configured NVIDIA driver is essential. The NVIDIA driver facilitates communication between the GPU and the operating system, enabling efficient execution of parallel computational tasks. This section outlines the detailed process of installing and configuring the NVIDIA driver across different operating systems.

1. Preparing for the Installation

Before initiating the installation process, ensure that you have administrative privileges on your machine. It's advisable to check the compatibility of the driver with your specific GPU model and CUDA version by referring to the NVIDIA documentation. Additionally, uninstall any current graphics drivers to avoid conflicts.

2. Installing the NVIDIA Driver on Windows

1. Download the appropriate driver from the NVIDIA Driver Download page. Select your GPU model and operating system to obtain the correct driver version.
2. Once downloaded, execute the installer by double-clicking the file.
3. Follow the installation prompts. Select 'Custom (Advanced)' installation to ensure a clean installation by checking the 'Perform a clean installation' box.
4. Reboot your system to finalize the installation.

3. Installing the NVIDIA Driver on Linux

- **Using the package manager:**

  1. For Ubuntu, run the following commands to add the NVIDIA package repositories and install the driver:

     ```
     sudo add-apt-repository ppa:graphics-drivers/ppa
     sudo apt update
     sudo apt install nvidia-driver-<version>
     sudo reboot
     ```

     Ensure you substitute '<version>' with the driver version compatible with your GPU and CUDA version.

2. For RHEL/CentOS, use the ‘dnf‘ or ‘yum‘ command:

```
sudo dnf install epel-release
sudo dnf config-manager --add-repo=https://developer.download.nvidia.
    com/compute/cuda/repos/rhel<VERSION>/x86_64/cuda-rhel<
    VERSION>.repo
sudo dnf clean expire-cache
sudo dnf install nvidia-driver-latest-dkms
sudo reboot
```

   Replace ‘<VERSION>‘ with your specific RHEL/CentOS version number.

- **Using the NVIDIA .run file:**

  1. Switch to runlevel 3 by running ‘sudo telinit 3‘ to avoid issues with the graphical environment.
  2. Make the installer executable and run it:

```
chmod +x NVIDIA-Linux-x86_64-<version>.run
sudo ./NVIDIA-Linux-x86_64-<version>.run
```

  Follow the on-screen prompts, and upon completion, reboot your system.

4. Installing the NVIDIA Driver on MacOS

For MacOS, the NVIDIA drivers are typically included in the Mac CUDA drivers that are specifically released by NVIDIA to support CUDA applications. Follow these steps:

1. Visit the NVIDIA Driver Download page and select 'Mac OS' in the operating system field.
2. Download the suitable driver package, then open the ‘.dmg‘ file and run the installer.
3. Follow the on-screen instructions to complete the installation, then reboot your machine.

5. Verifying the NVIDIA Driver Installation

After installing the driver, verify that it is correctly configured:

- **Windows:**

  1. Open the Device Manager by pressing Win + X and selecting Device Manager.

2. Expand the Display adapters section. Ensure that your NVIDIA GPU is listed and there are no warning indicators.

- **Linux:**

```
nvidia-smi
```

The output should display information about your GPU, driver version, and running processes.

```
+-----------------------------------------------------------------------------+
| NVIDIA-SMI 450.80.02    Driver Version: 450.80.02    CUDA Version: 11.0     |
|-------------------------------+----------------------+----------------------+
| GPU  Name        Persistence-M| Bus-Id        Disp.A | Volatile Uncorr. ECC |
| Fan  Temp  Perf  Pwr:Usage/Cap|         Memory-Usage | GPU-Util  Compute M. |
|===============================+======================+======================|
|   0  GeForce GTX 1080    On   | 00000000:01:00.0  On |                  N/A |
| 35%   57C    P2    29W / 180W |   5007MiB /  8119MiB |      0%      Default |
+-------------------------------+----------------------+----------------------+
```

- **MacOS:**

1. Open System Information by clicking the Apple logo and selecting About This Mac → System Report.
2. Under the Graphics/Displays section, ensure that your NVIDIA GPU is correctly listed.

Proper installation and verification of the NVIDIA driver ensure smooth execution of CUDA applications and optimal use of the GPU for computational tasks.

2.4 Installing a Supported Compiler

To harness the full capability of CUDA, it is crucial to use a compiler that is compatible with the CUDA Toolkit. The primary compiler supported by CUDA is the gcc compiler on Linux, clang on MacOS, and Microsoft Visual Studio on Windows. Ensuring a compatible compiler is installed constitutes a critical step in setting up the CUDA development environment. The following is a detailed guideline on installing and configuring the supported compiler for each operating system.

Linux

Most modern Linux distributions come with gcc pre-installed. However, we need to ensure that the installed version of gcc aligns with the CUDA Toolkit requirements. Specifically, CUDA 11.0 supports gcc versions 8.x to 9.x. You can check the installed version using the command:

```
gcc --version
```

If the installed version meets the requirements, you can proceed. If not, you will need to install the compatible version. The following commands showcase how to install gcc-8 on Ubuntu:

```
sudo apt-get update
sudo apt-get install -y gcc-8 g++-8
```

To use gcc-8 as the default compiler, you need to update the alternatives:

```
sudo update-alternatives --install /usr/bin/gcc gcc /usr/bin/gcc-8 50
sudo update-alternatives --install /usr/bin/g++ g++ /usr/bin/g++-8 50
sudo update-alternatives --config gcc
sudo update-alternatives --config g++
```

The above command will prompt you to choose the alternative configurations for gcc and g++, where you should select the option corresponding to gcc-8 and g++-8.

MacOS

For MacOS, clang is the supported compiler. The easiest way to install clang is through Xcode Command Line Tools. First, ensure that you have the latest version of Xcode installed. You can install Xcode from the Mac App Store. After installing Xcode, you can install the Command Line Tools using the following command:

```
xcode-select --install
```

This command will prompt a GUI to download and install the essential command-line tools, including clang. After installation, verify the installation and the version of clang:

```
clang --version
```

Ensure that the installed version matches the CUDA Toolkit requirements.

Windows

For Windows, the supported compiler for CUDA development is from Microsoft Visual Studio. CUDA 11.0 supports Microsoft Visual Studio 2017 and 2019. Follow these steps to install Microsoft Visual Studio 2019:

1. Download the installer from the official [Visual Studio website](https://visualstudio.microsoft.com/). 2. Run the installer and select the "Desktop development with C++" workload. 3. Install the required components.

After the installation, verify the integration with CUDA. Open Microsoft Visual Studio, create a new project, and add a new .cu file to see if the CUDA toolset is available directly from the Visual Studio environment.

To confirm successful integration, you can check for specific project properties and see if there is a "CUDA C++" option available in the "General" tab of project properties.

Configuration Files for Each Compiler

It is equally important to configure the compilers correctly within the CUDA development environment. For each of the supported compilers, ensure the environment variables and paths are correctly set.

- For Linux, update the PATH and LD_LIBRARY_PATH variables in .bashrc or .bash_profile:

```
export PATH=/usr/local/cuda-11.0/bin${PATH:+:${PATH}}
export LD_LIBRARY_PATH=/usr/local/cuda-11.0/lib64\
                        ${LD_LIBRARY_PATH:+:${LD_LIBRARY_PATH}}
```

- For MacOS, configuration is primarily handled through Xcode settings, but if using nvcc directly, ensure appropriate path settings similarly to Linux. - For Windows, environment variables should be set as part of the Visual Studio setup process, but double-check CUDA_PATH from the system environment variables to ensure it points to the correct CUDA Toolkit path.

Following these guidelines will ensure your system has a supported compiler ready for CUDA development.

2.5 Setting Up CUDA on Windows

To set up CUDA on a Windows system, it is imperative to follow a series of well-defined steps that include downloading and installing the CUDA Toolkit, configuring the NVIDIA driver, and setting up a supported compiler. Each step must be performed carefully to ensure the development environment functions properly.

First, download the CUDA Toolkit from the official NVIDIA website. The toolkit contains the necessary libraries, header files, and other development tools to create CUDA applications.

- Visit the NVIDIA CUDA Toolkit download page.
- Select your operating system under "Select Target Platform."

- Choose the CUDA Toolkit version you wish to install.
- Download the appropriate installer based on your system's architecture, typically x86_64 (64-bit).

Once the download is complete, execute the installer by double-clicking the file. The installation involves several prompts, requiring you to make specific selections. Follow these steps:

- Accept the End User License Agreement (EULA).
- Select the installation type, either 'Express' or 'Custom'. The 'Express' installation includes default options suitable for most users, while 'Custom' allows for more granular control.
- Ensure that the CUDA Toolkit, CUDA Samples, and documentation are selected for installation.
- Choose the installation path or accept the default path.
- Allow the installer to proceed and complete the installation.

After the CUDA Toolkit installation, the next step is to install the corresponding NVIDIA driver if it is not already present on your system. Most CUDA Toolkits bundle the driver with the installer; however, it can also be downloaded separately from the NVIDIA driver download webpage:

https://www.nvidia.com/Download/index.aspx

Make sure the driver version is compatible with the installed CUDA Toolkit version. Refer to the CUDA Toolkit documentation for driver compatibility requirements.

To verify proper driver installation, open the Device Manager and check that the NVIDIA GPU is listed under 'Display Adapters'. Alternatively, use the NVIDIA Control Panel:

- Right-click on the desktop and select 'NVIDIA Control Panel'.
- Navigate to 'System Information' to review the driver version.

A supported C++ compiler is necessary to compile your CUDA applications. The CUDA Toolkit supports specific versions of Microsoft Visual Studio. Verify the compatibility list from the NVIDIA documentation and install the corresponding Visual Studio version if not already installed. Once installed, configure Visual Studio to recognize the CUDA Toolkit paths:

- Open Visual Studio.
- Navigate to 'Tools' > 'Options'.
- Under 'Projects and Solutions' > 'VC++ Directories', add the CUDA Toolkit include and library paths.
- Typically, these paths are:
  ```
  C:\Program Files\NVIDIA GPU Computing Toolkit\CUDA\vX.X\include
  C:\Program Files\NVIDIA GPU Computing Toolkit\CUDA\vX.X\lib\x64
  ```

Replace vX.X with the installed CUDA version number. You may also need to add these paths to the 'Executable Directories' under the same VC++ Directories settings.

To ensure everything is set up correctly, compile and run one of the CUDA sample projects, included with the toolkit. These samples help verify that the configurations are correct and provide introductory examples on how to write CUDA programs.

Navigate to the CUDA Samples directory using the command line or File Explorer. This directory can be found at:

```
C:\ProgramData\NVIDIA Corporation\CUDA Samples\vX.X
```

Open a sample project, such as the 'vectorAdd' example, in Visual Studio and build the project:

```
cd "C:\ProgramData\NVIDIA Corporation\CUDA Samples\vX.X\1_Utilities\
    bandwidthTest"
bandwidthTest_vs2019.sln
```

This command launches the sample project solution in Visual Studio. Build the solution by selecting 'Build Solution' from the 'Build' menu or pressing Ctrl+Shift+B. If the build is successful, run the project by selecting 'Start Debugging' or pressing F5.

Upon execution, the output should display the performance results of the bandwidth test:

```
[CUDA Bandwidth Test] - Starting...
Running on...

 Device 0: GeForce GTX 1080Ti
 Quick Mode

Host to Device Bandwidth, 1 Device(s)
 PINNED Memory Transfers
   Transfer Size (Bytes) Bandwidth(GB/s)
   33554432              12.8

...

Result = PASS
```

This confirms that the CUDA environment is properly configured and the system is ready for CUDA development.

2.6 Setting Up CUDA on Linux

To establish a robust CUDA development environment on a Linux system, follow these systematic instructions which encompass the installation of the NVIDIA driver, the CUDA Toolkit, and the necessary libraries. Ensure compatibility between the versions of the driver and the toolkit to avoid runtime discrepancies.

Start by updating the system package repository to ensure the latest version of all packages. In the terminal, execute:

```
sudo apt-get update
```

Next, confirm that the Linux kernel is up to date:

```
sudo apt-get upgrade
```

Installing the NVIDIA Driver

It is imperative to install the appropriate NVIDIA driver for CUDA. Utilize the following commands to identify and install the suitable driver:

```
ubuntu-drivers devices
```

This command lists the available proprietary drivers. Install the recommended driver with:

```
sudo ubuntu-drivers autoinstall
```

Reboot the system to apply changes:

```
sudo reboot
```

After rebooting, verify the driver installation using:

```
nvidia-smi
```

The output should display the NVIDIA driver's version and GPU status.

Installing the CUDA Toolkit

Download the CUDA Toolkit from NVIDIA's official site. Ensure selecting the appropriate configuration matching your Linux distribution:

```
wget https://developer.download.nvidia.com/compute/cuda/repos/ubuntu2004/x86_64
    /cuda-repo-ubuntu2004_11.4.4-1_amd64.deb
```

Install the downloaded package and add the public GPG key:

```
sudo dpkg -i cuda-repo-ubuntu2004_11.4.4-1_amd64.deb
sudo apt-key adv --fetch-keys https://developer.download.nvidia.com/compute/cuda/
    repos/ubuntu2004/x86_64/7fa2af80.pub
```

Update the package repository again:

```
sudo apt-get update
```

Install the CUDA package:

```
sudo apt-get -y install cuda
```

To ensure the CUDA binaries are in the system's PATH, add the following lines to the ~/.bashrc file:

```
export PATH=/usr/local/cuda-11.4/bin${PATH:+:${PATH}}
export LD_LIBRARY_PATH=/usr/local/cuda-11.4/lib64\
                    ${LD_LIBRARY_PATH:+:${LD_LIBRARY_PATH}}
```

Apply the changes to the current session:

```
source ~/.bashrc
```

Verifying the Installation

Compile and run a simple CUDA program to validate installation. Navigate to the CUDA samples directory:

```
cd /usr/local/cuda-11.4/samples/1_Utilities/deviceQuery
make
```

Execute the compiled binary:

```
./deviceQuery
```

The output should indicate that the CUDA-capable device has been successfully detected:

```
Result = PASS
```

Managing Device Nodes

Ensure the NVIDIA device files are properly configured. Verify device nodes exist with:

```
ls /dev/nvidia*
```

To automate the creation of device nodes at boot, create or modify the nvidia.conf file:

```
sudo nano /etc/modprobe.d/nvidia.conf
```

Add the following content to the file:

```
alias char-major-195 nvidia
options nvidia NVreg_DeviceFileUID=0 NVreg_DeviceFileGID=0 NVreg_DeviceFileMode=0666
```

Reload the driver to apply changes:

```
sudo modprobe -r nvidia
sudo modprobe nvidia
```

Following these steps equips your Linux environment with the necessary tools and configurations for CUDA development. This setup is crucial for ensuring a seamless and productive programming experience.

2.7 Setting Up CUDA on MacOS

Setting up the CUDA development environment on macOS requires careful attention to system requirements and a series of precise steps to ensure successful installation. Here's a detailed guide to assist you in the process.

System Requirements: Before proceeding, verify that your macOS meets the following prerequisites:

- macOS 10.13 or later
- NVIDIA GPU with CUDA Compute Capability 3.0 or higher
- At least 1.5 GB of free disk space
- Minimum 4 GB of RAM

Driver Installation: The NVIDIA drivers are essential for CUDA to interact effectively with your GPU. Follow these steps to install the NVIDIA driver on macOS:

- Visit the official NVIDIA website and navigate to the "Drivers" section.
- Select your GPU model and macOS version to download the appropriate driver.
- Open the downloaded .dmg file and run the installer.
- Follow the on-screen instructions to complete the installation. You may need to allow the installer through the macOS security settings, which can be done by going to *System Preferences* → *Security & Privacy* and authorizing the installation.
- Restart your system after the installation completes to apply changes.

Installing Xcode: Xcode provides the necessary development tools and compilers to build CUDA applications on macOS.

- Open the App Store and search for "Xcode".
- Download and install Xcode.
- After installation, launch Xcode to complete the initial setup.
- Install Command Line Tools by running the following command in Terminal:

```
xcode-select --install
```

Installing CUDA Toolkit: The CUDA Toolkit can be downloaded from the NVIDIA website. Follow these steps:

- Visit the NVIDIA Developer website and navigate to the CUDA Toolkit page.
- Select macOS as the operating system and choose the version of the CUDA Toolkit you wish to install.
- Download the .dmg installer file.
- Open the downloaded .dmg file and follow the on-screen instructions to install the CUDA Toolkit.
- Add CUDA binaries to your PATH by editing your shell profile (e.g., .bash_profile or .zshrc) with the following command:

```
export PATH=/usr/local/cuda/bin:$PATH
```

- Refresh your terminal session by running:

```
source ~/.bash_profile % or ~/.zshrc, depending on your default shell
```

Verifying the Installation: After installation, it is necessary to verify that CUDA is correctly set up.

- Open Terminal and run the following command to check the CUDA version:

```
nvcc --version
```

- You should see an output similar to:

```
nvcc: NVIDIA (R) Cuda compiler driver
Built on Tue_Sep_15_23:24:52_PDT_2020
Cuda compilation tools, release 11.1, V11.1.74
```

- To ensure that the installed NVIDIA driver is working correctly, run:

```
nvidia-smi
```

- A successful installation will return information about your GPU and driver version:

NVIDIA-SMI 450.36.06	Driver Version: 450.36.06	CUDA Version: 11.1
GPU Name	Bus-Id Disp.A	Volatile Uncorr. ECC
Fan Temp Perf Pwr:Usage/Cap	Memory-Usage	GPU-Util Compute M.
		MIG M.
0 GeForce GTX 107... Off	00000000:01:00.0 Off	N/A
0% 33C P8 5W / 151W	0MiB / 8119MiB	0% Default
		N/A

Table 2.1: NVIDIA GPU Information

Handling Compilation and Execution Permissions: macOS has specific security policies related to executable permissions which might impact CUDA programs. Ensure correct permissions as follows:

- Change the permission of the CUDA samples or any CUDA executable files using:

```
chmod +x <filename>
```

- For smooth execution, you can run the CUDA samples to ensure everything is functioning properly. Navigate to the CUDA samples directory and compile the samples by executing:

```
cd /Developer/NVIDIA/CUDA-samples
make
```

- Run a sample program, such as:

```
./bin/x86_64/darwin/release/deviceQuery
```

- Check the output to see if your GPU is recognized and functioning correctly.

Following these steps carefully will set up a functional CUDA development environment on macOS, enabling you to compile, run, and optimize CUDA programs effectively.

2.8 Verifying the Installation

To ensure that the CUDA development environment has been correctly set up, it is essential to perform a series of verification steps. These steps will confirm that the CUDA Toolkit, NVIDIA driver, and compiler are properly installed and configured, and that they are functioning as expected.

The verification process can be broken down into the following tasks:

1. Confirming CUDA Toolkit Installation 2. Compiling and Running CUDA Samples 3. Checking Device Query 4. Verifying Driver and Runtime API

- **Confirming CUDA Toolkit Installation**

  After installing the CUDA Toolkit, you should verify that the installation was successful. You can do this by compiling a simple CUDA program.

  First, open a terminal or command prompt and navigate to the common installation directory of CUDA. By default, this directory is /usr/local/cuda/ on Linux, C:\Program

Files\NVIDIA GPU Computing Toolkit\CUDA on Windows, and /Developer/NVIDIA/CUDA-x.y on macOS.

Verify the installation by listing the contents of the directory to ensure that it contains the necessary files and subdirectories.

```
ls /usr/local/cuda/bin
```

The output should list several binaries such as *nvcc*, *cuda-gdb*, and *cuda-memcheck*.

- **Compiling and Running CUDA Samples**

  The CUDA Toolkit includes several sample programs that you can compile and run to ensure that your environment is set up correctly. These samples are provided in the samples directory within the CUDA installation path. Navigate to this directory and compile the samples using the following commands.

```
cd /usr/local/cuda/samples
make
```

  The make command will compile all the sample programs. You can run any of the compiled examples to test your setup. For instance, running the device query sample can provide valuable information about your GPU and its capabilities.

```
./bin/x86_64/linux/release/deviceQuery
```

  The output should be similar to the following:

```
Detected 1 CUDA Capable device(s)

Device 0: "Tesla V100-SXM2-32GB"
  CUDA Driver Version / Runtime Version          10.0 / 10.0
  CUDA Capability Major/Minor version number:    7.0
  Total amount of global memory:                 32510 MBytes (34193641472 bytes)
  (80) Multiprocessors, ( 64) CUDA Cores/MP:     5120 CUDA Cores
  ...
```

  This output indicates that the device is recognized and details various properties of the GPU.

- **Checking Device Query**

  The device query tool is essential for verifying that the CUDA-capable GPU is being detected correctly by the system. Running this tool provides information about all CUDA-capable devices available on the system.

  The 'deviceQuery' tool, executable from the previous step, will output information about the GPU, such as the CUDA driver version, runtime version, number of multiprocessors, CUDA cores, and available memory.

If the output matches the specifications of your GPU, then your CUDA environment is correctly set up.

- **Verifying Driver and Runtime API**

  Finally, it is crucial to ensure that the installed NVIDIA driver is compatible with the CUDA runtime. You can check this by running a simple program that utilizes the CUDA API to conduct a general test of the runtime environment.

  Create a basic CUDA program, save it as test.cu, and compile it.

```
#include <cuda_runtime.h>
#include <iostream>

__global__ void kernel()
{
    printf("Hello, CUDA!\n");
}

int main()
{
    kernel<<<1, 1>>>();
    cudaDeviceSynchronize();
    return 0;
}
```

  Compile and run the program using:

```
nvcc -o test test.cu
./test
```

  The output should be:

```
Hello, CUDA!
```

  The correct output confirms that the CUDA runtime and the NVIDIA driver are correctly installed and functioning properly.

Completing these verification steps will indicate a successful setup of your CUDA development environment, allowing you to move forward with confidence in your CUDA programming endeavors.

2.9 Introduction to CUDA Samples

Upon successfully installing the CUDA Toolkit, users gain access to a comprehensive set of CUDA samples. These pre-packaged examples demonstrate the range of functionality and performance enhancements achievable with CUDA. The samples serve as both an instructional aid for newcomers and a reference for experienced developers looking to implement specific features. These examples are installed alongside the CUDA Toolkit and can be found in the samples directory within the CUDA installation path.

The samples consist of various categories, including but not limited to:

- **0_Simple**: Fundamental examples illustrating basic CUDA operations.
- **1_Utilities**: Utility functions for various CUDA tasks.
- **2_Graphics**: Samples involving graphical CUDA applications.
- **3_Imaging**: Image processing examples using CUDA.
- **4_Finance**: Financial computations demonstrating CUDA's computational capabilities.
- **5_Simulations**: Simulation-oriented applications harnessing the power of CUDA.

To run these samples, navigate to the samples directory and build them using make on Linux or by opening the provided Visual Studio solutions on Windows. Here, we will demonstrate how to build and execute a sample on both platforms to solidify understanding.

Building and Running CUDA Samples on Linux

1. Open a terminal and navigate to the samples directory:

```
cd /usr/local/cuda/samples
```

2. Ensure the sample Makefile is properly configured. Most samples come with their own Makefile. Navigate to a specific sample directory, such as 0_Simple/vectorAdd:

```
cd 0_Simple/vectorAdd
```

3. Compile the sample using make:

```
make
```

4. Upon successful compilation, an executable file will be produced. To run the generated executable:

```
./vectorAdd
```

The output should resemble:

```
[Vector addition of 50000 elements]
Copy inputs to device
CUDA kernel launch with 196 blocks of 256 threads
Copy output data from the CUDA device to the host memory
Test PASSED
Done
```

Building and Running CUDA Samples on Windows

1. Open the NVIDIA CUDA Samples directory, typically found in C:\ProgramData\NVIDIA Corporation\CUDA Samples.

2. Navigate to a sample, for example, 0_Simple/vectorAdd, and locate the Visual Studio solution file (.sln).

3. Open the .sln file in Visual Studio. Make sure to select the correct build target (x64 Release or Debug) and build the sample by selecting Build → Build Solution.

4. After building successfully, the executable can be found in the Release or Debug directory within the sample folder. To run the executable:

```
vectorAdd.exe
```

Expected output:

```
[Vector addition of 50000 elements]
Copy inputs to device
CUDA kernel launch with 196 blocks of 256 threads
Copy output data from the CUDA device to the host memory
Test PASSED
Done
```

These instructions provide a foundation for working with CUDA samples on different operating systems. Each sample includes specific information in the associated README file, which details functionalities and additional requirements.

By exploring these samples, users can glean insights into various CUDA concepts and practices, facilitating the application of these principles to broader and more complex projects.

2.10 Writing and Running Your First CUDA Program

Writing and running your first CUDA program might seem intimidating initially, but following systematically will make the process straightforward. This section will guide you through writing a simple CUDA program to ensure the CUDA development environment is properly configured and to familiarize you with basic CUDA programming concepts.

Step 1: Create a New File
Start by creating a new file with a .cu extension, typically indicating a CUDA program. For example, you can name your file hello_cuda.cu.

Step 2: Write the CUDA Program
Let's write a simple CUDA program that prints "Hello, World from GPU!".

```
#include <stdio.h>

__global__ void helloFromGPU() {
    printf("Hello, World from GPU!\n");
}

int main() {
    // Launch the kernel with one block and one thread
    helloFromGPU<<<1, 1>>>();

    // Ensure all threads complete
    cudaDeviceSynchronize();

    return 0;
}
```

Explanation of the CUDA Program Code

- #include <stdio.h>: This standard header file allows the use of the printf function for output.
- __global__ void helloFromGPU(): The __global__ keyword indicates that this function is a CUDA kernel, meaning it will execute on the GPU. Inside this kernel, the printf function is used to print a message from the GPU.
- helloFromGPU«<1, 1»>();: The triple angle-bracket syntax «<1, 1»> is used to launch the kernel. It specifies the execution configuration: one block with one thread.
- cudaDeviceSynchronize(): This function is used to wait for the kernel to finish execution before proceeding. It ensures that the CPU

waits until the GPU has completed its execution, preventing premature termination of the program.

Step 3: Compile the CUDA Program
To compile the CUDA program, use the NVIDIA CUDA Compiler nvcc. Open your terminal or command prompt and navigate to the directory where the hello_cuda.cu file is located. Run the following command:

```
nvcc hello_cuda.cu -o hello_cuda
```

This command invokes nvcc, specifying the input CUDA file hello_cuda.cu and the output binary executable hello_cuda.

Step 4: Run the Compiled Program
Execute the compiled program by typing the following command in your terminal or command prompt:

```
./hello_cuda
```

Expected Output
The program should output the following text:

```
Hello, World from GPU!
```

Step 5: Validate and Troubleshoot
If the output matches the expected result, your first CUDA program has run successfully. If not, common issues might involve ensuring the CUDA toolkit and drivers are correctly installed. Check the following:

- Verify the CUDA toolkit path and environmental variables.
- Ensure the NVIDIA driver is up-to-date and compatible with the CUDA toolkit version.
- Check for any syntax errors or typos in your code.
- Utilize cudaGetErrorString with cudaError_t to obtain error messages that help diagnose runtime issues.

Incorporating these steps and understanding the basic structure of a CUDA program lays the foundation for more complex and advanced CUDA programming. The example provided demonstrates key concepts such as defining and launching kernels and synchronizing device and host operations. These core ideas are instrumental in writing efficient and functional CUDA programs.

Chapter 3

Basics of CUDA Programming

This chapter introduces the foundational aspects of CUDA programming, covering the structure of a CUDA program, the concept of CUDA threads, and the different types of memory in CUDA. It walks through writing your first kernel, compiling and running CUDA programs, and handling errors efficiently. The chapter also provides an overview of the CUDA API and libraries, culminating in a practical example of vector addition to solidify the concepts discussed.

3.1 Introduction to CUDA C

CUDA (Compute Unified Device Architecture) is a parallel computing platform and application programming interface (API) model created by NVIDIA. CUDA enables developers to speed up compute-intensive applications by harnessing the power of NVIDIA GPUs for the parallelizable parts of the computation. With CUDA C, programmers can write code that runs on the GPU with extensions to the C programming language.

The core concept of CUDA C revolves around the execution of functions, called *kernels*, on the GPU. These kernels are executed in parallel by multiple threads; each thread processes its own data and operates independently of the others, within the broader context of a grid and block architecture, which will be discussed in subsequent sections.

A fundamental aspect of understanding CUDA C is appreciating the structure and execution model. In the traditional sequential programming model, a single thread executes instructions one after another. Conversely, CUDA C employs a parallel execution model wherein kernels are executed by a multitude of threads simultaneously.

An Example CUDA C Code Structure:

Consider a simple CUDA C program that adds two vectors. This example aims to provide initial exposure to the CUDA C syntax and structure.

```
#include <cuda_runtime.h>
#include <stdio.h>

// Kernel to add elements of two arrays
__global__ void vectorAdd(const float *A, const float *B, float *C, int N) {
    int i = threadIdx.x + blockIdx.x * blockDim.x;
    if (i < N) {
        C[i] = A[i] + B[i];
    }
}

int main() {
    int N = 50000;
    size_t size = N * sizeof(float);

    // Allocate input vectors h_A and h_B in host memory
    float *h_A = (float *)malloc(size);
    float *h_B = (float *)malloc(size);
    float *h_C = (float *)malloc(size);

    // Initialize input vectors
    for (int i = 0; i < N; i++) {
        h_A[i] = rand() / (float)RAND_MAX;
        h_B[i] = rand() / (float)RAND_MAX;
    }

    // Allocate vectors in device memory
    float *d_A, *d_B, *d_C;
    cudaMalloc(&d_A, size);
    cudaMalloc(&d_B, size);
    cudaMalloc(&d_C, size);

    // Copy vectors from host memory to device memory
    cudaMemcpy(d_A, h_A, size, cudaMemcpyHostToDevice);
    cudaMemcpy(d_B, h_B, size, cudaMemcpyHostToDevice);

    // Invoke kernel
    int threadsPerBlock = 256;
    int blocksPerGrid = (N + threadsPerBlock - 1) / threadsPerBlock;
    vectorAdd<<<blocksPerGrid, threadsPerBlock>>>(d_A, d_B, d_C, N);

    // Copy result from device memory to host memory
    cudaMemcpy(h_C, d_C, size, cudaMemcpyDeviceToHost);

    // Verify result
```

```
    for (int i = 0; i < N; i++) {
        if (fabs(h_A[i] + h_B[i] - h_C[i]) > 1e-5) {
            fprintf(stderr, "Result verification failed at element %d!\n", i);
            exit(EXIT_FAILURE);
        }
    }

    // Free device memory
    cudaFree(d_A);
    cudaFree(d_B);
    cudaFree(d_C);

    // Free host memory
    free(h_A);
    free(h_B);
    free(h_C);

    printf("Test PASSED\n");
    return 0;
}
```

Explanation of the Example:

- #include <cuda_runtime.h> and #include <stdio.h>: Inclusion of necessary header files. cuda_runtime.h includes the runtime API functions.
- __global__ void vectorAdd(const float *A, const float *B, float *C, int N): Definition of a kernel function with the __global__-specifier, indicating it will be executed on the GPU.
- int i = threadIdx.x + blockIdx.x * blockDim.x;: Calculation of the global index i for the thread. threadIdx.x, blockIdx.x, and blockDim.x are built-in variables provided by CUDA.
- if (i < N) {...}: Ensures the thread index does not exceed the bounds of the array.
- C[i] = A[i] + B[i];: The core operation performed by each thread - adding corresponding elements of vectors A and B, and storing the result in C.
- int main() {...}: The main function where the host code is executed.
- float *h_A = (float *)malloc(size);: Allocation of host memory.
- cudaMalloc(&d_A, size);: Allocation of device memory.
- cudaMemcpy(d_A, h_A, size, cudaMemcpyHostToDevice);: Copying data from host to device memory.

- int threadsPerBlock = 256;: Setting the number of threads per block.
- vectorAdd«<blocksPerGrid, threadsPerBlock»>(d_A, d_B, d_C, N);: Kernel invocation with a specified number of blocks and threads.
- cudaMemcpy(h_C, d_C, size, cudaMemcpyDeviceToHost);: Copying the result back from device to host memory.
- cudaFree(d_A);: Deallocation of device memory.
- free(h_A);: Deallocation of host memory.

Each step of the example meticulously carries out the necessary procedures for successful CUDA programming: memory allocation, data transfer between host and device, kernel execution, and memory deallocation. Understanding and implementing these steps are crucial to efficient CUDA programming.

Executing the above CUDA program will result in a simple summation of two vectors, performed in parallel on the GPU. The output validation step ensures the correctness of computation, providing a prototype for developing more complex CUDA applications.

By examining this example, the fundamental syntax and program structure of CUDA C are reinforced. This foundation sets the stage for deeper exploration into the intricacies of parallel computing with CUDA.

3.2 CUDA Program Structure

CUDA (Compute Unified Device Architecture) leverages the GPU's parallel processing capabilities to execute computational tasks efficiently. A CUDA program consists of both host (CPU) and device (GPU) code. The division between host and device code is critical for harnessing the full power of a GPU. A well-structured CUDA program balances computations between the CPU and the GPU, ensuring optimal performance. This section details CUDA's program structure, laying the groundwork for writing efficient CUDA applications.

A typical CUDA program comprises the following key components:

- **Kernel Functions:** These functions are executed on the GPU.

Each function defines the operations to be performed by parallel threads.

- **Host Code:** This is the code that runs on the CPU, responsible for managing memory, launching kernels, and synchronizing operations.
- **Memory Management:** Involves allocating memory on the device, transferring data between the host and device, and deallocating memory.
- **Kernel Launch Configuration:** Specifies the grid and block dimensions for kernel execution, determining how threads are organized.

Kernel Functions

In CUDA, functions meant to run on the GPU are referred to as kernel functions. A kernel is declared using the __global__ keyword, indicating that the function will be executed on the device but called from the host.

```
__global__ void MyKernel(int *a, int *b, int *c) {
    int idx = threadIdx.x;
    c[idx] = a[idx] + b[idx];
}
```

The example above demonstrates a simple kernel, MyKernel, which adds two integer arrays element-wise. The special variable threadIdx.x provides the thread's index within its block, allowing concurrent threads to operate on different elements of the arrays.

Host Code

The host code manages the program flow, including memory allocation, data transfer between the host and device, and kernel execution. The host code typically follows these steps:

- Allocate memory on the device using cudaMalloc.
- Copy data from the host to the device using cudaMemcpy.
- Define the kernel launch configuration, specifying the grid and block dimensions.
- Launch the kernel.
- Copy the results back to the host.

- Free the memory allocated on the device using cudaFree.

Consider the following host code snippet that complements the previously defined MyKernel:

```
int main() {
    const int arraySize = 10;
    int a[arraySize] = {0, 1, 2, 3, 4, 5, 6, 7, 8, 9};
    int b[arraySize] = {9, 8, 7, 6, 5, 4, 3, 2, 1, 0};
    int c[arraySize] = {0};

    int *d_a, *d_b, *d_c;

    cudaMalloc((void**)&d_a, arraySize * sizeof(int));
    cudaMalloc((void**)&d_b, arraySize * sizeof(int));
    cudaMalloc((void**)&d_c, arraySize * sizeof(int));

    cudaMemcpy(d_a, a, arraySize * sizeof(int), cudaMemcpyHostToDevice);
    cudaMemcpy(d_b, b, arraySize * sizeof(int), cudaMemcpyHostToDevice);

    MyKernel<<<1, arraySize>>>(d_a, d_b, d_c);

    cudaMemcpy(c, d_c, arraySize * sizeof(int), cudaMemcpyDeviceToHost);

    cudaFree(d_a);
    cudaFree(d_b);
    cudaFree(d_c);

    for (int i = 0; i < arraySize; i++) {
        printf("%d + %d = %d\n", a[i], b[i], c[i]);
    }

    return 0;
}
```

The steps in this code can be correlated directly to the bullet points mentioned earlier. Here's a further detailed breakdown:

- cudaMalloc((void)&d_a, arraySize * sizeof(int)); This allocates memory on the GPU for array d_a. The cudaMalloc function requires a pointer to the allocated memory and the size in bytes.
- cudaMemcpy(d_a, a, arraySize * sizeof(int), cudaMemcpyHostToDevice); This copies the data from host memory (a) to device memory (d_a). The cudaMemcpy function is versatile and can transfer data in both directions (host-to-device or device-to-host), controlled by the fourth parameter.
- MyKernel«<1, arraySize»>(d_a, d_b, d_c); This launches the kernel. The «1, arraySize» syntax specifies the execution configuration. Here, it indicates the kernel will run with one block of arraySize threads.

- cudaFree(d_a); This deallocates the memory previously allocated on the GPU for array d_a. It is essential to free any allocated memory to prevent memory leaks.

Kernel Launch Configuration

The execution configuration «<gridDim, blockDim»> determines how threads are organized and executed in parallel. Here:

- gridDim specifies the number of blocks in the grid.
- blockDim specifies the number of threads in each block.

In the example, MyKernel«<1, arraySize»> launches a grid containing one block with arraySize threads. Each thread in the block executes a copy of the kernel, processing different elements of the arrays. Advanced configurations can involve multiple dimensions (up to three) for both grids and blocks, allowing for complex data structures and operations.

```
MyKernel<<<dim3 gridDim(2, 2, 1), dim3 blockDim(16, 16, 1)>>>(d_a, d_b, d_c);
```

In this scenario, the kernel runs with a 2x2 grid of blocks, and each block contains 16x16 (256) threads. This setup can be particularly useful for two-dimensional data like matrices.

Memory Management

CUDA provides several memory types, each suited for different purposes:

- **Global Memory:** Large, non-cached memory accessible by all threads.
- **Shared Memory:** Faster, smaller memory shared among threads within the same block.
- **Constant and Texture Memory:** Read-only memory spaces optimized for specific access patterns.

Effective memory management is essential for deriving maximum performance. Global memory is convenient due to its large size, but accessing it is slower compared to shared or constant memory. Utilizing shared memory for frequently accessed data reduces latency and enhances performance. Properly managing different types of memory requires understanding their characteristics and usage patterns.

Throughout this exploration of CUDA program structure, the integration of kernel functions, host code, kernel launch configuration, and memory management is critical for efficient CUDA programming. By mastering these elements, one can leverage the immense parallel processing power of GPUs to tackle complex computational tasks.

3.3 Understanding CUDA Threads

CUDA architecture is designed around the concept of executing many threads in parallel. A thread in CUDA is the smallest unit of execution, and understanding their organization, mapping, and execution is fundamental for efficient CUDA programming. Threads in CUDA are organized into grids of thread blocks, providing a way to handle large-scale parallel tasks effectively.

Thread Hierarchy: Each CUDA kernel, when launched, executes a grid of thread blocks. Each thread block, in turn, contains multiple threads. This hierarchical organization allows for fine-grained parallelism and scalability. Here's the breakdown of the hierarchy:

- **Grid:** The top-level structure, consisting of multiple thread blocks.
- **Thread Block:** A mid-level structure within the grid, consisting of multiple threads. Thread blocks are organized in a one-dimensional, two-dimensional, or three-dimensional structure.
- **Thread:** The basic unit of execution, organized within thread blocks. Threads may also be organized in one-dimensional, two-dimensional, or three-dimensional structures.

Defining Thread Organization in CUDA: Here is an example of how a kernel launch specifies the grid and thread block dimensions:

```
// Define grid and block dimensions
dim3 blockDim(16, 16); // 16x16 threads per block
dim3 gridDim(32, 32); // 32x32 blocks per grid

// Kernel launch
myKernel<<<gridDim, blockDim>>>(/* kernel parameters */);
```

In this example, each block consists of 16x16 threads, and the grid consists of 32x32 such blocks.

Thread Indexing: Within a kernel, each thread can determine its unique index using built-in variables. The most common variables are:

- **threadIdx:** This provides the index of the thread within its block. For example, threadIdx.x, threadIdx.y, and threadIdx.z.
- **blockIdx:** This provides the index of the block within the grid. For example, blockIdx.x, blockIdx.y, and blockIdx.z.
- **blockDim:** This provides the dimensions of the block. For example, blockDim.x, blockDim.y, and blockDim.z.
- **gridDim:** This provides the dimensions of the grid. For example, gridDim.x, gridDim.y, and gridDim.z.

Each thread can calculate a global index using these variables to identify its unique position in the entire grid:

```
int globalIdx = threadIdx.x + blockIdx.x * blockDim.x;
int globalIdy = threadIdx.y + blockIdx.y * blockDim.y;
```

Thread Synchronization: Synchronization between threads in the same block can be crucial to ensuring correct program execution. CUDA provides the __syncthreads() function, which acts as a barrier at which all threads in the block must wait until they all reach the barrier. This can be useful in scenarios where threads need to cooperate to complete a task.

```
__global__ void exampleKernel()
{
    // Perform some computation
    // All threads must reach this point before any can proceed
    __syncthreads();
    // Continue computation
}
```

However, it is important to note that __syncthreads() only works within a single block. Synchronizing across blocks requires more advanced techniques outside the scope of this section.

Thread Divergence: Thread divergence occurs when threads within the same block follow different execution paths due to conditional branching (e.g., if-else statements). Divergence can lead to reduced execution efficiency because the threads in a warp (a group of 32 threads) execute both branches serially. To minimize divergence:

- Align conditional branches among the threads as much as possible.
- Use predication to eliminate small branches.

Example With Thread Divergence:

```
__global__ void divergenceKernel()
{
    int idx = threadIdx.x + blockIdx.x * blockDim.x;
    if (idx % 2 == 0)
    {
        // Path A
    }
    else
    {
        // Path B
    }
}
```

In the above example, potential divergence is introduced by the if-else condition based on the thread index.

Using Threads Effectively: Effective use of threads is essential for optimizing CUDA programs. Strategies include:

- Maximizing occupancy by choosing appropriate block sizes that use hardware resources efficiently.
- Reducing thread divergence by organizing work to minimize conditional branches.
- Utilizing shared memory within a block for data that is repeatedly accessed by multiple threads.
- Balancing the workload to ensure that all threads have an approximately equal amount of work.

Understanding the intricacies of thread organization, indexing, synchronization, and divergence management is essential for writing efficient CUDA programs. By maximizing the parallel processing capabilities of the CUDA architecture, one can significantly improve the performance of compute-intensive applications.

3.4 Memory Types in CUDA

In CUDA programming, understanding the various types of memory available is essential for optimizing performance and ensuring efficient execution of your kernels. CUDA provides multiple memory spaces, each with distinct properties, access patterns, and use cases. The principal memory types in CUDA include global memory, shared memory, local memory, constant memory, and texture memory. Each of these memory types plays a crucial role in how CUDA threads interact with data, so a thorough understanding is necessary for writing efficient CUDA programs.

Global Memory: This is the largest and most fundamental memory space in CUDA, accessible by all threads, and has the highest latency and least bandwidth when compared to other memory types. Global memory is typically used for large data sets that need to be transferred between the host (CPU) and the device (GPU).

```
__global__ void kernelExample(float *a, int N) {
    int idx = threadIdx.x + blockIdx.x * blockDim.x;
    if (idx < N)
        a[idx] = a[idx] * 2.0f;
}
```

In the above kernel, the array a resides in global memory, and each thread retrieves and updates its corresponding element.

Shared Memory: This is an on-chip memory shared among threads of the same block. It has significantly lower latency compared to global memory, making it suitable for scenarios requiring fast data exchange among threads. Properly leveraging shared memory can drastically boost performance, especially when minimizing accesses to global memory.

```
__global__ void kernelWithSharedMemory(float *a, int N) {
    extern __shared__ float sharedData[];
    int idx = threadIdx.x + blockIdx.x * blockDim.x;

    if (idx < N) {
        sharedData[threadIdx.x] = a[idx];
        __syncthreads();
        sharedData[threadIdx.x] *= 2.0f;
        __syncthreads();
        a[idx] = sharedData[threadIdx.x];
    }
}
```

Here, the sharedData array is employed to temporarily store and manipulate data, reducing dependence on the slower global memory.

Local Memory: Despite its name, local memory is not cached and resides in the global memory space. It is designated for variables that are private to a thread, typically used for register spillover or when threads require their own copies of variables.

```
__global__ void kernelWithLocalMemory(float *a, float *b, int N) {
    int idx = threadIdx.x + blockIdx.x * blockDim.x;
    if (idx < N) {
        float temp = a[idx];
        temp += b[idx];
```

```
        a[idx] = temp * 2.0f;
    }
}
```

In this case, the variable temp is stored in local memory because it is unique to each thread.

Constant Memory: This read-only memory space is cached and offers high-bandwidth access when multiple threads simultaneously access the same address. It is ideal for storing data that doesn't change over the lifetime of the application, like coefficients in mathematical computations.

```
__constant__ float constData[256];

__global__ void kernelWithConstantMemory(float *a, int N) {
    int idx = threadIdx.x + blockIdx.x * blockDim.x;
    if (idx < N)
        a[idx] = a[idx] + constData[idx % 256];
}
```

The __constant__ qualifier indicates that constData resides in constant memory, which threads can read from efficiently if accessed uniformly.

Texture Memory: This read-only memory space is optimized for certain data access patterns, particularly useful in graphics applications for image data and linear algebra computations. Texture memory leverages a different cache hierarchy and is beneficial for spatial locality exploitation.

```
texture<float, cudaTextureType1D, cudaReadModeElementType> texRef;

__global__ void kernelWithTextureMemory(float *a, int N) {
    int idx = threadIdx.x + blockIdx.x * blockDim.x;
    if (idx < N)
        a[idx] = tex1Dfetch(texRef, idx);
}
```

Here, the texture reference texRef is used to fetch data, which the texture cache optimizes for spatial locality.

Each memory type in CUDA has its optimal scenarios and best practices. Global memory is best for large data arrays, shared memory for inter-thread communication within a block, local memory for thread-specific data, constant memory for data that doesn't change, and texture memory for spatially coherent data access. Careful planning and usage of these memory types can significantly enhance the performance and efficiency of CUDA programs.

3.5 Writing Your First Kernel

A CUDA kernel is a function executed on the GPU, which is called from the host (CPU) code and executed in parallel by multiple threads. Understanding how to write a kernel function is fundamental to leveraging the parallel processing capabilities of CUDA. This section will guide you through the process of writing your first CUDA kernel, elucidating the key components and their functionalities.

In CUDA, a kernel function is defined using the __global__ declaration specifier. This keyword indicates that the function will be executed on the device (GPU) and can be called from the host. The basic structure of a CUDA kernel function is as follows:

```
__global__ void myKernelFunction() {
    // Kernel code here
}
```

The myKernelFunction is the kernel, and it is typically called from the host code. When invoked, a certain number of threads are launched to execute this kernel in parallel. Let's walk through a concrete example to illustrate these concepts.

Consider the task of adding two vectors, A and B, each with N elements, and storing the result in a vector C. Here is how you can write and call a CUDA kernel to accomplish this task.

```
__global__ void vectorAdd(float *A, float *B, float *C, int N) {
    int i = threadIdx.x + blockDim.x * blockIdx.x;
    if (i < N) {
        C[i] = A[i] + B[i];
    }
}
```

In this kernel, each thread computes an index i to operate on. The index is determined using the thread index (threadIdx.x) within the block and the block index (blockIdx.x). The if condition ensures that out-of-bound accesses are prevented, especially when the total number of threads launched exceeds the size of the vectors.

Setting Up the Host Code

To utilize this kernel in a CUDA program, you'll need to set up the host code appropriately. Here is a step-by-step guide to complete the vector addition example:

- Allocate memory on the host and device.
- Copy data from host to device.
- Launch the kernel.
- Copy the result from device to host.
- Free the allocated memory.

Here's the complete host code for these steps:

```
#include <iostream>
#include <cuda_runtime.h>

__global__ void vectorAdd(float *A, float *B, float *C, int N) {
    int i = threadIdx.x + blockDim.x * blockIdx.x;
    if (i < N) {
        C[i] = A[i] + B[i];
    }
}

int main() {
    int N = 1000;
    size_t size = N * sizeof(float);

    // Allocate memory on the host
    float *h_A = (float *)malloc(size);
    float *h_B = (float *)malloc(size);
    float *h_C = (float *)malloc(size);

    // Initialize input vectors
    for (int i = 0; i < N; i++) {
        h_A[i] = i;
        h_B[i] = i * 2.0f;
    }

    // Allocate memory on the device
    float *d_A, *d_B, *d_C;
    cudaMalloc(&d_A, size);
    cudaMalloc(&d_B, size);
    cudaMalloc(&d_C, size);

    // Copy data from host to device
    cudaMemcpy(d_A, h_A, size, cudaMemcpyHostToDevice);
    cudaMemcpy(d_B, h_B, size, cudaMemcpyHostToDevice);

    // Launch the kernel
    int threadsPerBlock = 256;
    int blocksPerGrid = (N + threadsPerBlock - 1) / threadsPerBlock;
    vectorAdd<<<blocksPerGrid, threadsPerBlock>>>(d_A, d_B, d_C, N);

    // Copy result from device to host
    cudaMemcpy(h_C, d_C, size, cudaMemcpyDeviceToHost);

    // Check the result
    for (int i = 0; i < N; i++) {
        if (fabs(h_C[i] - (h_A[i] + h_B[i])) > 1e-5) {
            std::cerr << "Result verification failed at element " << i << std::endl;
            exit(EXIT_FAILURE);
```

```
        }
    }

    // Free device memory
    cudaFree(d_A);
    cudaFree(d_B);
    cudaFree(d_C);

    // Free host memory
    free(h_A);
    free(h_B);
    free(h_C);

    std::cout << "Test PASSED" << std::endl;
    return 0;
}
```

Upon executing this program, the vectors A and B are added element-wise by the CUDA kernel, and the result is verified in the host code.

Understanding Execution Configuration

The execution configuration («<Grid, Block»>) specifies the number of blocks and threads per block used to execute the kernel. The following parameters are crucial:

- Grid: Defines the number of blocks in the grid.
- Block: Defines the number of threads in each block.

In the example, blocksPerGrid ensures that we cover all elements in the vectors. The calculation (N + threadsPerBlock - 1) / threadsPerBlock ensures that we have enough blocks to handle the vector size N. This approach prevents potential underutilization of GPU resources.

Executing this host code launches the vectorAdd kernel with sufficient threads to process the entire data. Each thread calculates its unique index, accesses the corresponding elements from vectors A and B, performs the addition, and stores the result in vector C.

```
Test PASSED
```

3.6 Compiling and Running CUDA Programs

To execute a CUDA program, we need to understand the compilation and execution process specific to the CUDA environment. The compilation of a CUDA program is distinct from standard C/C++ compilation as it involves generating device code for the GPU and host code for the CPU. We will use the NVIDIA CUDA Compiler, nvcc, which is designed to handle this process seamlessly.

The Role of nvcc

The nvcc compiler is a command-line tool that simplifies the compilation of CUDA programs. It splits the source code into host code (C/C++) and device code (CUDA C), compiling each part with the appropriate compiler and then linking them together. Consider the following example of a simple CUDA program:

```
#include <stdio.h>

__global__ void add(int *a, int *b, int *c) {
    int index = threadIdx.x;
    c[index] = a[index] + b[index];
}

int main(void) {
    int a[5] = {1, 2, 3, 4, 5};
    int b[5] = {10, 20, 30, 40, 50};
    int c[5];

    int *d_a, *d_b, *d_c;
    int size = 5 * sizeof(int);

    // Allocate device memory
    cudaMalloc((void **)&d_a, size);
    cudaMalloc((void **)&d_b, size);
    cudaMalloc((void **)&d_c, size);

    // Copy arrays from host memory to device memory
    cudaMemcpy(d_a, a, size, cudaMemcpyHostToDevice);
    cudaMemcpy(d_b, b, size, cudaMemcpyHostToDevice);

    // Launch add kernel on GPU with N threads
    add<<<1, 5>>>(d_a, d_b, d_c);

    // Copy result back to host memory
    cudaMemcpy(c, d_c, size, cudaMemcpyDeviceToHost);

    // Free device memory
    cudaFree(d_a);
    cudaFree(d_b);
    cudaFree(d_c);

    printf("Result: ");
    for(int i = 0; i < 5; i++) {
        printf("%d ", c[i]);
    }
    printf("\n");

    return 0;
}
```

Compiling the CUDA Program

To compile the above CUDA program, you can use the following command:

```
nvcc -o vector_add vector_add.cu
```

The nvcc command takes care of compiling both the host and device code. The -o option specifies the name of the output executable file. The input file is vector_add.cu, where .cu is the conventional file extension for CUDA source files.

Running the Compiled Program

Once compiled, you can run the executable just like any other C or C++ program:

```
./vector_add
```

The expected output of the program should be the addition of corresponding elements of the arrays, displayed as:

```
Result: 11 22 33 44 55
```

Handling Compilation Errors

While compiling, you may encounter errors. Common issues include syntax errors, undeclared variables, and incorrect usage of CUDA API functions. nvcc will provide error messages that indicate the line number and type of error. Consider the example of an error due to undefined host function decoration:

```
vector_add.cu(24): error: identifier "cudadMalloc" is undefined
```

This error indicates a typo in the cudaMalloc function call. Correcting the function name will resolve this error.

Compilation Flags

nvcc supports various flags for different purposes:

- -arch=<arch>: Specifies the compute capability of the target GPU architecture.
- -G: Enables debugging information in the generated device code.
- -maxrregcount=<N>: Limits the number of registers to N per thread.

- -ptx: Generates PTX code instead of an executable.

For example, if you want to compile a program with debugging information, use:

```
nvcc -G -g -O0 -o vector_add_debug vector_add.cu
```

Compatibility Considerations

Ensure that the CUDA toolkit version is compatible with the NVIDIA driver version and your GPU architecture. Compatibility issues can lead to compilation or runtime failures. Refer to the official NVIDIA CUDA documentation for compatibility guidelines.

In the CUDA compilation and execution workflow, the nvcc compiler plays a pivotal role, orchestrating the compilation of both host and device code, and ensuring they work seamlessly together. Understanding and correctly handling the commands and options provided by nvcc is essential for efficient and error-free compilation of CUDA programs.

3.7 CUDA Error Handling

Error handling in CUDA programming is critical for ensuring the reliability and stability of applications. Unlike traditional sequential programming languages, CUDA requires error handling mechanisms that account for the parallel nature of its execution environment. Effective error handling helps in diagnosing issues early, minimizing debugging time, and promoting efficient use of GPU resources. This section focuses on the types of errors that may occur in CUDA programs and the techniques available to handle them efficiently.

CUDA uses a range of error codes and functions to detect and manage errors. These error codes correspond to different types of problems that may arise during the execution of CUDA programs, such as memory access violations, misconfigurations of kernel launches, and issues with device compatibility. The primary method for retrieving the last error that occurred is through the function cudaGetLastError().

The following example demonstrates the use of cudaGetLastError() in a simple CUDA program:

```
#include <stdio.h>
#include <cuda_runtime.h>
```

```
__global__ void kernelFunc() {
    // Intentional error: accessing invalid memory
    int *p = NULL;
    *p = 10;
}

int main() {
    kernelFunc<<<1, 1>>>();

    cudaError_t err = cudaGetLastError();
    if (err != cudaSuccess) {
        printf("CUDA error: %s\n", cudaGetErrorString(err));
    }

    return 0;
}
```

In this example, the kernelFunc() makes an illegal memory access by dereferencing a NULL pointer. After the kernel execution, cudaGetLastError() is called to retrieve the last error that occurred. If an error is detected, the program prints out a descriptive error string obtained from cudaGetErrorString(err).

CUDA provides two major error-checking approaches: explicit error checking and implicit error checking. Explicit error checking involves manually querying error status after each CUDA API call or kernel launch by using functions like cudaGetLastError() or cudaPeekAtLastError(). Implicit error checking incorporates error-checking mechanisms directly within the program flow, often leveraging macros for brevity and readability.

To implement explicit error checking at various stages of a program, each CUDA API call or kernel launch can be followed directly by an error check:

```
cudaMalloc((void**)&d_a, size);
cudaError_t err = cudaGetLastError();
if (err != cudaSuccess) {
    printf("CUDA error: %s\n", cudaGetErrorString(err));
    // Handle error (e.g., cleanup and abort)
}
// Continue with program
```

Explicit error checking is comprehensive, but it can clutter the codebase with multiple repeated checks. Implicit error checking can help streamline this process using a macro, simplifying the program logic:

```
#define CUDA_CALL(func) \
    { \
        cudaError_t err = (func); \
        if (err != cudaSuccess) { \
            printf("CUDA error at %s:%d: %s\n", __FILE__, __LINE__, \
                    cudaGetErrorString(err)); \
```

```
            exit(EXIT_FAILURE); \
        } \
    }

int main() {
    int* d_a;
    size_t size = 1024;

    CUDA_CALL(cudaMalloc((void**)&d_a, size));

    kernelFunc<<<1, 1>>>();
    CUDA_CALL(cudaGetLastError());

    return 0;
}
```

The macro CUDA_CALL encapsulates the error checking, making the core code more readable and maintaining a consistent error-handling strategy. This approach enables a cleaner and more maintainable codebase, especially in large projects.

CUDA also defines synchronous and asynchronous error handling. Synchronous errors occur immediately during the API call and are detected right away. Asynchronous errors may arise from concurrent operations, like kernel executions, and their detection is deferred until an explicit synchronization point, such as cudaDeviceSynchronize(), cudaMemcpy(), or cudaStreamSynchronize().

Consider the following program to highlight asynchronous error checking:

```
__global__ void faultyKernel(int* data) {
    int idx = threadIdx.x;
    if (idx == 0) data = NULL;
    data[idx] = 10;
}

int main() {
    int *d_data;
    size_t size = 256 * sizeof(int);

    cudaError_t err = cudaMalloc((void**)&d_data, size);
    if (err != cudaSuccess) {
        printf("CUDA error: %s\n", cudaGetErrorString(err));
    }

    faultyKernel<<<1, 256>>>(d_data);
    cudaDeviceSynchronize(); // Ensure kernel execution completes

    err = cudaGetLastError();
    if (err != cudaSuccess) {
        printf("CUDA error after kernel execution: %s\n", cudaGetErrorString(err));
    }

    cudaFree(d_data);
    return 0;
}
```

In this code, faultyKernel writes to NULL for the first thread. Since the kernel executes asynchronously, cudaDeviceSynchronize() ensures the program waits for the kernel to complete before checking for errors using cudaGetLastError().

Handling errors correctly in a CUDA application involves combining techniques to detect issues both synchronously and asynchronously, ensuring the program can report and manage problems effectively. By implementing rigorous error checking practices, developers can enhance the robustness and reliability of CUDA-based applications.

3.8 CUDA API Basics

The CUDA Application Programming Interface (API) provides a foundation for developing parallel applications in C or C++ by extending these languages with minimal syntax additions. In this section, we will cover key elements of the CUDA API, focusing on essential concepts that form the basis of CUDA programming.

1. Basic CUDA API Components

The CUDA API is divided into several main components that interact to enable efficient parallel computing on NVIDIA GPUs. These components include:

- **Execution Configuration:** Specifies the organization of threads and thread blocks for a kernel launch.
- **Kernel Functions:** Special functions that execute on the GPU.
- **Memory Management:** Functions for managing different types of memory in CUDA.
- **Error Handling:** Mechanisms for handling and reporting errors arising during CUDA execution.

2. Execution Configuration Syntax

The execution configuration defines how kernel functions are called. It specifies the thread hierarchy for a kernel launch, consisting of a grid of thread blocks. The syntax for launching a kernel is as follows:

```
kernel_function<<<gridDim, blockDim>>>(arguments);
```

Here, gridDim and blockDim are instances of the dim3 type that define the dimensions of the grid and blocks, respectively. For example:

```
dim3 gridSize(16, 16);
dim3 blockSize(16, 16);
kernel_function<<<gridSize, blockSize>>>(arguments);
```

This configuration specifies a grid of 16×16 thread blocks, where each block contains 16×16 threads.

3. Kernel Functions

Kernel functions are declared using the __global__ qualifier and can only be called from the host (CPU). An example of a simple kernel function is given below:

```
__global__ void addVectors(float* A, float* B, float* C, int N) {
    int idx = threadIdx.x + blockDim.x * blockIdx.x;
    if (idx < N) {
        C[idx] = A[idx] + B[idx];
    }
}
```

In this function, each thread calculates the index idx and performs vector addition for the elements at that index.

4. Memory Management

CUDA provides various types of memory, such as global, shared, and constant memory. Efficient memory management is crucial for achieving high performance in CUDA applications. Some of the fundamental memory management functions are:

- cudaMalloc: Allocates memory on the device.

  ```
  cudaMalloc((void**)&devicePtr, size);
  ```

- cudaFree: Frees previously allocated device memory.

  ```
  cudaFree(devicePtr);
  ```

- cudaMemcpy: Copies data between host and device memory.

  ```
  cudaMemcpy(devicePtr, hostPtr, size, cudaMemcpyHostToDevice);
  cudaMemcpy(hostPtr, devicePtr, size, cudaMemcpyDeviceToHost);
  ```

5. Error Handling

CUDA provides a robust mechanism for error handling. After calling a CUDA function, the developer can check for errors using the cudaGetLastError function:

```
cudaError_t err = cudaGetLastError();
if (err != cudaSuccess) {
    printf("CUDA Error: %s\n", cudaGetErrorString(err));
}
```

This way, any errors that occur during the execution of CUDA functions can be identified and appropriate actions can be taken.

6. Synchronization

Synchronization ensures that all threads within a block have completed executing before allowing further progress. The intrinsic function __syncthreads is used for this purpose:

```
__syncthreads();
```

__syncthreads is useful in scenarios where threads within a block must collaborate and share data through shared memory.

The CUDA API is a powerful tool that provides extensive control over parallel execution on NVIDIA GPUs. By mastering its various components, developers can fully harness the computational power of these devices for a wide array of applications.

3.9 Using CUDA Libraries

CUDA libraries provide an extensive set of APIs designed to simplify and optimize the development of parallel applications on NVIDIA GPUs. Seasoned developers leverage these libraries to achieve significant performance improvements and write less code by reusing extensively optimized kernels. This section delves into the essential libraries available in the CUDA ecosystem, their functionalities, and how to integrate them into your applications efficiently.

cuBLAS (CUDA Basic Linear Algebra Subroutines) is a GPU-accelerated library for dense linear algebra. It provides highly optimized routines for matrix and vector operations, echoing the functionality of the legacy BLAS library. Below is an example of how to multiply two matrices using cuBLAS:

```
#include <stdio.h>
#include <cublas_v2.h>

int main() {
    cublasHandle_t handle;
    cublasCreate(&handle);
```

```
    // Allocating memory and initializing matrices A, B, and C
    float *A, *B, *C;
    // Assume matrices are already allocated and initialized

    const float alpha = 1.0f;
    const float beta = 0.0f;

    cublasSgemm(handle, CUBLAS_OP_N, CUBLAS_OP_N,
                M, N, K,
                &alpha,
                A, M,
                B, K,
                &beta,
                C, M);

    // Cleanup
    cublasDestroy(handle);
    return 0;
}
```

In this example, cublasSgemm performs the matrix multiplication $C = \alpha \times A \times B + \beta \times C$. Here, M, N, and K denote the dimensions of the matrices, and alpha and beta are scaling factors.

cuFFT is another significant library tailored for signal processing, particularly Fast Fourier Transforms (FFT). cuFFT accelerates the computation of FFTs, enabling real-time signal processing applications. Here's an example illustrating how to compute the FFT of a complex signal using cuFFT:

```
#include <stdio.h>
#include <cufft.h>

int main() {
    cufftHandle plan;
    cuComplex *data;

    // Assume 'data' is a complex array allocated and initialized

    cufftPlan1d(&plan, N, CUFFT_C2C, 1);
    cufftExecC2C(plan, data, data, CUFFT_FORWARD);

    // Cleanup
    cufftDestroy(plan);
    return 0;
}
```

The command cufftPlan1d creates a 1D FFT plan for an array of length N. This plan specifies the configuration for the FFT computation. cufftExecC2C executes the FFT in the forward direction, transforming the data in place.

cuRAND is the CUDA library dedicated to random number generation. It provides a suite of functions for generating high-quality pseudo-random and quasi-random numbers. Below is a simple example of generating uniformly distributed numbers using cuRAND:

```
#include <stdio.h>
#include <curand.h>

int main() {
    curandGenerator_t gen;
    float *devData;

    // Assume 'devData' is an array of floats allocated on the device

    curandCreateGenerator(&gen, CURAND_RNG_PSEUDO_DEFAULT);
    curandSetPseudoRandomGeneratorSeed(gen, 1234ULL);
    curandGenerateUniform(gen, devData, 1000);

    // Cleanup
    curandDestroyGenerator(gen);
    return 0;
}
```

In this snippet, curandCreateGenerator initializes a new random number generator, and curandSetPseudoRandomGeneratorSeed seeds it with 1234ULL. curandGenerateUniform fills the device array devData with 1000 uniformly distributed floats.

cuSPARSE offers routines for handling sparse matrices effectively. When working with sparse matrices, cuSPARSE ensures that memory usage is minimized while maintaining high computational speed. Here's how to perform a sparse matrix-vector multiplication:

```
#include <stdio.h>
#include <cusparse.h>

int main() {
    cusparseHandle_t handle;
    cusparseCreate(&handle);

    // Assume 'csrVal', 'csrRowPtr', 'csrColInd' are properly allocated and initialized
    // Assume 'x' and 'y' are vectors

    const float alpha = 1.0f;
    const float beta = 0.0f;

    cusparseScsrmv(handle, CUSPARSE_OPERATION_NON_TRANSPOSE,
                   rows, cols, nnz, &alpha,
                   desc, csrVal, csrRowPtr, csrColInd,
                   x, &beta, y);

    // Cleanup
    cusparseDestroy(handle);
    return 0;
}
```

Here, cusparseScsrmv multiplies the sparse matrix, represented in CSR format by csrVal, csrRowPtr, csrColInd, with a dense vector x and stores the result in y. nnz denotes the number of non-zero elements in the sparse matrix.

These examples illustrate the power and convenience of CUDA libraries in accelerating complex computations on GPUs. Utilizing these libraries can lead to significant performance gains with minimal code changes, enabling developers to focus on higher-level algorithmic design rather than low-level memory and thread management.

3.10 Practical Example: Vector Addition

Vector addition is a foundational operation in parallel computing and serves as an excellent starting point for getting hands-on experience with CUDA programming. This section will guide you through implementing and understanding vector addition using CUDA in C.

In this example, we will add two vectors A and B (each of size N) to produce a resultant vector C, where each element $C_i = A_i + B_i$. Below is a step-by-step explanation followed by the corresponding code.

The first step involves defining the kernel function. A CUDA kernel is a function that runs on the GPU and is called from the host (CPU) code. Let's define the kernel for vector addition:

```
// Kernel function to add the elements of two arrays
__global__
void vectorAdd(const float *A, const float *B, float *C, int N) {
    int i = blockDim.x * blockIdx.x + threadIdx.x;
    if (i < N) {
        C[i] = A[i] + B[i];
    }
}
```

Here, the keyword __global__ specifies that vectorAdd is a kernel function. The function parameters include pointers to the input vectors A and B, the output vector C, and the size of the vectors N. Each thread in the grid computes a single element of the output vector. The index i is calculated using the block and thread indices.

Next, we'll write the host code to manage memory and launch the kernel. This includes allocating memory on the GPU, copying data from the host to the device, launching the kernel, copying the results back to the host, and freeing the allocated memory. Below is the complete host code for vector addition:

```
#include <cuda.h>
#include <stdio.h>
```

```
// Check for CUDA errors
#define CUDA_CHECK_RETURN(value) { \
    cudaError_t _m_cudaStat = value; \
    if (_m_cudaStat != cudaSuccess) { \
        fprintf(stderr, "Error %s at line %d in file %s\n", \
            cudaGetErrorString(_m_cudaStat), __LINE__, __FILE__); \
        exit(1); \
    } }

int main(void) {
    int N = 1<<20; // 1M elements

    size_t size = N * sizeof(float);

    // Allocate input vectors h_A and h_B in host memory
    float *h_A = (float *)malloc(size);
    float *h_B = (float *)malloc(size);
    float *h_C = (float *)malloc(size);

    // Initialize input vectors
    for (int i = 0; i < N; i++) {
        h_A[i] = 1.0f;
        h_B[i] = 2.0f;
    }

    // Allocate vectors in device memory
    float *d_A, *d_B, *d_C;
    CUDA_CHECK_RETURN(cudaMalloc((void **)&d_A, size));
    CUDA_CHECK_RETURN(cudaMalloc((void **)&d_B, size));
    CUDA_CHECK_RETURN(cudaMalloc((void **)&d_C, size));

    // Copy vectors from host memory to device memory
    CUDA_CHECK_RETURN(cudaMemcpy(d_A, h_A, size,
        cudaMemcpyHostToDevice));
    CUDA_CHECK_RETURN(cudaMemcpy(d_B, h_B, size,
        cudaMemcpyHostToDevice));

    // Invoke kernel with N threads
    int threadsPerBlock = 256;
    int blocksPerGrid = (N + threadsPerBlock - 1) / threadsPerBlock;
    vectorAdd<<<blocksPerGrid, threadsPerBlock>>>(d_A, d_B, d_C, N);

    // Check for any errors launching the kernel
    CUDA_CHECK_RETURN(cudaGetLastError());

    // Copy result from device memory to host memory
    CUDA_CHECK_RETURN(cudaMemcpy(h_C, d_C, size,
        cudaMemcpyDeviceToHost));

    // Verify result
    for (int i = 0; i < N; i++) {
        if (fabs(h_C[i] - (h_A[i] + h_B[i])) > 1e-5) {
            fprintf(stderr, "Result verification failed at element %d!\n", i);
            exit(1);
        }
    }
    printf("Test PASSED\n");

    // Free device memory
    CUDA_CHECK_RETURN(cudaFree(d_A));
    CUDA_CHECK_RETURN(cudaFree(d_B));
    CUDA_CHECK_RETURN(cudaFree(d_C));
```

```
    // Free host memory
    free(h_A);
    free(h_B);
    free(h_C);

    return 0;
}
```

The host code proceeds as follows: 1. **Memory Allocation**: Allocate memory for vectors h_A, h_B, and h_C on the host using malloc. Allocate corresponding vectors d_A, d_B, and d_C on the device using cudaMalloc. 2. **Initialization**: Initialize the input vectors h_A and h_B on the host. 3. **Memory Copy**: Copy the initialized vectors from the host to the device using cudaMemcpy. 4. **Kernel Launch**: Define the execution configuration by specifying the number of blocks and threads per block. Then, launch the kernel. 5. **Error Checking**: Ensure the kernel launch was successful by checking for errors. 6. **Result Copy**: Copy the resultant vector d_C from the device to the host. 7. **Verification**: Verify the results to ensure the operation was performed correctly. This includes checking if each element in the resultant vector equals the sum of the corresponding elements from the input vectors. 8. **Memory Deallocation**: Free the allocated memory on both the device and the host to avoid memory leaks.

This complete example demonstrates essential CUDA programming concepts from kernel definition to execution.

Chapter 4

Memory Management in CUDA

This chapter delves into the intricacies of memory management in CUDA, starting with an overview of the memory hierarchy and the roles of global, shared, constant, and texture memory. It covers memory allocation and deallocation, as well as memory copy operations. Key topics include memory access patterns and memory coalescing, essential for optimizing GPU performance. The chapter concludes with guidance on optimized memory usage and an introduction to unified memory in CUDA.

4.1 Overview of Memory Hierarchy in CUDA

Understanding the memory hierarchy in CUDA is essential for effectively leveraging the computational power of NVIDIA GPUs. CUDA (Compute Unified Device Architecture) provides a rich memory model that allows developers to exploit various types of memory, each with its own scope, lifetime, and performance characteristics. The memory hierarchy in CUDA consists of several levels: global memory, shared memory, constant memory, texture memory, registers, and local memory.

Global Memory is the largest memory space available on the GPU, typically amounting to several gigabytes. It is accessible by all threads and provides a unified address space across the entire GPU. Despite its large size, global memory has high latency and lower bandwidth compared to other types of memory. As such, it is crucial to optimize access patterns to achieve memory coalescing and minimize costly access delays. Allocation and deallocation of global memory are handled using CUDA runtime functions such as cudaMalloc and cudaFree.

Shared Memory is partitioned per block and is a low-latency memory space shared among threads within the same block. Each streaming multiprocessor (SM) hosts a fixed amount of shared memory, which can be used to facilitate fast data exchange and synchronization among threads. This memory is especially valuable for implementing algorithms that require frequent inter-thread communication. However, shared memory is limited in size, and its efficient use is critical for maximizing performance. Shared memory allocation is specified during kernel launch, and its usage is governed by the __shared__ keyword.

Constant Memory is a read-only memory space accessible by all threads, designed for storing data that does not change throughout the kernel execution. It supports low-latency access when all threads in a warp read the same location, thanks to the underlying caching mechanism. Constant memory is allocated and initialized using cudaMemcpyToSymbol and declared via the __constant__ keyword. Its small size (typically 64KB) limits its use to storing small but frequently accessed constants.

Texture Memory is another read-only memory, optimized for spatial locality and benefiting from a special texture cache. It is ideal for applications involving image processing and other tasks requiring random access patterns. Texture memory is accessed through texture references and is beneficial for algorithms that can exploit its caching and filtering capabilities.

Registers are the fastest and smallest memory space, assigned to individual threads. They store per-thread variables and are directly managed by the CUDA compiler. The number of registers per SM is limited, and exceeding this limit can result in register spilling, where excess variables are stored in slower local memory. Efficient register usage is key for achieving high performance, as registers enable rapid access to frequently used data.

Local Memory refers to memory local to each thread but stored in the global memory space. It is used for variables that exceed register storage capacity or are dynamically indexed. Despite its name, local memory incurs the same high latency as global memory; thus, its usage should be minimized where possible.

CUDA's memory hierarchy also includes various caches, such as the **L1 and L2 caches**, which serve to reduce access latencies to global and local memory. These caches can dynamically store frequently accessed data, improving memory throughput. The L1 cache is shared by all threads within an SM, while the L2 cache is shared across the entire GPU. Understanding cache behavior is crucial for optimizing memory access patterns.

The effective use of CUDA's memory hierarchy involves balancing the trade-offs between size, latency, and bandwidth. Developers must consider these aspects to optimize data placement and access strategies, ensuring maximal utilization of the GPU's computational resources. Proper memory management can significantly impact the performance of CUDA applications, making it a cornerstone of high-performance parallel computing on GPUs.

4.2 Global Memory

Global memory in CUDA, often referred to as device memory, is the most abundant yet the slowest memory accessible by all threads across the entire grid. Each CUDA-enabled GPU contains several gigabytes of global memory, which is used to store large datasets and arrays. Understanding how to effectively manage and access global memory is crucial for optimizing CUDA programs.

Global memory is allocated and deallocated similarly to how memory is managed in traditional C programming, using functions such as cudaMalloc and cudaFree. However, the performance implications of global memory access in a massively parallel environment necessitate a diligent approach.

Allocation and Deallocation: To allocate memory on the GPU, the cudaMalloc function is used. This function allocates memory of the specified size, returning a pointer to the allocated space. Its usage is akin to the malloc function in standard C.

```
int *d_array;
cudaMalloc((void**)&d_array, size * sizeof(int));
```

The above code allocates space for an array of integers on the device. The pointer d_array is used to reference this memory in subsequent CUDA kernel calls.

Deallocating global memory involves the cudaFree function, which releases the memory space previously allocated by cudaMalloc.

```
cudaFree(d_array);
```

Proper memory deallocation is essential to avoid memory leaks and ensure the efficient usage of GPU resources.

Data Transfer Between Host and Device: Data in global memory is not directly accessible by the host (CPU); it must be transferred between host and device memory explicitly. The cudaMemcpy function facilitates this data transfer. Its parameters include source pointer, destination pointer, size of data to transfer, and the direction of transfer (e.g., cudaMemcpyHostToDevice or cudaMemcpyDeviceToHost).

```
cudaMemcpy(d_array, h_array, size * sizeof(int), cudaMemcpyHostToDevice);
```

In this example, data is copied from the host array h_array to the device array d_array. To transfer data back from the device to the host, the direction flag would be switched to cudaMemcpyDeviceToHost.

Access Characteristics and Performance: Global memory access characteristics are a pivotal aspect of performance optimization. Global memory has higher latency compared to other memory types like shared or constant memory. Therefore, minimizing global memory access latency is essential for achieving optimal performance.

One effective strategy for minimizing access latency is through memory coalescing, where consecutive threads (within a warp) access consecutive memory locations in global memory. To achieve this, ensure that memory accesses are aligned and within a small contiguous block, typically a multiple of 32 bytes, as typical warp size in NVIDIA GPUs is 32 threads. Properly coalesced memory accesses can significantly reduce the overall memory access time compared to non-coalesced accesses.

```
int idx = threadIdx.x + blockIdx.x * blockDim.x;
d_array[idx] = d_array[idx] * 2;
```

The above kernel ensures that each thread accesses a unique, contiguous position in the device array d_array, resulting in coalesced memory access.

Handling Memory Access Patterns: Understanding memory access patterns is critical for enhancing the performance of global memory operations. Strided or random access patterns can lead to significant performance degradation. Strided access occurs when threads access memory locations that are spaced apart from each other by a fixed interval. This can lead to non-coalesced access, increasing memory transaction count.

```
int idx = threadIdx.x + blockIdx.x * blockDim.x;
d_array[2 * idx] = d_array[2 * idx] * 2; // Example of strided access
```

In the above kernel, threads access every other element in the array, resulting in inefficient, non-coalesced memory access. It's advisable to restructure data and access patterns to maintain contiguity and alignments conducive to optimal memory access.

Optimization through Caching: The architecture of modern NVIDIA GPUs includes an L2 cache, which can store frequently accessed global data, potentially reducing access time for data residing in global memory. While this caching is handled automatically by the hardware, programmers can strategically design data structures and access patterns to maximize cache efficiency.

Assigning commonly accessed data to variables in registers or shared memory is another effective optimization technique. Registers offer the fastest storage with per-thread scope, while shared memory offers high-speed, low-latency access with a broader scope shared among threads in a block.

Global memory management in CUDA programming is a fundamental skill that requires an understanding of hardware behavior, memory hierarchy, and optimal access patterns. Proficient handling of global memory, paired with mindful allocation, deallocation, and access strategies, significantly contributes to the performance and efficiency of CUDA applications.

4.3 Shared Memory

Shared memory in CUDA is a special type of memory that resides on-chip and is shared among threads within the same block. This memory provides low-latency, high-bandwidth access compared to global memory, making it a crucial feature for achieving optimal performance in CUDA applications. Understanding the proper usage and management of shared memory is essential for CUDA programmers to leverage its full potential.

Within a block, threads can share data through shared memory without the need for costly memory transactions to global memory. Each block has access to its own distinct shared memory, and the size of shared memory per block is limited, typically on the order of 48 KB per block, though this can vary depending on the hardware generation and configuration.

To illustrate the importance and utility of shared memory, let us consider the matrix multiplication example. When multiplying two matrices, efficient use of shared memory can significantly reduce the number of global memory accesses, thereby improving performance.

Below is an example of matrix multiplication using shared memory in CUDA:

```
__global__ void matrixMulCUDA(float *C, float *A, float *B, int width) {
    // Allocate shared memory
    __shared__ float As[BLOCK_SIZE][BLOCK_SIZE];
    __shared__ float Bs[BLOCK_SIZE][BLOCK_SIZE];

    int bx = blockIdx.x;
    int by = blockIdx.y;
    int tx = threadIdx.x;
    int ty = threadIdx.y;

    // Calculate the row index of the P element and M matrix
    int Row = by * BLOCK_SIZE + ty;
    // Calculate the column index of P and N matrix
    int Col = bx * BLOCK_SIZE + tx;

    float Cvalue = 0.0;

    // Loop over the A and B matrices to multiply them
    for (int m = 0; m < width / BLOCK_SIZE; ++m) {
        // Load elements into shared memory
        As[ty][tx] = A[Row * width + (m * BLOCK_SIZE + tx)];
        Bs[ty][tx] = B[(m * BLOCK_SIZE + ty) * width + Col];

        // Synchronize to ensure all threads have loaded their data
        __syncthreads();

        // Perform partial multiplication
        for (int k = 0; k < BLOCK_SIZE; ++k) {
            Cvalue += As[ty][k] * Bs[k][tx];
        }

        // Synchronize again to ensure partial results are updated before loading new
            values
        __syncthreads();
    }

    // Write the result to the output matrix
    C[Row * width + Col] = Cvalue;
}
```

In this example, the use of shared memory is demonstrated with two matrices, ‘As‘ and ‘Bs‘, each mapped to blocks of the input matrices ‘A‘ and ‘B‘, respectively. Each thread within a block loads a single element from global memory into shared memory. After synchronization with '__syncthreads()', which ensures all threads within the block have completed their respective memory loads, the threads collaboratively compute partial products. This process is repeated for each tile of the matrices, and final results are stored back into global memory.

The benefits of using shared memory include:

- Reduced Global Memory Access: By loading data into shared memory once per block and reusing it, the number of global memory accesses is significantly reduced.
- Increased Memory Throughput: Shared memory offers higher bandwidth compared to global memory, leading to faster data access and execution.
- Efficient Synchronization: Threads within a block can efficiently synchronize their work using shared memory.

It is important to note some key considerations when working with shared memory:

- Bank Conflicts: Shared memory is divided into banks, and accessing memory addresses that correspond to the same bank can cause serialization of accesses. To avoid bank conflicts, ensure that threads access diverse memory banks whenever possible.
- Memory Allocation: The amount of shared memory available per block is limited, and excessive usage can affect the number of concurrent blocks that fit into a streaming multiprocessor (SM). This is managed via the '__shared__' specifier and can be dynamically configured using the 'cudaFuncSetAttribute' API.
- Lifetime and Scope: Shared memory is only valid for the duration of the block's execution and is scoped to the block itself. Data in shared memory is not persistent beyond the end of the block's execution.

To visualize the impact of bank conflicts, consider an example with sequential and strided access patterns:

```
__global__ void sequentialAccessPattern(float *input, float *output) {
    __shared__ float sharedData[256];
    int tid = threadIdx.x;
    sharedData[tid] = input[tid];
```

```
    __syncthreads();

    output[tid] = sharedData[tid];
}

__global__ void stridedAccessPattern(float *input, float *output) {
    __shared__ float sharedData[256];
    int tid = threadIdx.x;
    sharedData[tid * 4] = input[tid * 4];
    __syncthreads();

    output[tid * 4] = sharedData[tid * 4];
}
```

In the 'sequentialAccessPattern' kernel, threads access shared memory sequentially, which generally avoids bank conflicts if the data size and number of threads are aligned with the memory bank structure. In contrast, the 'stridedAccessPattern' kernel specifies a stride factor of 4, potentially introducing bank conflicts if multiple threads attempt to access the same memory bank simultaneously. To mitigate this, appropriate padding and memory access patterns should be employed.

The efficient utilization of shared memory can substantially improve CUDA application performance by maximizing memory throughput and minimizing latency. By carefully designing memory access patterns and managing shared memory allocation, one can achieve significant speed-ups in parallel computations.

4.4 Constant and Texture Memory

Constant and texture memory in CUDA offer specialized types of memory that optimize certain types of data access patterns, particularly for specific classes of applications. Both types of memory are read-only caches designed to enhance data locality and improve performance for operations that involve frequent data retrieval.

Constant Memory is an area of memory that remains unchanged throughout the execution of a kernel. Its principal advantage is that all threads read the same data, which allows it to be efficiently cached. Constant memory is beneficial for data that is read frequently but rarely modified. This memory type is particularly efficient when all or the majority of threads access the same element of constant memory simultaneously, exploiting the broadcast capability of the constant cache.

To declare and initialize constant memory in CUDA, use the `__constant__` keyword. Below is an example:

```
__constant__ float constData[256];
```

The host can copy data to constant memory using the cudaMemcpyToSymbol function. For example:

```
float h_constData[256];
// Initialize h_constData...
cudaMemcpyToSymbol(constData, h_constData, sizeof(float) * 256);
```

The kernel can then access this data as follows:

```
__global__ void myKernel() {
    float value = constData[threadIdx.x]; // Reading from constant memory
}
```

Texture Memory, on the other hand, is designed to handle spatial locality in data access patterns. It includes hardware support for specific types of memory access that are common in graphics and image processing applications. Textures can be bound to linear memory or CUDA arrays, supporting a variety of data formats.

To use texture memory, declare a texture reference and bind it to a memory region:

```
texture<float, 1, cudaReadModeElementType> texRef;
```

Before invoking the kernel, bind the texture reference to some linear memory in the host code:

```
float* d_data;
cudaMalloc(&d_data, sizeof(float) * 256);
// Initialize d_data...
cudaBindTexture(NULL, texRef, d_data, sizeof(float) * 256);
```

In the kernel, you can access texture data using the tex1Dfetch function:

```
__global__ void myTextureKernel() {
    float value = tex1Dfetch(texRef, threadIdx.x);
}
```

Texture memory provides several advantages, including hardware-accelerated filtering, addressing, and optimized caching for 2D and 3D spatial locality. It is especially effective for applications like image processing, where data points from neighboring locations are often accessed together.

Both constant and texture memory have their respective use cases. Constant memory is ideal for cases where the same value will be read by many threads, benefiting from broadcast efficiency. Texture memory excels in scenarios involving spatial locality and the need for specific filtering and addressing capabilities.

Constraints associated with these types of memory impact their utility. Constant memory is limited to 64 KB, and poorly coalesced accesses can still lead to inefficient memory transactions. Texture memory, while highly efficient for certain access patterns, demands understanding of binding and management, which can introduce complexity into the development process.

In practice, leveraging constant and texture memory effectively can result in substantial performance improvements, particularly in applications with the appropriate access patterns. Understanding their distinct characteristics and specific API requirements is crucial for achieving optimal performance and efficient memory utilization.

4.5 Memory Allocation and Deallocation

Efficient memory management is a cornerstone of CUDA programming, as it directly impacts the performance of GPU-accelerated applications. This section addresses how to allocate and deallocate memory on the GPU, ensuring efficient communication between the host (CPU) and device (GPU).

Memory allocation in CUDA typically involves using functions from the CUDA runtime API. The primary functions for this purpose are:

- cudaMalloc
- cudaFree
- cudaMallocHost
- cudaMallocManaged

cudaMalloc is analogous to the standard C malloc function but operates on the GPU device memory. It allocates a specified size of linear memory on the device.

```
cudaError_t cudaMalloc(void **devPtr, size_t size);
```

Here, devPtr is a pointer to the allocated device memory, and size is the size of memory allocation in bytes. The function returns cudaSuccess if the allocation is successful.

Example usage of cudaMalloc:

```
#include <cuda_runtime.h>
#include <stdio.h>

int main() {
    int *dev_a;
    size_t size = 10 * sizeof(int);
    cudaError_t err = cudaMalloc((void**)&dev_a, size);

    if (err != cudaSuccess) {
        printf("cudaMalloc failed: %s\n", cudaGetErrorString(err));
        return -1;
    }

    // Use dev_a...

    cudaFree(dev_a);
    return 0;
}
```

To deallocate the memory allocated by cudaMalloc, we use cudaFree:

```
cudaError_t cudaFree(void *devPtr);
```

As seen in the example, devPtr is the pointer to the device memory to be freed. cudaFree ensures that memory no longer needed is returned to the heap, making it available for future allocations.

cudaMallocHost allocates page-locked (pinned) memory on the host, which is essential for efficient data transfer between host and device.

```
cudaError_t cudaMallocHost(void **ptr, size_t size);
```

Here, ptr is the pointer to the allocated host memory, and size is the size of the memory to allocate in bytes.

Example usage:

```
#include <cuda_runtime.h>
#include <stdio.h>

int main() {
    int *host_a;
    size_t size = 10 * sizeof(int);
    cudaError_t err = cudaMallocHost((void**)&host_a, size);

    if (err != cudaSuccess) {
        printf("cudaMallocHost failed: %s\n", cudaGetErrorString(err));
        return -1;
    }

    // Use host_a...

    cudaFreeHost(host_a);
    return 0;
}
```

Deallocation of page-locked host memory is handled by cudaFreeHost:

```
cudaError_t cudaFreeHost(void *ptr);
```

Unified memory, managed by CUDA through cudaMallocManaged, allows memory to be accessed by both the CPU and GPU without explicit data transfer calls.

```
cudaError_t cudaMallocManaged(void **devPtr, size_t size);
```

In this call, devPtr is the pointer to the allocated managed memory, and size specifies the allocation size in bytes.

Example usage of cudaMallocManaged:

```
#include <cuda_runtime.h>
#include <stdio.h>

int main() {
    int *unified_a;
    size_t size = 10 * sizeof(int);
    cudaError_t err = cudaMallocManaged((void**)&unified_a, size);

    if (err != cudaSuccess) {
        printf("cudaMallocManaged failed: %s\n", cudaGetErrorString(err));
        return -1;
    }

    // Use unified_a...

    cudaFree(unified_a);
    return 0;
}
```

In this context, cudaFree frees the managed memory allocated by cudaMallocManaged.

Understanding these functions is crucial for developing applications that efficiently utilize GPU resources. The subsequent step involves ensuring that allocated memory is coherently accessed and efficiently transferred between host and device, topics covered in upcoming sections.

4.6 Memory Copy Operations

Efficient memory management is critical for achieving high performance in CUDA programs. Memory copy operations allow the transfer of data between the host (CPU) and the device (GPU). Understanding how to perform these operations efficiently can lead to significant performance enhancements. This section will explore the mechanisms provided by CUDA for memory copy operations and the best practices for their use.

Host to Device and Device to Host Copies

The primary functions used for memory copy operations in CUDA are *cudaMemcpy* and its variants. These functions facilitate the copying of memory from host to device, device to host, and device to device.

The syntax for the basic *cudaMemcpy* function is as follows:

```
cudaError_t cudaMemcpy(void *dst, const void *src, size_t count, cudaMemcpyKind
    kind);
```

dst refers to the destination memory address, *src* to the source memory address, *count* specifies the number of bytes to copy, and *kind* indicates the direction of the copy operation. The *kind* parameter can take the following values:

- **cudaMemcpyHostToDevice**: Copies data from host memory to device memory.
- **cudaMemcpyDeviceToHost**: Copies data from device memory to host memory.
- **cudaMemcpyDeviceToDevice**: Copies data from one location in device memory to another.
- **cudaMemcpyHostToHost**: Copies data from one location in host memory to another.

Example: Host to Device Copy

Below is an example of copying data from host to device:

```
#include <cuda_runtime.h>
#include <stdio.h>

int main() {
    int N = 100;
    size_t size = N * sizeof(int);

    // Allocate host memory
    int *h_array = (int *)malloc(size);
    // Initialize host array
    for (int i = 0; i < N; ++i) {
        h_array[i] = i;
    }

    // Allocate device memory
    int *d_array;
```

```
    cudaMalloc((void **)&d_array, size);

    // Copy data from host to device
    cudaMemcpy(d_array, h_array, size, cudaMemcpyHostToDevice);

    // Free device memory
    cudaFree(d_array);

    // Free host memory
    free(h_array);

    return 0;
}
```

Asynchronous Memory Copy

For advanced applications, asynchronous memory copies can be performed using functions such as *cudaMemcpyAsync*. These functions allow overlapping of memory copy operations with kernel executions, which can lead to improved overall performance.

The syntax for *cudaMemcpyAsync* is:

```
cudaError_t cudaMemcpyAsync(void *dst, const void *src, size_t count,
    cudaMemcpyKind kind, cudaStream_t stream);
```

Example: Asynchronous Host to Device Copy

Below is an example of an asynchronous memory copy operation:

```
#include <cuda_runtime.h>
#include <stdio.h>

int main() {
    int N = 100;
    size_t size = N * sizeof(int);

    // Allocate host memory
    int *h_array = (int *)malloc(size);
    for (int i = 0; i < N; ++i) {
        h_array[i] = i;
    }

    // Allocate device memory
    int *d_array;
    cudaMalloc((void **)&d_array, size);

    // Create a stream
    cudaStream_t stream;
    cudaStreamCreate(&stream);

    // Copy data from host to device asynchronously
    cudaMemcpyAsync(d_array, h_array, size, cudaMemcpyHostToDevice, stream);

    // Synchronize the stream
    cudaStreamSynchronize(stream);

    // Destroy the stream
    cudaStreamDestroy(stream);
```

```
    // Free device memory
    cudaFree(d_array);

    // Free host memory
    free(h_array);

    return 0;
}
```

Pinned Memory

Using pinned (page-locked) memory for host allocations can significantly enhance the performance of memory copy operations. Pinned memory is allocated using *cudaHostAlloc* and is subject to different caching and paging policies, leading to faster data transfers.

```
cudaError_t cudaHostAlloc(void **pHost, size_t size, unsigned int flags);
```

Example: Utilizing Pinned Memory

Below is an example utilizing pinned memory to improve performance:

```
#include <cuda_runtime.h>
#include <stdio.h>

int main() {
    int N = 100;
    size_t size = N * sizeof(int);

    // Allocate pinned host memory
    int *h_array;
    cudaHostAlloc((void **)&h_array, size, cudaHostAllocDefault);

    for (int i = 0; i < N; ++i) {
        h_array[i] = i;
    }

    // Allocate device memory
    int *d_array;
    cudaMalloc((void **)&d_array, size);

    // Copy data from host to device
    cudaMemcpy(d_array, h_array, size, cudaMemcpyHostToDevice);

    // Free device memory
    cudaFree(d_array);

    // Free pinned host memory
    cudaFreeHost(h_array);

    return 0;
}
```

Efficient use of memory copy operations is a crucial aspect of developing high-performance CUDA applications. By carefully choosing between synchronous and asynchronous memory copies, leveraging streams, and utilizing pinned memory, programmers can significantly optimize data transfer times and enhance overall application performance.

4.7 Memory Access Patterns

Effective memory access patterns are critical to achieving high performance in CUDA programming. By understanding and optimizing these patterns, developers can fully exploit the parallelism offered by GPUs. In this section, we will discuss various memory access patterns and their impact on program performance.

A fundamental concept in CUDA is the execution of threads in groups called warps. A warp consists of 32 threads that execute instructions in a SIMD (Single Instruction, Multiple Data) fashion. When a warp accesses memory, all threads in the warp perform the access simultaneously. Thus, the pattern of these accesses significantly influences performance.

Coalesced vs Uncoalesced Accesses

Memory transactions in global memory are most efficient when threads access contiguous memory locations in a coalesced manner. Coalescing occurs when memory accesses by threads within a warp can be combined into as few transactions as possible. Uncoalesced accesses, on the other hand, result in more memory transactions and thus increased memory latency.

Consider the following example where we access an array in a coalesced manner:

```
__global__ void coalescedAccess(float *data) {
    int idx = threadIdx.x + blockDim.x * blockIdx.x;
    data[idx] = data[idx] + 1.0f;
}
```

In this example, all threads within a warp access contiguous elements of the array data, resulting in coalesced memory accesses. The memory controller can combine these accesses into a single transaction, thus improving performance.

Contrast this with uncoalesced access:

```
__global__ void uncoalescedAccess(float *data) {
    int idx = threadIdx.x + blockDim.x * blockIdx.x;
    data[idx * 2] = data[idx * 2] + 1.0f;
}
```

Here, each thread accesses non-contiguous memory locations (every other element), leading to uncoalesced accesses and hence, multiple memory transactions for a single warp. This pattern incurs higher latency and degraded performance.

Bank Conflicts in Shared Memory

Shared memory is an essential resource that provides low-latency, high-bandwidth memory access. However, performance can be degraded by bank conflicts. Shared memory is divided into banks, and each bank can service only one address per cycle. When multiple threads in a warp access different addresses within the same bank, a bank conflict occurs, serializing the accesses.

Consider an example of shared memory access:

```
__global__ void sharedMemoryAccess(float *data) {
    __shared__ float sdata[32];
    int idx = threadIdx.x;
    sdata[idx] = data[idx];
    __syncthreads();
    data[idx] = sdata[idx] + 1.0f;
}
```

If threads within a warp access contiguous elements in sdata, there are no bank conflicts. However, if the access pattern changes such that consecutive threads access elements that map to the same bank, conflicts arise:

```
__global__ void sharedMemoryBankConflict(float *data) {
    __shared__ float sdata[128];
    int idx = threadIdx.x;
    sdata[4 * idx] = data[4 * idx];
    __syncthreads();
    data[4 * idx] = sdata[4 * idx] + 1.0f;
}
```

Here, every fourth element is accessed by consecutive threads, potentially leading to bank conflicts and reduced performance.

Strided Access Patterns

Strided memory access patterns occur when threads access memory locations separated by a constant stride. Such access patterns can lead to inefficient memory utilization and degradation in performance. For instance, if each thread accesses an element with a stride greater than one, it can cause uncoalesced global memory accesses:

```
__global__ void stridedAccess(float *data, int stride) {
    int idx = threadIdx.x + blockDim.x * blockIdx.x;
    data[idx * stride] = data[idx * stride] + 1.0f;
}
```

If the stride is greater than one, this access pattern may result in a significant number of uncoalesced accesses, causing high memory latency.

To minimize the impact of strided access, one can adjust the algorithm to utilize shared memory more effectively or reorganize the data layout to enhance spatial locality and achieve more coalesced accesses.

Memory Alignment

Memory alignment plays a vital role in ensuring efficient data transfers and avoiding unnecessary overhead. CUDA's global memory operations are optimized for accesses to aligned memory addresses. Ensuring that data structures start at aligned addresses can help optimize memory transactions.

```
struct AlignedData {
    float x;
    float y;
    float z;
    float w;
} __align__(16);
```

The structure AlignedData is aligned to 16 bytes, making it suitable for efficient memory transactions. Misaligned accesses, on the other hand, can result in multiple transactions, hampering performance.

Prefetching and Cache Utilization

Modern GPUs leverage caching mechanisms for global memory. Effective utilization of these caches can significantly boost performance. Prefetching data that will be used in subsequent computations into shared memory or using the __ldg() intrinsic to take advantage of read-only data caches can help optimize memory bandwidth.

```
__global__ void cacheAccess(float *data) {
    int idx = threadIdx.x + blockDim.x * blockIdx.x;
    float value = __ldg(&data[idx]);
    data[idx] = value + 1.0f;
}
```

The __ldg() intrinsic allows loading data through the read-only cache, which can be particularly useful for data that does not change during kernel execution, optimizing cache utilization and memory bandwidth.

By understanding and applying these principles of memory access patterns, developers can craft CUDA programs that make efficient use of the GPU's memory hierarchy, leading to improved performance and scalability.

4.8 Memory Coalescing

Memory coalescing in CUDA is crucial for achieving high memory bandwidth and optimal performance. When threads in a warp access contiguous memory locations in a coordinated manner, the memory transactions are combined, or coalesced, reducing the number of memory transactions between the device memory and the GPU. This section focuses on the principles of memory coalescing, the different access patterns that affect coalescing, and specific strategies to optimize memory access.

Coalescing requirements have evolved through different generations of NVIDIA GPUs. For compute capability 1.x devices, strict requirements were necessary for access patterns to be coalesced, demanding contiguous memory addresses by consecutive threads in a half-warp. For compute capability 2.x and later, these requirements have been relaxed, allowing more flexibility and efficiency.

To illustrate the concept, consider the following example where each thread in a warp accesses a unique element in an array of integers:

```
__global__ void coalesced_example(int *d_array) {
    int idx = blockIdx.x * blockDim.x + threadIdx.x;
    d_array[idx] = d_array[idx] + 1;
}
```

In the above kernel, if blockDim.x is a multiple of the warp size (e.g., 32), and d_array is aligned in memory, the memory accesses by threads will be coalesced. Each thread in the warp accesses a consecutive memory location, and therefore, the memory transactions can be grouped together.

Non-coalesced memory accesses occur when threads in a warp access memory locations that are not contiguous or not properly aligned. This scenario is common in cases where threads access multi-dimensional arrays in row-major or column-major order, which may lead to inefficient memory transactions:

```
__global__ void non_coalesced_example(float *d_matrix, int num_cols) {
    int row = blockIdx.y * blockDim.y + threadIdx.y;
    int col = blockIdx.x * blockDim.x + threadIdx.x;
    int index = row * num_cols + col;
    d_matrix[index] = d_matrix[index] + 1.0f;
}
```

If num_cols is not a multiple of the warp size and threads access elements in a non-contiguous manner, memory coalescing will be suboptimal. Specifically, row-major access patterns can lead to non-coalesced access since each thread in a warp accesses different rows in the matrix.

To improve memory coalescing, consider using shared memory to reorder data access patterns or restructure data layouts. One approach is to transpose the matrix within shared memory so that data accessed by the warp is contiguous:

```
__global__ void coalesced_transpose(float *d_in, float *d_out, int num_rows, int
    num_cols) {
    __shared__ float tile[32][33]; // 32x32 tile

    int x = blockIdx.x * blockDim.x + threadIdx.x;
    int y = blockIdx.y * blockDim.y + threadIdx.y;

    // Load data into shared memory with a coalesced access pattern
    if (x < num_cols && y < num_rows) {
        int input_idx = y * num_cols + x;
        tile[threadIdx.y][threadIdx.x] = d_in[input_idx];
    }

    __syncthreads();

    // Write data from shared memory to global memory in a coalesced access pattern
    x = blockIdx.y * blockDim.y + threadIdx.x;
    y = blockIdx.x * blockDim.x + threadIdx.y;
    if (x < num_rows && y < num_cols) {
        int output_idx = y * num_rows + x;
        d_out[output_idx] = tile[threadIdx.x][threadIdx.y];
    }
}
```

In this kernel, the matrix is transposed within a shared memory tile. Memory accesses are coalesced when reading from d_in and writing to d_out because the threads in the warp access contiguous memory locations. The shared memory tile dimensions are chosen to be non-power-of-two to avoid bank conflicts.

Strategies to optimize memory coalescing include ensuring data is aligned to 128 bytes (the size of a memory transaction for single-precision floats), using sequential thread access patterns, and leveraging shared memory to re-arrange data layout.

Ensuring efficient memory coalescing significantly impacts the performance of CUDA applications. Utilizing the flexibility provided by the modern GPU architecture and employing techniques such as data alignment and shared memory usage can lead to substantial improvements in memory throughput and overall efficiency.

4.9 Optimizing Memory Usage

Optimizing memory usage in CUDA is pivotal for achieving efficient and high-performance GPU applications. Effective memory management involves not only judicious allocation and deallocation but also understanding and utilizing different types of memory to minimize latency and maximize throughput. This section will explore advanced strategies for optimizing memory usage by leveraging memory hierarchy, access patterns, and coalescing principles.

The CUDA memory hierarchy includes global, shared, constant, and texture memory. Each type of memory has unique characteristics and optimal usage scenarios. Proper management and utilization of these memory types can significantly enhance the performance of CUDA applications.

1. Minimize Global Memory Access: Global memory is relatively slow compared to other memory types. Hence, minimizing its usage is essential for performance improvement. One effective method is to use shared memory, which is significantly faster, as an intermediary buffer. Below is an example illustrating this concept.

```
// Kernel using global memory inefficiently
__global__ void globalMemoryKernel(float* input, float* output, int size) {
    int idx = blockIdx.x * blockDim.x + threadIdx.x;
    if (idx < size) {
        output[idx] = input[idx] * 2.0f;
    }
}

// Kernel optimized with shared memory
__global__ void sharedMemoryKernel(float* input, float* output, int size) {
    extern __shared__ float s_data[];
    int idx = blockIdx.x * blockDim.x + threadIdx.x;

    // Load data into shared memory
    if (idx < size) {
        s_data[threadIdx.x] = input[idx];
    }
    __syncthreads();

    // Perform computation using shared memory buffer
    if (idx < size) {
        output[idx] = s_data[threadIdx.x] * 2.0f;
    }
}
```

In the above example, the second kernel demonstrates how shared memory can be utilized to buffer data and reduce the number of slow global memory accesses.

2. Memory Coalescing: Memory coalescing is critical for efficient global memory access. When threads in a warp access consecutive memory addresses, the accesses can be coalesced into fewer transactions, resulting in improved performance.

```
// Non-coalesced access
__global__ void nonCoalescedKernel(float* data) {
    int idx = blockIdx.x * blockDim.x + threadIdx.x;
    data[idx * 2] = data[idx * 2] * 2.0f; // Non-sequential access pattern
}

// Coalesced access
__global__ void coalescedKernel(float* data) {
    int idx = blockIdx.x * blockDim.x + threadIdx.x;
    data[idx] = data[idx] * 2.0f; // Sequential access pattern
}
```

In the above kernels, nonCoalescedKernel accesses memory in a stride pattern, causing inefficient memory transactions. Conversely, coalescedKernel accesses memory sequentially, enabling coalesced transactions and reducing access latency.

3. Efficient Use of Shared Memory: Although shared memory can reduce global memory accesses, efficient usage is crucial. Shared memory is limited in size, and inappropriate use can lead to bank conflicts, decreasing performance. Proper indexing and avoiding conflicts are vital.

```
__global__ void bankConflictsKernel(float* input, float* output) {
    __shared__ float s_data[32];
    int tid = threadIdx.x;
    // This leads to bank conflicts
    s_data[tid] = input[tid * warpSize];
    __syncthreads();
    output[tid] = s_data[tid];
}

__global__ void noBankConflictsKernel(float* input, float* output) {
    __shared__ float s_data[32];
    int tid = threadIdx.x;
    // Avoid bank conflicts by proper indexing
    s_data[tid * warpSize + threadIdx.x] = input[tid];
    __syncthreads();
    output[tid] = s_data[tid];
}
```

bankConflictsKernel encounters bank conflicts due to the naive indexing strategy, whereas noBankConflictsKernel demonstrates a strategy that avoids such conflicts by offsetting indices.

4. Leveraging Constant and Texture Memory: Constant memory is cached and can speed up read-only data access when all threads read the same value. Texture memory provides caching and interpolation, beneficial for computations involving spatial locality.

```
__constant__ float constData[256];

__global__ void constantMemoryKernel(float* output, int size) {
    int idx = blockIdx.x * blockDim.x + threadIdx.x;
    if (idx < size) {
        output[idx] = constData[idx % 256] * 2.0f;
    }
}
```

5. Use of Unified Memory: Unified memory simplifies memory management by allowing a shared memory space accessible by both the CPU and GPU. While it simplifies development, transferring large datasets or frequent transfers can introduce latency. Performance developers can optimize by explicitly managing data locality.

```
#include <cuda_runtime.h>

__global__ void unifiedMemoryKernel(float* data, int size) {
    int idx = blockIdx.x * blockDim.x + threadIdx.x;
    if (idx < size) {
        data[idx] = data[idx] * 2.0f;
    }
}

int main() {
    float* data;
    int size = 1000;

    cudaMallocManaged(&data, size * sizeof(float));
    // Initialize data

    unifiedMemoryKernel<<<(size + 255) / 256, 256>>>(data, size);
    cudaDeviceSynchronize();

    // Use data on CPU

    cudaFree(data);
    return 0;
}
```

Effective memory usage in CUDA not only enhances performance but also influences the overall efficiency of the application. By minimizing global memory usage, employing efficient memory access patterns, leveraging the advantages of shared, constant, and texture memory, and using unified memory judiciously, developers can significantly optimize GPU programs. Understanding these principles and applying them correctly elevates the proficiency of CUDA programming.

4.10 Unified Memory in CUDA

Unified Memory in CUDA is a memory management system that provides a simple, higher-level abstraction for programmers to handle memory allocation and deallocation. It allows the CPU and GPU to access a common memory space without the need for explicit memory copy operations between host and device. This enhances ease of use and can reduce the complexity of memory management tasks traditionally associated with CUDA programming.

In CUDA, Unified Memory is achieved through the use of managed memory, which allows data to be automatically migrated between the host and device as needed. The CUDA runtime handles the underlying memory transfers, ensuring data coherency. This concept was introduced to alleviate the challenges of managing separate memory spaces, thereby improving programmer productivity and code maintainability.

To allocate Unified Memory, the cudaMallocManaged function is used. This function allocates managed memory that is accessible by both the CPU and GPU. Below is the syntax for this function:

```
cudaError_t cudaMallocManaged(void **devPtr, size_t size, unsigned int flags =
    cudaMemAttachGlobal);
```

Parameters:

- devPtr: Pointer to the allocated device memory.
- size: Size of the allocation in bytes.
- flags: Scope of visibility of the allocated memory (optional). By default, cudaMemAttachGlobal is used.

Example:

The following example demonstrates how to allocate Unified Memory using cudaMallocManaged and perform a simple vector addition on the GPU:

```
#include <cuda_runtime.h>
#include <iostream>

__global__ void vectorAdd(float *A, float *B, float *C, int N) {
    int idx = threadIdx.x + blockDim.x * blockIdx.x;
    if (idx < N) {
        C[idx] = A[idx] + B[idx];
    }
```

```
}

int main() {
    int N = 1<<20; // 1 million elements
    size_t size = N * sizeof(float);

    // Allocate Unified Memory
    float *A, *B, *C;
    cudaMallocManaged(&A, size);
    cudaMallocManaged(&B, size);
    cudaMallocManaged(&C, size);

    // Initialize vectors on the host
    for (int i = 0; i < N; ++i) {
        A[i] = static_cast<float>(i);
        B[i] = static_cast<float>(i);
    }

    // Define grid and block dimensions
    int threadsPerBlock = 256;
    int blocksPerGrid = (N + threadsPerBlock - 1) / threadsPerBlock;

    // Launch kernel
    vectorAdd<<<blocksPerGrid, threadsPerBlock>>>(A, B, C, N);
    cudaDeviceSynchronize();

    // Verify results
    for (int i = 0; i < N; ++i) {
        if (C[i] != A[i] + B[i]) {
            std::cerr << "Error at index " << i << std::endl;
            break;
        }
    }

    // Free memory
    cudaFree(A);
    cudaFree(B);
    cudaFree(C);

    return 0;
}
```

In this example, cudaMallocManaged is used to allocate managed memory for the vectors A, B, and C. This memory is then accessible by both the CPU and GPU. The kernel vectorAdd performs element-wise addition of the vectors on the GPU. After kernel execution, cudaDeviceSynchronize is called to ensure that all GPU operations are complete before the host accesses the results.

One significant advantage of Unified Memory is its ability to simplify memory management, especially in complex applications. However, it is important to consider potential performance implications. Since the CUDA runtime must manage data migration between the host and device, improper access patterns can lead to performance degradation due to frequent and costly memory transfers.

CUDA 6.0 introduced Unified Memory, and later versions have improved its performance and capabilities. CUDA 8.0 and above provide enhanced support for multi-GPU systems and improved data migration policies, providing more control to programmers over memory access patterns.

Additionally, from CUDA 9.0 onwards, the introduction of cudaMallocManaged with support for non-default flags allows for more nuanced control of memory visibility and migration. For instance:

```
// Allocate managed memory with device-specific visibility
cudaMallocManaged(&A, size, cudaMemAttachHost);
cudaMallocManaged(&B, size, cudaMemAttachGlobal);
```

In summary, Unified Memory simplifies CUDA programming by abstracting the details of managing separate memory spaces. While it offers significant ease of use, understanding its implications on performance is crucial. Developers should carefully assess the access patterns and ensure that memory transfers are minimized to maintain optimal performance.

Chapter 5

CUDA Thread Hierarchy and Execution Model

This chapter explores the thread hierarchy and execution model in CUDA, explaining the organization of threads, blocks, and grids. It covers thread indexing and mapping, the configuration of block and grid dimensions, and thread synchronization techniques using functions like __syncthreads(). The concepts of warp and warp divergence are discussed, along with the overall execution model in CUDA, including kernel launches. The chapter concludes with a practical example of matrix multiplication to illustrate these concepts.

5.1 Understanding Thread Hierarchy

In CUDA, the thread hierarchy is a critical concept that dictates how threads are organized and executed. Understanding this hierarchy is fundamental to effectively leveraging the computational power of GPUs for parallel processing. The thread hierarchy in CUDA is structured into three main components: threads, thread blocks, and grids.

Each component in the hierarchy serves a specific role in the execution model:

- **Threads**: These are the individual units of execution. Each thread executes a single instance of the kernel code. Threads are the basic parallel execution units and perform calculations independently.

- **Thread Blocks**: Threads are grouped into thread blocks. A thread block is a collection of concurrently executing threads that can cooperate by sharing data through shared memory and synchronizing their execution to coordinate memory accesses. The size of a thread block is defined by its dimensions, which can be one, two, or three-dimensional.

- **Grid**: Thread blocks are organized into a grid. A grid can be one, two, or three-dimensional, and it defines how blocks are distributed across the GPU for execution. Each block within a grid executes independently.

Threads: Each thread in CUDA has a unique identifier, which can be accessed using built-in variables. These identifiers are crucial for indexing the data each thread will process, ensuring that parallel tasks do not interfere with each other.

The built-in variables for a thread include:

- threadIdx.x, threadIdx.y, threadIdx.z: Represent the thread index within a block.

The combination of these indices allows multidimensional access patterns, which are particularly useful when dealing with data structures like matrices or multi-dimensional arrays.

Thread Blocks: Each thread block has a unique identifier within a grid, accessible using the built-in variable blockIdx. Thread blocks can also be multi-dimensional, and their dimensions are specified by blockDim.x, blockDim.y, and blockDim.z, respectively.

Here is an example illustrating how threads and thread blocks can be indexed within a kernel function:

```
__global__ void exampleKernel() {
    int tx = threadIdx.x; // Thread index within the block
    int ty = threadIdx.y; // Thread index within the block
    int bx = blockIdx.x; // Block index within the grid
    int by = blockIdx.y; // Block index within the grid
    int block_width = blockDim.x; // Width of a thread block
    int block_height = blockDim.y; // Height of a thread block

    int global_index_x = bx * block_width + tx; // Global index calculation
    int global_index_y = by * block_height + ty; // Global index calculation
}
```

Grids: The grid is the top-level structure that organizes thread blocks. Each grid can contain many thread blocks, and the total number of thread blocks is determined by the grid dimensions, accessible via gridDim.x, gridDim.y, and gridDim.z.

Consider the following complete example demonstrating a 2D grid of 2D blocks accessing a 2D data array:

```
__global__ void process2DGrid(float *data, int width, int height) {
    // Calculate thread's row and column within the entire grid
    int row = blockIdx.y * blockDim.y + threadIdx.y;
    int col = blockIdx.x * blockDim.x + threadIdx.x;

    if (row < height && col < width) {
        // Perform some operation on data[row * width + col]
        data[row * width + col] = ...
    }
}

int main() {
    int width = 1024; // Width of the 2D data array
    int height = 1024; // Height of the 2D data array
    float *d_data;

    // Allocate memory on the device
    cudaMalloc((void**)&d_data, width * height * sizeof(float));

    // Define grid and block dimensions
    dim3 threadsPerBlock(16, 16);
    dim3 numBlocks((width + threadsPerBlock.x - 1) / threadsPerBlock.x,
                   (height + threadsPerBlock.y - 1) / threadsPerBlock.y);

    // Launch kernel
    process2DGrid<<<numBlocks, threadsPerBlock>>>(d_data, width, height);

    // Free device memory
    cudaFree(d_data);

    return 0;
}
```

The thread hierarchy enables a structured approach to breaking down problems into smaller, parallelizable tasks. By dividing the problem space into grids of blocks and subsequently into threads, CUDA ensures that the GPU resources are used efficiently. This organization facilitates scalable parallelism, allowing CUDA applications to target a wide range of GPU architectures, from systems with a few cores to those with thousands.

5.2 Threads, Blocks, and Grids

In CUDA programming, understanding the organization of threads, blocks, and grids is fundamental. This hierarchical structure allows for scalable parallel execution on NVIDIA GPUs.

A **thread** in CUDA is the smallest unit of execution. Each thread executes a single instance of the kernel function. Threads are organized into **blocks**, which are groups of threads that can communicate and synchronize with one another through shared memory. Blocks are further organized into a **grid**, which represents the entire computational domain for a particular kernel launch.

Threads are lightweight processes managed by the GPU. They have their own register and local memory space. Threads within a block can communicate and synchronize using the __syncthreads() function to ensure data consistency.

Blocks are one-dimensional, two-dimensional, or three-dimensional arrays of threads. Each block has a unique identifier accessible within the kernel through the blockIdx.x, blockIdx.y, and blockIdx.z variables. The dimensions and size of blocks are specified during the kernel launch using the dim3 type for flexibility. Blocks within a grid can execute concurrently, but they do not have built-in synchronization mechanisms; therefore, reliance on atomic operations or multiple kernel launches is required for synchronization between blocks.

Grids are collections of blocks that define the overall computation to be carried out by the kernel. The grid can also be one, two, or three-dimensional. The size of the grid is specified at kernel launch using the dim3 type. Every block within the grid has a unique identifier, which can be extracted within the kernel using gridDim.x, gridDim.y, and gridDim.z variables to determine the grid's dimensions.

The following example demonstrates the declaration of a kernel and its subsequent launch with configurable block and grid dimensions:

```
__global__ void exampleKernel(float *data, int width) {
    int blockID = blockIdx.x + blockIdx.y * gridDim.x;
    int threadID = blockID * (blockDim.x * blockDim.y)
                   + threadIdx.y * blockDim.x + threadIdx.x;

    if (threadID < width) {
        data[threadID] = exampleOperation(threadID);
    }
}

int main(){
    dim3 blockDims(16, 16);
```

```
    dim3 gridDims((width + blockDims.x - 1) / blockDims.x,
                  (height + blockDims.y - 1) / blockDims.y);
    exampleKernel<<<gridDims, blockDims>>>(data, width);
    return 0;
}
```

In the above code snippet, the exampleKernel is launched with configurable block and grid dimensions. The block identifier (blockID) and thread identifier (threadID) within the grid and block are calculated to define unique indices for each thread to process the data.

Proper selection of block and grid dimensions is vital for maximizing GPU resource utilization. The optimal number of threads per block is usually a multiple of the warp size (32 threads), enabling efficient execution on the CUDA cores.

The constraint to bear in mind:

- The maximum number of threads per block varies depending on the GPU architecture but is typically 1024.

- Shared memory and register limits per block, influencing the occupancy of blocks on the multiprocessors.

When designing CUDA programs, the choice of block and grid dimensions should account for the problem size and the available GPU resources to achieve the highest performance. Experimentation and profiling tools like NVIDIA's Nsight Compute can assist in identifying the optimal configuration.

The design of the thread hierarchy has implications for memory access patterns and overall performance. Coalesced memory access can lead to significant performance gains. Ensuring threads within a warp access contiguous memory addresses enables more efficient memory transactions.

The reader should now understand the foundational aspects of CUDA's thread hierarchy: threads, blocks, and grids. Building upon this, subsequent sections will delve deeper into how to index and map threads, crucial for designing efficient CUDA kernels. Understanding the thread hierarchy is essential for exploiting the full potential of CUDA-enabled GPUs and achieving high-performance computing.

5.3 Thread Indexing and Mapping

In CUDA programming, efficient utilization of the GPU requires a thorough understanding of how threads are indexed and mapped. This understanding facilitates the development of algorithms that fully leverage the parallel processing capabilities of the GPU. Considerable attention should be paid to the layout of threads, blocks, and grids since they influence memory access patterns and computational efficiency.

Each thread is uniquely identified within its block. The CUDA runtime provides built-in variables that help in determining these unique identifiers. For a one-dimensional block of threads, the identifier of a thread within a block can be accessed using the threadIdx.x variable. When working with two or three-dimensional blocks, the threadIdx structure also includes .y and .z components.

For accessing the thread index, observe the following conventional example for a one-dimensional block:

```
int tid = threadIdx.x;
```

In a multi-dimensional configuration:

```
int tid_x = threadIdx.x;
int tid_y = threadIdx.y;
int tid_z = threadIdx.z;
```

These indices allow for precise control over the individual threads within a block. However, indexing does not stop at the block level. Blocks themselves are part of a larger grid, and identifying each block within the grid is crucial for complex parallel tasks. The grid index can be retrieved using the blockIdx variable, which, similar to threadIdx, includes .x, .y, and .z components for two and three-dimensional grids.

To compute an overall thread index across multiple blocks, consider both block and thread indices:

```
int unique_tid = blockIdx.x * blockDim.x + threadIdx.x;
```

In this equation, blockDim.x represents the number of threads per block, and multiplying it by the block index blockIdx.x gives the starting position of the block's threads within the grid. Adding threadIdx.x gives the final unique thread index.

Extending this to two and three-dimensional configurations:

```
int unique_tid_x = blockIdx.x * blockDim.x + threadIdx.x;
```

```
int unique_tid_y = blockIdx.y * blockDim.y + threadIdx.y;

int unique_tid = unique_tid_y * (gridDim.x * blockDim.x) + unique_tid_x;
```

Here, gridDim.x corresponds to the total number of blocks in the x dimension of the grid. This computation initializes the unique thread ID based on a flattened two-dimensional indexing scheme.

Understanding these indexing techniques is vital for mapping thread indices to data structures properly. Suppose a situation where each thread is responsible for processing one element of a linear array; the above indexing ensures each thread operates on a distinct array element.

```
__global__ void processArray(float *array, int N) {
    int tid = blockIdx.x * blockDim.x + threadIdx.x;
    if (tid < N) {
        array[tid] = array[tid] * 2.0f;
    }
}
```

This example kernel function doubles the values in an array. It first calculates the global thread index and ensures that the index is within bounds (i.e., tid < N). This prevents out-of-bounds memory access, which could lead to undefined behavior or crashes.

Moreover, thread indexing and mapping are critical when dealing with more complex data structures like matrices. Consider mapping threads to a two-dimensional matrix, using a two-dimensional grid and block:

```
__global__ void processMatrix(float *matrix, int width, int height) {
    int x = blockIdx.x * blockDim.x + threadIdx.x;
    int y = blockIdx.y * blockDim.y + threadIdx.y;

    if (x < width && y < height) {
        int index = y * width + x;
        matrix[index] = matrix[index] * 2.0f;
    }
}
```

The width and height variables represent the matrix dimensions. The global thread indices x and y are computed considering both block and grid dimensions. Index calculation ensures that every matrix element is processed by a unique thread and bounds checking prevents invalid access.

Proper indexing directly affects performance, ensuring memory accesses are coalesced where possible and diverse computational resources are effectively utilized. Mapping threads to data structures lays the foundation for implementing efficient parallel algorithms, from simple array manipulations to complex numerical simulations, relying on properly calculated and managed thread indices.

5.4 Block and Grid Dimensions

In CUDA programming, the dimensions of blocks and grids are critical for the proper execution of parallel algorithms. Understanding how to configure these dimensions appropriately can significantly impact the performance and efficiency of your CUDA programs.

A block in CUDA is defined as a group of threads that can cooperate among themselves using shared memory and can synchronize their execution to coordinate memory access. The configuration of blocks and grids must be explicitly defined during the launch of a kernel. This configuration is specified through the use of the dim3 type, which facilitates the setting of one, two, or three-dimensional thread blocks and grids.

Defining Block Dimensions

Block dimensions are typically defined using a dim3 variable that specifies the number of threads in the x, y, and z dimensions:

```
dim3 blockDim(8, 8, 8); // Defines a block with 512 threads (8x8x8)
```

A block can contain up to 1024 threads, which can be arranged in either one, two, or three dimensions. It is crucial to choose block dimensions that effectively map to the problem space and leverage the GPU's capabilities. The following example demonstrates defining a 2D block:

```
dim3 blockDim2D(32, 32); // Defines a 2D block with 1024 threads (32x32)
```

Defining Grid Dimensions

Grid dimensions are also defined using the dim3 type, specifying the number of blocks in the x, y, and z dimensions:

```
dim3 gridDim(16, 16); // Defines a grid with 256 blocks (16x16)
```

Each block within the grid is uniquely identified by its block index, which can be accessed within the kernel using the built-in blockIdx variable. It is essential to set the grid dimensions such that they cover the entire problem space.

Example of Configuring Block and Grid Dimensions

Consider a case where we need to perform an operation on a 1024x1024 matrix. We can choose a block size of 16x16 threads, resulting in each block covering a 16x16 submatrix. To cover the entire 1024x1024 matrix, we require a grid size that contains sufficient blocks:

```
dim3 blockDim(16, 16); // 16x16 threads per block
dim3 gridDim(64, 64); // 64x64 blocks to cover 1024x1024 elements
```

Kernel Launch Configuration

When a kernel is launched, the block and grid dimensions are specified to determine the parallel execution configuration:

```
myKernel<<<gridDim, blockDim>>>(deviceArray);
```

Within the kernel, each thread can calculate its unique global index by combining the block and thread indices:

```
__global__ void myKernel(float *array)
{
    int globalIdx = blockIdx.x * blockDim.x + threadIdx.x;
    int globalIdy = blockIdx.y * blockDim.y + threadIdx.y;

    // Access the array using these global indices
    float value = array[globalIdy * WIDTH + globalIdx];
    // Perform computations and store results back to global memory
}
```

The variables blockIdx.x and blockIdx.y provide the block indices in the x and y dimensions, whereas threadIdx.x and threadIdx.y provide the thread indices within the block. These indices are used to compute the global position of each thread, ensuring proper indexing and access to array elements.

Optimizing Block and Grid Dimensions

Choosing optimal block and grid dimensions requires balancing several factors, including the total number of threads, memory access patterns, GPU architecture, and the nature of the computation. Systems with high computational requirements or memory bandwidth constraints benefit from maximizing occupancy by configuring block and grid dimensions that allow for full utilization of the GPU's resources.

For example, solving a real-world problem might involve experimenting with different configurations and profiling the performance of each to identify the optimal setup. Tools like NVIDIA's nvprof or NSight can assist in analyzing the execution and determining the most efficient configuration.

Understanding the interplay between blocks and grids and their dimensions allows for the effective formulation of algorithms that harness the full power of CUDA and improve computational performance. Configuring these dimensions correctly is a fundamental skill for all CUDA developers.

5.5 Thread Synchronization

In CUDA programming, thread synchronization is a crucial concept that ensures threads within a block coordinate and complete certain operations safely and consistently. Synchronization is necessary when threads within a block need to share data or coordinate their tasks to avoid race conditions and ensure data integrity. This section delves into the mechanisms available for thread synchronization and the scenarios where they are essential.

CUDA provides several methods for synchronizing threads within a block. Among these, the primary mechanism is the __syncthreads() function. The __syncthreads() function acts as a synchronization barrier within a block, where all threads must reach this barrier before any are allowed to proceed.

The __syncthreads() function is a built-in CUDA function, and it plays a crucial role when threads need to collaborate, especially in scenarios involving shared memory. When a __syncthreads() call is made, it ensures that:

- All threads in the block wait at the barrier until every thread in the block has reached the barrier.
- All writes to shared memory made by any thread prior to the barrier are visible to other threads after they pass the barrier.

The proper use of __syncthreads() is vital to avoid data hazards, which can occur when multiple threads read from and write to the same memory locations without proper synchronization. Let's examine an example that illustrates the need for synchronization.

Consider a scenario where we need to perform a reduction operation, such as summing all elements in an array. Each thread in a block will sum a subset of the array elements stored in shared memory. Here is a CUDA kernel demonstrating efficient reduction using __syncthreads():

```
__global__ void reduce(int *g_idata, int *g_odata, unsigned int n) {
    extern __shared__ int sdata[];

    unsigned int tid = threadIdx.x;
    unsigned int i = blockIdx.x * blockDim.x + threadIdx.x;

    if (i < n) {
        sdata[tid] = g_idata[i];
    } else {
        sdata[tid] = 0;
    }
    __syncthreads();

    for (unsigned int s = 1; s < blockDim.x; s *= 2) {
        if (tid % (2 * s) == 0) {
            sdata[tid] += sdata[tid + s];
        }
        __syncthreads();
    }

    if (tid == 0) {
        g_odata[blockIdx.x] = sdata[0];
    }
}
```

In this example, each block of threads performs a partial reduction in shared memory. The shared memory array sdata is used to store partial sums, and synchronization is achieved using __syncthreads() at key points within the kernel.

As illustrated:

- The data is first loaded into shared memory from global memory by each thread. Before any further operations, a synchronization barrier is established using __syncthreads() to ensure all threads have loaded their respective data into shared memory.
- During the reduction loop, we use __syncthreads() inside the iterative loop to guarantee that all threads have completed their current step of the reduction before proceeding to the next.

Failure to use __syncthreads() properly can result in incorrect results, as threads may access partially updated data from other threads, leading to race conditions.

While __syncthreads() is effective within a block, it does not provide synchronization across different blocks. The kernel launch acts as a global synchronization point. However, when more explicit inter-block synchronization is required, such as when a multi-kernel approach needs synchronization across kernel launches, developers can use CUDA streams and events.

CUDA events are used to mark points in the code so that the host can monitor the progress of device operations. An example of using CUDA events for synchronization is as follows:

```
cudaEvent_t start, stop;
cudaEventCreate(&start);
cudaEventCreate(&stop);

cudaEventRecord(start, 0);
kernelA<<<grid, block>>>();
cudaEventRecord(stop, 0);

cudaEventSynchronize(stop); // Wait for kernelA to complete

kernelB<<<grid, block>>>();
```

In the code above:

- cudaEventRecord(start, 0) and cudaEventRecord(stop, 0) record events before and after kernelA.
- cudaEventSynchronize(stop) ensures that the host code waits until kernelA has finished executing before launching kernelB.

Carefully managing synchronization is essential to ensuring the correctness and performance of CUDA applications. Misuse of synchronization primitives can lead to deadlocks, inefficient execution, or incorrect program results. Therefore, comprehension and appropriate application of synchronization mechanisms are mandatory for effective parallel programming in CUDA.

5.6 Using __syncthreads() Function

The __syncthreads() function is a crucial synchronization primitive in CUDA programming, enabling coordination between threads within the same block. This collective operation ensures that all threads in a block reach the same point in the code before any are allowed to proceed, guaranteeing that shared data accessed by multiple threads is consistently updated. Understanding and correctly utilizing __syncthreads() is essential for avoiding race conditions and ensuring data integrity in parallel computations.

In CUDA, each block of threads executes independently, and they have access to a shared memory space. When threads within a block need to communicate or share results, synchronization is necessary to ensure the correct sequence of operations. The __syncthreads() function serves this purpose by acting as a barrier synchronization point, where all threads in the block must wait until every thread has reached the barrier.

Consider the following kernel code that sums the elements of an array within each block using shared memory:

```
__global__ void blockSumKernel(float *input, float *output, int n) {
    extern __shared__ float sharedData[];
    int tid = threadIdx.x;
    int bid = blockIdx.x;
    int idx = bid * blockDim.x + tid;

    if (idx < n) {
        sharedData[tid] = input[idx];
    } else {
        sharedData[tid] = 0.0f;
    }

    __syncthreads();

    for (int s = 1; s < blockDim.x; s *= 2) {
        if (tid % (2 * s) == 0) {
            sharedData[tid] += sharedData[tid + s];
        }
        __syncthreads();
    }

    if (tid == 0) {
        output[bid] = sharedData[0];
    }
}
```

In this example, the kernel function blockSumKernel computes the sum of elements in the input array in parallel, storing the sum of each block in the output array. An explanation of the various elements and their roles follows:

- **Shared Memory Declaration:** The line extern __shared__ float sharedData[]; declares a shared memory array. The size of this array is specified when launching the kernel.
- **Thread and Block Indexing:** The variables tid and bid store the thread index within the block and the block index within the grid, respectively. idx is the global index for element access in the input array.
- **Loading Data into Shared Memory:** Each thread loads one element of the input array into sharedData. If idx extends beyond the array bounds, the thread loads 0.0f.
- **First __syncthreads() Call:** The first call to __syncthreads() ensures that all threads have completed the data loading stage

before proceeding. This prevents data inconsistency in shared memory when accessed in the subsequent steps.

- **Reduction Loop:** The reduction loop performs the summation in a tree-based manner. During each iteration, threads at even indices add the value of the thread s steps ahead. The inner __syncthreads() ensures that the additions in the current step are completed before moving to the next step.

- **Storing the Result:** Finally, the first thread in the block (thread 0) stores the block's sum in the output array.

The correct placement of __syncthreads() is essential to ensure data correctness and avoid race conditions. Misplacing __syncthreads() or failing to use it when necessary can lead to unpredictable results.

To illustrate a potential issue, consider a subtle modification to the reduction loop where __syncthreads() is omitted:

```
for (int s = 1; s < blockDim.x; s *= 2) {
    if (tid % (2 * s) == 0) {
        sharedData[tid] += sharedData[tid + s];
    }
    // __syncthreads(); // Uncommenting this line prevents race conditions!
}
```

Without the internal __syncthreads(), threads might read incomplete data from sharedData[], resulting in incorrect computations. This emphasizes the necessity of using __syncthreads() correctly to prevent race conditions.

Another essential consideration is that __syncthreads() only synchronizes threads within the same block. It cannot synchronize threads across different blocks. Therefore, for inter-block synchronization, other techniques such as atomic operations or multi-kernel launches are needed.

Profiling tools such as NVIDIA Visual Profiler (nvprof) or NVIDIA Nsight can help in optimizing and debugging synchronization-related issues by providing insights into the execution timeline and thread behavior.

Proper use of __syncthreads() facilitates reliable and efficient parallel programs by ensuring ordered execution of critical code sections. This synchronization function becomes a foundational component when designing algorithms that leverage shared memory for performance improvements in CUDA applications.

5.7 Warp and Warp Divergence

A fundamental concept in CUDA programming that significantly impacts the performance of applications is that of warps and warp divergence. Understanding the execution of warps and handling warp divergence effectively are crucial for writing efficient CUDA code.

In CUDA, a warp is defined as a group of 32 threads that execute the same instruction simultaneously. This synchronous execution model is a key aspect of the Single Instruction Multiple Threads (SIMT) architecture employed by NVIDIA GPUs. Warps are the basic unit of scheduling in CUDA, meaning that the CUDA scheduler dispatches instructions to warps rather than individual threads.

CUDA threads within a block are organized into warps sequentially. For instance, in a block consisting of 64 threads, there are two warps: the first warp will contain threads 0 to 31, and the second warp will include threads 32 to 63. This structured organization allows for the efficient mapping of parallel tasks.

Warp Divergence occurs when threads within a warp take different execution paths due to conditional branches, such as $\mathrm{if\text{-}else}$ statements. When warp divergence happens, the warp serially executes each branch path taken by any thread within the warp, disabling threads that are not on that path. This serialization leads to reduced parallel efficiency, as the number of active threads is less than the warp size (32 threads).

Consider the following example of code with potential warp divergence:

```
__global__ void warp_divergence_example(int *data, int threshold) {
    int idx = threadIdx.x + blockIdx.x * blockDim.x;
    if (data[idx] < threshold) {
        data[idx] = data[idx] * 2;
    } else {
        data[idx] = data[idx] + 1;
    }
}
```

In this example, if the condition $\mathrm{data}[\mathrm{idx}] < \mathrm{threshold}$ results in different paths for threads within the same warp, warp divergence occurs.

One way to mitigate warp divergence is to minimize conditional branches within warps. Where feasible, we can employ alternative coding strategies, such as the use of boolean masks, to harmonize the execution paths of threads within a warp. For example, using a boolean mask can refactor the above function to:

```
__global__ void optimized_warp_divergence(int *data, int threshold) {
    int idx = threadIdx.x + blockIdx.x * blockDim.x;
    int temp = (data[idx] < threshold) ? (data[idx] * 2) : (data[idx] + 1);
    data[idx] = temp;
}
```

In this refactored version, the ternary operator (?:) ensures that the same execution path is followed for all threads within the warp, thereby avoiding warp divergence.

Understanding the implications of warp divergence is essential for optimizing code performance, especially for algorithms with complex branching logic. Warps that experience significant divergence may exhibit poor performance due to increased execution time caused by serialized instruction processing.

It is also important to recognize scenarios where warp divergence cannot be entirely avoided, and instead, the focus should shift towards minimizing its impact. For instance, algorithms with inherent conditional logic, such as those in graph traversal or dynamic simulations, might not be able to completely eliminate divergence. In such cases, careful planning of thread block sizes and ensuring balanced workloads between threads can help mitigate performance degradation.

A more advanced technique to handle warp divergence involves distinguishing between coherent and non-coherent branching. Coherent branching suggests that the majority of the warp's threads are likely to follow the same execution path, e.g., when processing large contiguous data sets where nearby threads exhibit similar behavior. For non-coherent branching, often associated with more random or sparse data accesses, restructuring the algorithm or data layout can be useful.

Designing efficient CUDA code demands a deep comprehension of the mechanics of warps and how divergence affects parallel execution. By structuring code to maintain similar execution paths among threads within a warp, we can achieve higher performance and better utilization of the GPU's computational resources. Additionally, being mindful of the nature of the branching logic and exploring refactoring opportunities can serve as effective strategies to mitigate the adverse effects of warp divergence.

5.8 Execution Model in CUDA

CUDA's execution model enables efficient parallel computation by organizing threads into structured units and orchestrating their execution on the GPU. Understanding this execution model is crucial for harnessing the full potential of CUDA-enabled devices.

At its core, the CUDA execution model is hierarchically structured into grids, blocks, and threads. A **grid** comprises one or multiple blocks, and each block contains multiple threads. This hierarchy ensures scalable parallelism, making it possible to adapt to various computational needs and GPU architectures.

A kernel is defined as a function that runs on the GPU, executed by many threads in parallel. When a kernel is launched, multiple threads are organized into blocks, and these blocks form a grid. Each thread within a block has a unique *threadIdx* identifier, while each block within a grid has a unique *blockIdx* identifier. These indices allow threads to access specific elements of their domain, facilitating data parallelism.

Let's consider a simple kernel example to illustrate this:

```
__global__ void add(int *a, int *b, int *c) {
    int index = threadIdx.x;
    c[index] = a[index] + b[index];
}
```

In this kernel, each thread calculates the sum of corresponding elements from arrays a and b, storing the result in array c. Here, *threadIdx.x* provides each thread with an index that it uses to access elements of the arrays.

When launching a kernel, the number of blocks and the number of threads per block must be specified. The «<»> syntax is utilized for this purpose:

```
add<<<numBlocks, threadsPerBlock>>>(a, b, c);
```

CUDA supports setting these parameters in three dimensions to map onto the data's natural structure. For example, for image processing tasks on a 2D image, one may set the grid as a 2D grid and blocks as 2D blocks:

```
dim3 threadsPerBlock(16, 16);
dim3 numBlocks((width + threadsPerBlock.x - 1) / threadsPerBlock.x,
               (height + threadsPerBlock.y - 1) / threadsPerBlock.y);
add<<<numBlocks, threadsPerBlock>>>(a, b, c);
```

Upon launching the kernel, the CUDA runtime system takes over, allocating threads to various Streaming Multiprocessors (SMs) on the GPU. Each block is assigned to an SM, which further schedules the execution of the threads within the block. This scheduling is based on warps, groups of 32 threads that execute the same instruction simultaneously.

Warp management is essential for efficient execution. When all threads in a warp perform the same operation, they execute in lockstep. Divergence occurs when threads within a warp follow different execution paths due to conditional statements, leading to serialized execution of different paths, which can hinder performance.

Another aspect of the execution model involves memory hierarchy. CUDA threads have access to several memory types:

- **Local Memory**: Private to each thread.
- **Shared Memory**: Shared among threads within a block, allowing fast data exchange.
- **Global Memory**: Accessible by all threads in a grid, but slower than shared memory.

An efficient CUDA program minimizes use of global memory due to its latency and leverages shared memory for inter-thread communication within blocks.

The CUDA execution model provides features for synchronization. For instance, __syncthreads() is used to synchronize threads within a block, ensuring that all threads reach a certain point before any thread proceeds. This is crucial when threads share data through shared memory:

```
__global__ void matrixMul(int *a, int *b, int *c, int width) {
    __shared__ int sharedA[16][16]; // assuming 16x16 threads per block
    __shared__ int sharedB[16][16];

    int tx = threadIdx.x;
    int ty = threadIdx.y;

    int value = 0;
    for (int i = 0; i < width / 16; i++) {
        sharedA[ty][tx] = a[ty * width + (i * 16 + tx)];
        sharedB[ty][tx] = b[(i * 16 + ty) * width + tx];
        __syncthreads();

        for (int j = 0; j < 16; j++) {
            value += sharedA[ty][j] * sharedB[j][tx];
        }
        __syncthreads();
```

```
    }
    c[ty * width + tx] = value;
}
```

In this matrix multiplication kernel, __syncthreads() ensures that all threads correctly read data from shared memory before proceeding with computation. This synchronization avoids race conditions, providing correct results.

Managing execution dependencies, memory hierarchy, and synchronization efficiently is foundational for high-performance CUDA programming. Understanding the execution model is integral to designing efficient parallel algorithms suited to the architecture of GPU devices.

5.9 Launching CUDA Kernels

Launching a CUDA kernel is a fundamental aspect of programming with NVIDIA's CUDA architecture. Kernels are functions written in the CUDA language, typically a subset of C/C++ with extensions, that execute on the GPU. Using CUDA kernels leverages the massive parallelism inherent in GPU architecture. To launch a kernel, one must understand the syntax and the relationship between the host (CPU) and the device (GPU).

The syntax for launching a CUDA kernel in C/C++ is as follows:

```
kernel<<<dim3 gridDim, dim3 blockDim, size_t sharedMem, cudaStream_t stream
    >>>(parameters);
```

This snippet outlines the core components needed for kernel execution: - kernel: This is the name of the CUDA function to be executed on the GPU. - «<dim3 gridDim, dim3 blockDim»>: Configuration parameters that define the execution hierarchy, where gridDim specifies the number of blocks in the grid and blockDim specifies the number of threads in each block. - size_t sharedMem: This optional parameter specifies the amount of shared memory dynamically allocated per block. - cudaStream_t stream: This denotes the stream in which the kernel is issued. By default, if not specified, kernels are issued in the null stream.

Consider a simple example of a kernel function. This kernel will add two arrays, A and B, element by element and store the result in the array C:

```
__global__ void vectorAdd(int *A, int *B, int *C, int N) {
    int idx = threadIdx.x + blockIdx.x * blockDim.x;
```

```
    if (idx < N) {
        C[idx] = A[idx] + B[idx];
    }
}
```

The above kernel function utilizes the built-in variables threadIdx.x, blockIdx.x, and blockDim.x to compute a unique index for each thread. This index is then used to perform the addition operation for each corresponding element of arrays A and B.

Suppose we want to launch this kernel for an array of size N. The host code might look as follows:

```
int N = 1000000;
int *d_A, *d_B, *d_C;
size_t size = N * sizeof(int);

// Allocate device memory
cudaMalloc((void **)&d_A, size);
cudaMalloc((void **)&d_B, size);
cudaMalloc((void **)&d_C, size);

// Copy data from host to device
cudaMemcpy(d_A, h_A, size, cudaMemcpyHostToDevice);
cudaMemcpy(d_B, h_B, size, cudaMemcpyHostToDevice);

// Kernel launch parameters
dim3 blockDim(256);
dim3 gridDim((N + blockDim.x - 1) / blockDim.x);

// Launch the kernel
vectorAdd<<<gridDim, blockDim>>>(d_A, d_B, d_C, N);

// Copy result back to host
cudaMemcpy(h_C, d_C, size, cudaMemcpyDeviceToHost);

// Free device memory
cudaFree(d_A);
cudaFree(d_B);
cudaFree(d_C);
```

Several crucial steps are involved in this host code:

- **Device Memory Allocation**: The arrays d_A, d_B, and d_C are allocated in the device memory using cudaMalloc.
- **Memory Transfer**: The contents of the host arrays h_A and h_B are copied to the device arrays d_A and d_B using cudaMemcpy.
- **Kernel Configuration**: The execution configuration is specified by initializing dim3 objects for blockDim and gridDim. In this example, each block has 256 threads, and the number of blocks is calculated to ensure all elements in the array are processed.

- **Kernel Launch**: The kernel is launched with the specified execution configuration using vectorAdd«<gridDim, blockDim»>(d_A, d_B, d_C, N).

- **Result Transfer**: The result stored in d_C is copied back to the host memory array h_C.

- **Memory De-allocation**: The device memory allocated for d_A, d_B, and d_C is freed using cudaFree.

Additionally, handling CUDA errors using cudaGetErrorString and cudaError_t variables is good practice, ensuring robust and error-free execution. An example illustrating this practice is shown below:

```
vectorAdd<<<gridDim, blockDim>>>(d_A, d_B, d_C, N);
cudaError_t err = cudaGetLastError();
if (err != cudaSuccess) {
    fprintf(stderr, "Failed to launch vectorAdd kernel (error code %s)!\n",
            cudaGetErrorString(err));
    exit(EXIT_FAILURE);
}
```

Checking for errors after launching the kernel ensures early detection and mitigation of potential issues during kernel execution.

By understanding and implementing these steps, one can effectively launch and manage CUDA kernels, facilitating efficient and parallel computation on the GPU.

5.10 Practical Example: Matrix Multiplication

Matrix multiplication, also known as matrix product, is the most fundamental operation in various scientific computations, including graphics, simulations, and neural networks. This section presents a detailed, practical implementation of matrix multiplication using CUDA to leverage GPU capabilities. We will explore the manipulation of matrix data on the host and device, efficient memory access patterns, and synchronization aspects to ensure accurate computations.

Consider two matrices A and B with dimensions $M \times K$ and $K \times N$, respectively. The resultant matrix C will have dimensions $M \times N$.

$$C[i][j] = \sum_{k=0}^{K-1} A[i][k] \times B[k][j]$$

To perform this computation on a GPU, we must undertake the following steps:

1. Allocate memory on the host (CPU) and device (GPU). 2. Transfer matrix data from the host to the device. 3. Define and execute a CUDA kernel to perform the matrix multiplication. 4. Transfer the resultant matrix back to the host. 5. Free the allocated memory on the device.

Below are the CUDA kernel and host code implementations for matrix multiplication.

```
#include <stdio.h>
#include <cuda.h>

#define TILE_WIDTH 16

__global__ void matrixMulKernel(float *d_A, float *d_B, float *d_C, int M, int N,
    int K) {
    __shared__ float ds_A[TILE_WIDTH][TILE_WIDTH];
    __shared__ float ds_B[TILE_WIDTH][TILE_WIDTH];

    int bx = blockIdx.x; int by = blockIdx.y;
    int tx = threadIdx.x; int ty = threadIdx.y;

    int Row = by * TILE_WIDTH + ty;
    int Col = bx * TILE_WIDTH + tx;

    float Cvalue = 0.0;

    for (int t = 0; t < (K-1)/TILE_WIDTH + 1; ++t) {
        if (Row < M && t * TILE_WIDTH + tx < K)
            ds_A[ty][tx] = d_A[Row * K + t * TILE_WIDTH + tx];
        else
            ds_A[ty][tx] = 0.0;

        if (Col < N && t * TILE_WIDTH + ty < K)
            ds_B[ty][tx] = d_B[(t * TILE_WIDTH + ty) * N + Col];
        else
            ds_B[ty][tx] = 0.0;

        __syncthreads();

        for (int i = 0; i < TILE_WIDTH; ++i)
            Cvalue += ds_A[ty][i] * ds_B[i][tx];

        __syncthreads();
    }

    if (Row < M && Col < N)
        d_C[Row * N + Col] = Cvalue;
}

void matrixMultiply(float *h_A, float *h_B, float *h_C, int M, int N, int K) {
    int size_A = M * K * sizeof(float);
```

```
    int size_B = K * N * sizeof(float);
    int size_C = M * N * sizeof(float);

    float *d_A, *d_B, *d_C;

    cudaMalloc(&d_A, size_A);
    cudaMalloc(&d_B, size_B);
    cudaMalloc(&d_C, size_C);

    cudaMemcpy(d_A, h_A, size_A, cudaMemcpyHostToDevice);
    cudaMemcpy(d_B, h_B, size_B, cudaMemcpyHostToDevice);

    dim3 dimBlock(TILE_WIDTH, TILE_WIDTH);
    dim3 dimGrid((N-1)/TILE_WIDTH + 1, (M-1)/TILE_WIDTH + 1);

    matrixMulKernel<<<dimGrid, dimBlock>>>(d_A, d_B, d_C, M, N, K);

    cudaMemcpy(h_C, d_C, size_C, cudaMemcpyDeviceToHost);

    cudaFree(d_A);
    cudaFree(d_B);
    cudaFree(d_C);
}

int main() {
    int M = 64; int K = 64; int N = 64;

    float *h_A = (float*)malloc(M * K * sizeof(float));
    float *h_B = (float*)malloc(K * N * sizeof(float));
    float *h_C = (float*)malloc(M * N * sizeof(float));

    for (int i = 0; i < M * K; ++i)
        h_A[i] = 1.0;

    for (int i = 0; i < K * N; ++i)
        h_B[i] = 1.0;

    matrixMultiply(h_A, h_B, h_C, M, N, K);

    for (int i = 0; i < M * N; ++i) {
        if (i % N == 0) printf("\n");
        printf("%f ", h_C[i]);
    }
    printf("\n");

    free(h_A); free(h_B); free(h_C);
    return 0;
}
```

The matrixMulKernel function is the CUDA kernel performing the matrix multiplication. It utilizes shared memory for efficient memory access. Each thread block computes a $TILE\_WIDTH \times TILE\_WIDTH$ sub-matrix of C by loading corresponding sub-matrices of A and B into shared memory, multiplying them, and accumulating the results.

When defining the matrixMulKernel, threads within a block are indexed by threadIdx.x and threadIdx.y. Blocks are indexed by blockIdx.x and blockIdx.y. Shared memory arrays, ds_A and ds_B, are employed for storing sub-matrices of A and B. This reduces global memory access latency and bandwidth requirements.

The threads within the block load elements of A and B into shared memory in a coalesced manner. Synchronization using __syncthreads() ensures all threads have completed the data loading before proceeding to computation. The loop iterates through the tiles of A and B, computing partial sums for each tile.

In the host function matrixMultiply, memory allocation is performed for matrices A, B, and C on both the host and device. cudaMemcpy transfers matrix data between host and device. The kernel is executed using a grid of thread blocks, and the results are copied back to the host.

Upon successful execution, this code multiplies the matrices A and B and stores the result in matrix C, printing the resultant matrix to the console.

```
16.000000 16.000000 16.000000 16.000000 16.000000 16.000000 16.000000 16.000000
16.000000 16.000000 16.000000 16.000000 16.000000 16.000000 16.000000 16.000000
...
16.000000 16.000000 16.000000 16.000000 16.000000 16.000000 16.000000 16.000000
```

This output verifies that every element of the resultant matrix C is indeed the sum of products of corresponding elements of A and B. When A and B are filled with 1.0, the resultant matrix C has all elements equal to K.

Chapter 6

CUDA Kernel Functions

This chapter focuses on CUDA kernel functions, detailing their definition and how to launch them. It covers kernel execution configuration, passing parameters, and utilizing shared and constant memory within kernels. Error handling in kernel execution is discussed, along with strategies for optimizing kernel performance. A case study on image processing kernels is provided to demonstrate practical implementation and optimization techniques.

6.1 Introduction to Kernel Functions

In the context of CUDA, a kernel function represents the fundamental unit of parallel execution on the GPU. Unlike conventional functions in C or C++, kernel functions are designed to be executed by multiple threads concurrently, leveraging the parallel architecture of modern GPUs. This enables significant performance improvements for data-parallel tasks.

To define a kernel function in CUDA, the __global__ declaration specifier is used. This specifier indicates that the function will be executed on the device (GPU) and can be called from the host (CPU). Here is a simple example of a kernel function that adds two arrays element-wise:

```
__global__ void add(int *a, int *b, int *c, int N) {
    int index = threadIdx.x + blockIdx.x * blockDim.x;
    if (index < N) {
        c[index] = a[index] + b[index];
    }
```

```
}
```

In this code snippet, the __global__ specifier is followed by the void keyword, signaling that the kernel function does not return a value. It takes four parameters: pointers to the input arrays a and b, the output array c, and an integer N representing the number of elements in each array.

The built-in variables threadIdx, blockIdx, and blockDim are used to determine the global index of the thread within the grid. The expression:

$$\text{index} = \text{threadIdx.x} + \text{blockIdx.x} * \text{blockDim.x};$$

computes a unique index for each thread. This ensures that the addition operation covers the entire range of array elements when enough threads are launched.

When invoking this kernel function from the host, a specific syntax is used to configure the execution parameters. This is done through the «<»> operator. For our example, the kernel launch might look like this:

```
int N = 1024;
int blockSize = 256;
int numBlocks = (N + blockSize - 1) / blockSize;

add<<<numBlocks, blockSize>>>(d_a, d_b, d_c, N);
```

Here, blockSize is set to 256, meaning each block will contain 256 threads. The total number of blocks, numBlocks, is computed such that there are enough blocks to cover all elements in the array a, b, and c. The kernel function add is then launched with these parameters, specifying the grid and block dimensions.

CUDA kernels execute in a Single Instruction Multiple Threads (SIMT) architecture, where multiple threads execute the same instruction but on different data. Each thread has a unique ID given by the combination of threadIdx, blockIdx, and blockDim, allowing threads to process distinct data elements simultaneously.

Proper management of threads and blocks is crucial for optimizing performance and ensuring the efficient utilization of GPU resources. This involves understanding how to decompose a problem into parallel tasks that can be executed by threads and appropriately configuring the grid and block dimensions.

Equally important is the handling of kernel parameters. When passing pointers or other variables to a kernel, it is essential to ensure that the device memory has been allocated and initialized properly. Memory management operations, such as cudaMalloc and cudaMemcpy, are employed to facilitate this process. For instance:

```
int *d_a, *d_b, *d_c;
cudaMalloc(&d_a, N * sizeof(int));
cudaMalloc(&d_b, N * sizeof(int));
cudaMalloc(&d_c, N * sizeof(int));

cudaMemcpy(d_a, h_a, N * sizeof(int), cudaMemcpyHostToDevice);
cudaMemcpy(d_b, h_b, N * sizeof(int), cudaMemcpyHostToDevice);
```

In the example above, memory is allocated on the device for arrays d_a, d_b, and d_c. Data from host arrays h_a and h_b is then copied to the corresponding device arrays using cudaMemcpy with the cudaMemcpyHostToDevice flag.

These operations ensure that the data required by the kernel function is present in the device memory, enabling efficient execution without the overhead of data transfer during kernel execution.

When the kernel completes execution, results can be transferred back to the host using:

```
cudaMemcpy(h_c, d_c, N * sizeof(int), cudaMemcpyDeviceToHost);
```

Thus, the host array h_c contains the output of the kernel function, suitable for subsequent operations or verification.

The effective use of kernel functions in CUDA entails a good grasp of the underlying parallel computation model, efficient memory management, and proper configuration of the execution grid. This lays the foundation for writing high-performance CUDA applications that leverage the power of GPUs.

6.2 Defining a Kernel Function

A kernel function in CUDA is a globally defined function that is executed on the GPU. These functions are decorated with the __global__ keyword and are the entry points for GPU execution. Unlike standard C functions, kernel functions are designed to be executed in a parallel manner across multiple threads on the GPU.

To define a kernel function, use the following syntax:

```
__global__ void kernelFunction(parameters) {
    // Kernel code here
}
```

The __global__ keyword indicates that the function will be executed on the device (GPU) and can be called from the host (CPU).

- **Return Type:** Kernel functions must have a void return type because the execution of a kernel involves thousands of threads, making it impractical to return values directly.
- **Function Name:** The name follows standard C naming conventions. It should be intuitive and indicative of the function's purpose.
- **Parameters:** Parameters are passed from the host to the device. They can be of any type that is supported by device code. It's crucial to remember that passing parameters by value is the default behavior.

Here's a simple example of a kernel function that adds two arrays:

```
__global__ void addArrays(int *a, int *b, int *c, int n) {
    int index = threadIdx.x + blockIdx.x * blockDim.x;
    if(index < n) {
        c[index] = a[index] + b[index];
    }
}
```

In this example, addArrays is a kernel function that adds corresponding elements of two arrays a and b, storing the result in array c. Each thread computes one element of the arrays.

Thread Indexing To correctly distribute work among the threads, CUDA provides built-in variables that help identify each thread's unique index within a block and across the entire grid. These include:

- threadIdx.x: Index of the thread within the block.
- blockIdx.x: Index of the block within the grid.
- blockDim.x: Dimension (size) of the block.
- gridDim.x: Dimension (size) of the grid.

In the example above, threadIdx.x provides the unique index within its block, and blockIdx.x gives the block's index within the grid. The expression threadIdx.x + blockIdx.x * blockDim.x calculates the unique index of the thread within the entire grid.

Conditional Execution Conditional statements often control execution flow within kernel functions. The $\text{if}(\text{index} < \text{n})$ statement ensures that threads outside the bounds of the arrays do not perform out-of-bound accesses, which could lead to undefined behavior.

Parameter Passing Parameters to kernel functions can include pointers to device memory. For example, in our addArrays function, int *a, *b, *c are pointers to integer arrays in device memory. These pointers need to be allocated and initialized in device memory before launching the kernel.

Memory Considerations When defining a kernel function, it is essential to consider memory hierarchy and access patterns:

- Global Memory: Accessible by all threads but has higher latency.
- Shared Memory: Shared among threads of the same block and has lower latency.
- Registers: Fastest access time but are limited in number.

Efficient memory usage can significantly affect kernel performance. For instance, using shared memory for frequently accessed data within a block can reduce global memory accesses and improve efficiency.

Synchronization Proper synchronization is often required. CUDA provides __syncthreads() to synchronize threads within a block, ensuring that all threads have reached the same point before continuing execution. This is crucial in cases where threads need to share data through shared memory.

```
__global__ void exampleKernel() {
    __shared__ int sharedData[blockDim.x];
    int index = threadIdx.x;
    sharedData[index] = index;
    __syncthreads();
    if(index == 0) {
        // Only the first thread in the block executes this code
        int sum = 0;
        for(int i = 0; i < blockDim.x; i++) {
            sum += sharedData[i];
        }
    }
}
```

In this example, each thread writes its index to sharedData. The __syncthreads() function ensures that all threads have completed their write operations before any thread reads from sharedData.

Understanding these principles is fundamental for developing efficient CUDA kernel functions. These building blocks pave the way for more complex kernel programming, optimizing resource use, and achieving high performance in GPU computation tasks.

6.3 Launching Kernel Functions

In CUDA programming, once you have defined a kernel function, the next step is to launch it. Launching a kernel function involves specifying the execution configuration, which includes the grid and block dimensions. This configuration dictates how many threads will execute the kernel function and how these threads are organized. Additionally, the process of launching involves passing parameters to the kernel. Understanding these elements is crucial for writing efficient CUDA code. This section provides a detailed examination of the kernel launch syntax, components of execution configuration, and parameter passing mechanisms.

The syntax for launching a kernel is unique in CUDA C/C++ and uses triple angle brackets «< »>. This syntax, often referred to as the "execution configuration", is placed after the kernel name in the function call. For example:

```
// Kernel function definition
__global__ void myKernel(int* d_array) {
    // Kernel code
}

// Kernel function launch
myKernel<<<gridDim, blockDim>>>(d_array);
```

In the example above, myKernel«<gridDim, blockDim»>(d_array); launches the kernel myKernel with the execution configuration consisting of gridDim and blockDim. The parameters to be passed into the kernel function follow the execution configuration inside the usual function call parentheses.

Grid and Block Dimensions

The execution configuration is broken down into two main components: grid dimensions (gridDim) and block dimensions (blockDim).

- **Grid Dimensions**: The grid dimensions specify the number of blocks in the grid. It is defined using the dim3 data type, which allows for three-dimensional indexing. The simplest specification can be done using an integer value for a one-dimensional grid, or a dim3 object for two- or three-dimensional grids.

```
int gridDim = 16; // One-dimensional grid with 16 blocks
dim3 gridDim2(4, 4); // Two-dimensional grid with 4x4 blocks
dim3 gridDim3(2, 2, 2); // Three-dimensional grid with 2x2x2 blocks
```

- **Block Dimensions**: The block dimensions specify the number of threads in each block. It is also defined using the dim3 data type. Similar to grid dimensions, an integer value can specify a one-dimensional block, or a dim3 object can specify multi-dimensional blocks.

```
int blockDim = 64; // One-dimensional block with 64 threads
dim3 blockDim2(8, 8); // Two-dimensional block with 8x8 threads
dim3 blockDim3(4, 4, 4); // Three-dimensional block with 4x4x4 threads
```

The choice of grid and block dimensions depends on the problem's nature and the GPU's architecture. Practical considerations include maximizing the number of active threads, ensuring memory coalescing, and minimizing thread divergence.

Example: Vector Addition

Consider a simple example where we perform vector addition. In this example, we define and launch a kernel to add two vectors.

```
// Kernel function to add two vectors
__global__ void vectorAdd(const float* A, const float* B, float* C, int N) {
    int i = blockIdx.x * blockDim.x + threadIdx.x;
    if (i < N) {
        C[i] = A[i] + B[i];
    }
}

#define N 1024

int main() {
    // Allocate memory on host
    float h_A[N], h_B[N], h_C[N];

    // Allocate memory on device
    float *d_A, *d_B, *d_C;
    cudaMalloc((void**)&d_A, N * sizeof(float));
    cudaMalloc((void**)&d_B, N * sizeof(float));
    cudaMalloc((void**)&d_C, N * sizeof(float));

    // Copy data from host to device
    cudaMemcpy(d_A, h_A, N * sizeof(float), cudaMemcpyHostToDevice);
    cudaMemcpy(d_B, h_B, N * sizeof(float), cudaMemcpyHostToDevice);
```

```
    // Define grid and block dimensions
    dim3 blockDim(256);
    dim3 gridDim((N + blockDim.x - 1) / blockDim.x);

    // Launch the kernel
    vectorAdd<<<gridDim, blockDim>>>(d_A, d_B, d_C, N);

    // Copy result from device to host
    cudaMemcpy(h_C, d_C, N * sizeof(float), cudaMemcpyDeviceToHost);

    // Free device memory
    cudaFree(d_A);
    cudaFree(d_B);
    cudaFree(d_C);

    return 0;
}
```

In this example, the kernel vectorAdd is launched with gridDim and blockDim defined to suit the problem size. The formula used to calculate gridDim ensures that all elements of the vectors are processed by the kernel. The kernel index computation int i = blockIdx.x * blockDim.x + threadIdx.x; identifies the unique index of the thread within the vector.

Additional Parameters in Kernel Launch

CUDA allows for a third optional parameter in the execution configuration: shared memory size and a fourth for stream association. The extended syntax is as follows:

```
kernel<<<gridDim, blockDim, sharedMemSize, stream>>>(parameters);
```

- **sharedMemSize**: Specifies the size of dynamic shared memory required per block in bytes.

```
int sharedMemSize = 1024; // 1024 bytes of dynamic shared memory
kernel<<<gridDim, blockDim, sharedMemSize>>>(parameters);
```

- **stream**: Specifies the CUDA stream in which to execute the kernel.

```
cudaStream_t stream;
cudaStreamCreate(&stream);
kernel<<<gridDim, blockDim, sharedMemSize, stream>>>(parameters);
```

These additional parameters provide flexibility for optimizing kernel execution. Properly configuring and launching a kernel are fundamental steps in CUDA programming. By understanding the components and nuances involved, developers can harness the full potential of GPU computing.

6.4 Kernel Execution Configuration

When launching a kernel function in CUDA, it is essential to configure the execution parameters properly to achieve optimal performance and efficient resource utilization. This section discusses the various aspects of kernel execution configuration, including grid and block dimensions, and how these configurations influence the behavior of kernel execution.

The configuration of kernel execution is specified using the «< » syntax, which includes three main parameters: the number of thread blocks per grid, the number of threads per block, and an optional shared memory size. The general syntax for launching a kernel function in CUDA can be seen as:

```
kernel_function<<<numBlocks, numThreads, sharedMemSize, stream>>>(
    function_arguments);
```

Here, the parameters are defined as follows: - numBlocks: Specifies the number of blocks in the grid. - numThreads: Specifies the number of threads in each block. - sharedMemSize (optional): Specifies the amount of shared memory per block in bytes. - stream (optional): Specifies the stream identifier for asynchronous operations.

Grid and Block Dimensions:

One of the key components of kernel execution configuration is determining the grid and block dimensions. Grids and blocks can be defined in one, two, or three dimensions. The CUDA runtime provides the dim3 type to facilitate these multi-dimensional configurations.

For example:

```
dim3 numBlocks(16, 16, 1);
dim3 numThreads(16, 16, 1);
kernel_function<<<numBlocks, numThreads>>>(function_arguments);
```

Threads and Thread Indexing:

Within each block, threads are uniquely indexed by their thread IDs. The thread ID in each dimension (x, y, z) can be accessed using the built-in variable threadIdx. Similarly, the block ID in each grid dimension can be accessed using blockIdx. Combined with the block dimension (blockDim), these indices enable each thread to calculate its unique index across the entire grid.

A common approach to calculate a unique global thread ID for a 1D grid and 1D block can be illustrated as:

```
int globalIdx = blockIdx.x * blockDim.x + threadIdx.x;
```

For 2D and 3D grid/block configurations, these calculations extend naturally:

```
int globalIdx = blockIdx.x * blockDim.x + threadIdx.x;
int globalIdy = blockIdx.y * blockDim.y + threadIdx.y;
```

Shared Memory Configuration:

Shared memory is a powerful feature in CUDA that enables threads within the same block to share data efficiently. The optional sharedMemSize parameter in the kernel launch configuration allows specifying the amount of dynamically allocated shared memory. This can be accessed within the kernel function using the __shared__ keyword.

For example:

```
__global__ void kernel_function(float* data) {
    extern __shared__ float shared_data[];
    // kernel implementation utilizing shared_data
}
```

In the kernel launch:

```
int sharedMemSize = sizeof(float) * numElements;
kernel_function<<<numBlocks, numThreads, sharedMemSize>>>(data);
```

Choosing Optimal Grid and Block Sizes:

The decision to choose the optimal grid and block sizes depends on various factors including the problem size, the underlying hardware architecture, and memory access patterns. Key considerations include:

- **Occupancy:** This is the ratio of active warps per multiprocessor to the maximum number of warps supported. Higher occupancy often leads to better performance but is not the only factor. - **Execution Configuration:** For many problems, launching more smaller blocks may provide better load balancing, while fewer larger blocks can reduce kernel launch overhead but may underutilize some hardware resources. - **Memory Coalescing:** Properly configuring threads to optimize global memory accesses can significantly impact performance. Misaligned or uncoalesced memory accesses result in lower memory bandwidth utilization.

Example: Matrix Multiplication Kernel Configuration:

Consider an example where we are implementing a simple matrix multiplication. An optimal block size, leveraging shared memory for partial results, and calculating thread indices will be crucial for performance.

The kernel function might look like:

```
__global__ void matrixMul(float* A, float* B, float* C, int N) {
    __shared__ float Asub[BLOCK_SIZE][BLOCK_SIZE];
    __shared__ float Bsub[BLOCK_SIZE][BLOCK_SIZE];

    int blockRow = blockIdx.y;
    int blockCol = blockIdx.x;

    float Cvalue = 0.0;

    for (int m = 0; m < (N / BLOCK_SIZE); ++m) {
        Asub[threadIdx.y][threadIdx.x] = A[blockRow * BLOCK_SIZE + threadIdx.y] *
              N + (m * BLOCK_SIZE + threadIdx.x)];
        Bsub[threadIdx.y][threadIdx.x] = B[(m * BLOCK_SIZE + threadIdx.y) * N +
             blockCol * BLOCK_SIZE + threadIdx.x];
        __syncthreads();

        for (int e = 0; e < BLOCK_SIZE; ++e)
            Cvalue += Asub[threadIdx.y][e] * Bsub[e][threadIdx.x];
        __syncthreads();
    }

    C[(blockRow * BLOCK_SIZE + threadIdx.y) * N + blockCol * BLOCK_SIZE +
        threadIdx.x] = Cvalue;
}
```

Launching the kernel with appropriate dimension configuration:

```
dim3 dimBlock(BLOCK_SIZE, BLOCK_SIZE);
dim3 dimGrid(N / dimBlock.x, N / dimBlock.y);

matrixMul<<<dimGrid, dimBlock>>>(A, B, C, N);
```

In this configuration, $\mathrm{BLOCK\_SIZE}$ could be set to 16 or 32, and the grid dimensions ($\mathrm{dimGrid}$) are set to cover all elements of the resultant matrix C.

By carefully configuring the kernel execution parameters, developers can ensure efficient utilization of the GPU resources, leading to improvements in performance and scalability of CUDA applications.

6.5 Kernel Function Parameters

In CUDA, kernel functions can accept a diverse range of parameters, which allows them to operate on data arrays, structures, and other types, significantly contributing to the flexibility of GPU programming. Correctly handling and passing these parameters is crucial for the efficient functioning of kernel executions.

Kernel function parameters in CUDA are passed by value. This means that when a kernel is launched, the values of the arguments provided to the kernel function are copied from the host to the device. However, this rule applies differently to various data types, especially considering the pointer types.

When working with pointers, the device code must have access to the memory locations to which the pointers refer. Consequently, pointers passed as parameters to a kernel function often point to arrays in device memory, necessitating careful management of memory allocation and data transfer. Below is a simple example of a kernel function that uses parameters including an array and a scalar value.

```
__global__ void addScalarToArray(float* d_array, float scalar, int length) {
    int idx = blockIdx.x * blockDim.x + threadIdx.x;
    if (idx < length) {
        d_array[idx] += scalar;
    }
}
```

In this example, d_array is a pointer to a float array in device memory, scalar is a float value, and length is an integer that indicates the length of the array. The kernel adds the scalar value to each element of the array. All the parameters are passed by value; hence, only the addresses of the array and the actual values of the scalar and length are transferred to the device.

Managing Device Memory

Before calling the kernel function, it is essential to allocate memory on the device and transfer data from the host to the device, if necessary. This is typically done using CUDA memory management functions such as cudaMalloc, cudaMemcpy, and cudaFree. The following code snippet demonstrates this process for the earlier example.

```
#include <cuda_runtime.h>
#include <stdio.h>

int main() {
    int length = 1000;
```

```
    size_t size = length * sizeof(float);
    float scalar = 5.0f;

    // Allocate host memory and initialize
    float* h_array = (float*)malloc(size);
    for (int i = 0; i < length; i++) {
        h_array[i] = static_cast<float>(i);
    }

    // Allocate device memory
    float* d_array;
    cudaMalloc(&d_array, size);

    // Copy data from host to device
    cudaMemcpy(d_array, h_array, size, cudaMemcpyHostToDevice);

    // Define block and grid dimensions
    int blockSize = 256;
    int gridSize = (length + blockSize - 1) / blockSize;

    // Launch the kernel
    addScalarToArray<<<gridSize, blockSize>>>(d_array, scalar, length);

    // Copy result back to host
    cudaMemcpy(h_array, d_array, size, cudaMemcpyDeviceToHost);

    // Cleanup
    cudaFree(d_array);
    free(h_array);

    return 0;
}
```

cudaMalloc is used to allocate memory on the device, and cudaMemcpy transfers data from host memory to device memory. After the kernel execution, cudaMemcpy is again used to transfer the modified data back to the host. Finally, cudaFree releases the allocated device memory.

Passing Complex Data Structures

It is also possible to pass more complex data types, such as structs, to kernel functions. These structures are typically defined in a header file that is shared between the host and the device code, ensuring consistency. Consider the following example where a struct containing multiple data types is passed to a kernel:

```
struct Data {
    float* d_array;
    int length;
};

__global__ void processData(Data d, float scalar) {
    int idx = blockIdx.x * blockDim.x + threadIdx.x;
    if (idx < d.length) {
        d.d_array[idx] *= scalar;
    }
}
```

In this case, the struct Data contains a pointer to a float array and an integer representing the array length. The kernel processData operates on the array by multiplying each element by the scalar value.

The host code for managing memory and launching the kernel would look similar to the earlier example, with additional steps for setting up the struct:

```
#include <cuda_runtime.h>
#include <stdio.h>

int main() {
    int length = 1000;
    size_t size = length * sizeof(float);
    float scalar = 2.0f;

    // Allocate host memory and initialize
    float* h_array = (float*)malloc(size);
    for (int i = 0; i < length; i++) {
        h_array[i] = static_cast<float>(i);
    }

    // Allocate device memory
    float* d_array;
    cudaMalloc(&d_array, size);

    // Copy data from host to device
    cudaMemcpy(d_array, h_array, size, cudaMemcpyHostToDevice);

    // Create struct and set fields
    Data d;
    d.d_array = d_array;
    d.length = length;

    // Define block and grid dimensions
    int blockSize = 256;
    int gridSize = (length + blockSize - 1) / blockSize;

    // Launch the kernel
    processData<<<gridSize, blockSize>>>(d, scalar);

    // Copy result back to host
    cudaMemcpy(h_array, d_array, size, cudaMemcpyDeviceToHost);

    // Cleanup
    cudaFree(d_array);
    free(h_array);

    return 0;
}
```

Performance Considerations

Efficient handling of kernel parameters can significantly impact performance. Excessive copying of large data structures or frequent memory transfers between the host and device can lead to substantial overhead. To mitigate these issues, it is essential to:

- Minimize the data transferred between host and device by consolidating operations and optimizing data structures.
- Use cudaMemcpyAsync for overlapping computation and data transfer, where appropriate.
- Exploit shared and constant memory to reduce access times within kernels.

By carefully managing kernel parameters, developers can optimize the performance of their CUDA applications, ensuring efficient use of GPU resources.

6.6 Shared Memory and Kernel Functions

Shared memory in CUDA provides a mechanism for threads within the same block to efficiently share data amongst each other. It is a user-managed cache that resides on-chip, thus offering significantly lower latency than global memory. Proper utilization of shared memory can markedly improve the performance of your applications, particularly when memory access patterns exhibit spatial or temporal locality.

To declare shared memory within a kernel, you utilize the __shared__ qualifier. Shared memory is declared inside the kernel function and is accessible by all threads within the block. Below is an example of a simple kernel function that uses shared memory:

```
__global__ void exampleKernel(float *d_in, float *d_out) {
    __shared__ float sharedData[BLOCK_SIZE];

    int tid = threadIdx.x;

    // Load data into shared memory
    sharedData[tid] = d_in[tid];
    __syncthreads();

    // Perform operations on shared data
    sharedData[tid] *= 2.0f;
    __syncthreads();

    // Write the results back to global memory
    d_out[tid] = sharedData[tid];
}
```

In this example, sharedData is an array residing in shared memory, enabling fast read/write operations by threads within the same block. The synchronization function __syncthreads() ensures that all threads within the block have written their data to shared memory before any thread can proceed, preserving data consistency.

The usage of shared memory is beneficial in scenarios such as data reuse and reduction operations. Consider an example of performing a sum reduction over an array. By utilizing shared memory, we can significantly reduce the number of global memory accesses, as demonstrated in the following kernel:

```
__global__ void sumReduction(float *d_in, float *d_out, int size) {
    __shared__ float sharedData[BLOCK_SIZE];

    int tid = threadIdx.x;
    int gid = blockIdx.x * blockDim.x + tid;

    if (gid < size) {
        sharedData[tid] = d_in[gid];
    } else {
        sharedData[tid] = 0.0f;
    }
    __syncthreads();

    for (unsigned int s = blockDim.x / 2; s > 0; s >>= 1) {
        if (tid < s) {
            sharedData[tid] += sharedData[tid + s];
        }
        __syncthreads();
    }

    if (tid == 0) {
        d_out[blockIdx.x] = sharedData[0];
    }
}
```

In this code, the sumReduction kernel loads data from global memory into shared memory, performs the reduction within the block, and writes the result back to global memory. This design minimizes global memory accesses, leveraging the lower latency of shared memory to enhance performance.

Another crucial aspect of shared memory usage involves bank conflicts. Shared memory is divided into banks, and simultaneous access to different addresses in the same bank by multiple threads leads to serialization, degrading performance. To avoid bank conflicts, one can carefully align memory access patterns. For example, padding the shared memory array can help circumvent conflicts:

```
__global__ void optimizedKernel(float *d_in, float *d_out) {
    __shared__ float sharedData[BLOCK_SIZE + 1]; // Padding to avoid bank
        conflicts

    int tid = threadIdx.x;

    // Load data into shared memory
```

```
    sharedData[tid] = d_in[tid];
    __syncthreads();

    // Perform operations on shared data
    sharedData[tid] *= 2.0f;
    __syncthreads();

    // Write the results back to global memory
    d_out[tid] = sharedData[tid];
}
```

In this example, adding a single extra element to the shared memory array mitigates bank conflicts by ensuring that no two neighboring threads access the same bank simultaneously.

Calculating the appropriate size for shared memory is also essential for optimal performance. The amount of shared memory available per multiprocessor is limited. Therefore, excessive usage can limit the number of resident thread blocks, potentially reducing occupancy and impacting performance. The size of shared memory can be dynamically specified using the third execution configuration parameter in the kernel launch:

```
exampleKernel<<<blocks, threads, sharedMemSize>>>(d_in, d_out);
```

Here, sharedMemSize denotes the amount of shared memory in bytes allocated per block, and adjusting this parameter allows flexible management based on different use cases.

Understanding these principles and applying them judiciously can unlock significant performance improvements in your CUDA applications by efficiently using the low-latency shared memory architecture.

6.7 Using Constant Memory in Kernels

Constant memory in CUDA allows developers to provide read-only access to variables that do not change their values during the execution of a kernel. This memory is cached, which can lead to significant performance improvements when the same memory locations are accessed multiple times within a kernel. Utilizing constant memory effectively can optimize the performance of your CUDA applications, especially when working with data that is frequently read but rarely modified.

Declaration and Allocation of Constant Memory

Constant memory is declared in global scope using the __constant_-

_ qualifier. This memory needs to be allocated and initialized on the host before being accessed by the device.

```
__constant__ float constArray[256];
```

In the host code, constant memory is copied from the host to the device using the cudaMemcpyToSymbol function.

```
float h_array[256];
// Initialize h_array with values
cudaMemcpyToSymbol(constArray, h_array, sizeof(float) * 256);
```

Accessing Constant Memory in Kernels

Constant memory can be accessed inside the kernel using the same variable name declared with the __constant__ qualifier.

```
__global__ void kernelFunction() {
    int idx = threadIdx.x;
    float value = constArray[idx];
    // Utilize value in computations
}
```

When a global variable declared as constant is accessed inside a kernel, the memory access pattern significantly affects performance. Ideally, all threads within a warp should read the same memory location to take full advantage of constant memory caching.

Performance Considerations

The CUDA architecture includes a small constant memory cache per multiprocessor. When threads in a warp access different locations in constant memory, this results in multiple transactions, thus decreasing the cache's effectiveness. However, if all threads in a warp (or even better, all threads in a block) access the same memory location, the transaction can be satisfied by a single read from the constant cache. This property makes constant memory particularly useful for sharing common constants like coefficients used in calculations across all threads.

Consider a scenario involving a kernel that applies a coefficient to each element in an input array.

```
__global__ void applyCoefficient(float *input, float *output) {
    int idx = blockIdx.x * blockDim.x + threadIdx.x;
    output[idx] = input[idx] * constArray[0];
}
```

Here, constArray[0] is accessed by all threads, which makes good use of the constant memory cache, ensuring a high cache hit rate.

Example: Computation of Weighted Sum

To demonstrate the practical application of constant memory, consider the computation of a weighted sum of elements where the weights remain constant throughout the kernel execution.

```
__constant__ float weights[256];

__global__ void weightedSum(const float *input, float *output, int N) {
    int idx = blockIdx.x * blockDim.x + threadIdx.x;
    float sum = 0.0f;
    for (int i = 0; i < 256; ++i) {
        sum += input[idx + i * N] * weights[i];
    }
    output[idx] = sum;
}
```

In this example, since the weights array does not change and is used by all threads, placing it in constant memory ensures efficient access and leverages the constant cache. The loop iterates over 256 elements of the input data, each multiplied by their corresponding constant weight.

Advantages and Limitations

Constant memory is best utilized under conditions where there is a high level of reusability for the read-only data across multiple threads. However, this memory space is limited (typical sizes are 64KB), and excessive use without considering the access patterns can still result in performance bottlenecks.

For applications involving frequently accessed constants across multiple kernels, such as transformation matrices in graphics applications or statistical coefficients in scientific simulations, constant memory offers an optimized solution.

Proper utilization of constant memory can enhance kernel performance by reducing the number of global memory accesses and leveraging cache efficiency, thus enabling more efficient CUDA applications.

6.8 Error Handling in Kernel Execution

Efficient error handling is crucial for robust and fault-tolerant CUDA applications. Various types of errors can occur during kernel execution, including launch failures, memory access violations, or resource allocation errors. This section delves into strategies and best practices for identifying, managing, and mitigating these errors to ensure stable and reliable CUDA programs.

1. Introduction to CUDA Error Codes

CUDA provides a comprehensive set of error codes defined in the cudaError_t enumerated type. These error codes are returned by most CUDA runtime functions to indicate the success or failure of an operation. Key error codes include:

- cudaSuccess – indicates successful completion of an operation.
- cudaErrorInvalidValue – indicates an invalid value passed as a parameter.
- cudaErrorMemoryAllocation – indicates a failure to allocate the requested memory.
- cudaErrorLaunchFailure – indicates a kernel launch failure.

2. Checking and Handling Errors

CUDA functions typically return an error code that should be checked immediately after the function call. It's essential to propagate these errors properly to diagnose and fix problems effectively. A common approach is to define a macro for error checking:

```
#define cudaCheckError(ans) { cudaAssert((ans), __FILE__, __LINE__); }
inline void cudaAssert(cudaError_t code, const char *file, int line, bool abort=true)
{
   if (code != cudaSuccess)
   {
      fprintf(stderr,"CUDA Error: %s %s %d\n", cudaGetErrorString(code), file, line);
      if (abort) exit(code);
   }
}
```

This macro, cudaCheckError, wraps CUDA function calls and handles error checking by reporting the filename and line number where the error occurred.

3. Synchronous and Asynchronous Error Handling

Kernel launches and many CUDA operations are asynchronous; thus, errors may not be reported immediately. To ensure all preceding CUDA operations have completed and to check for errors, use cudaDeviceSynchronize():

```
kernelFunction<<<gridDim, blockDim>>>(...);
cudaCheckError(cudaPeekAtLastError()); // Check for launch errors
cudaCheckError(cudaDeviceSynchronize()); // Check for runtime errors
```

cudaPeekAtLastError() checks for errors from the most recent launch, while cudaDeviceSynchronize() ensures the device has completed all operations and checks for any errors.

4. Error Handling in Memory Operations

Memory-related errors are common in CUDA programming. Functions such as cudaMalloc() and cudaMemcpy() may fail due to insufficient memory or invalid copy sizes:

```
void* d_ptr;
cudaError_t err = cudaMalloc(&d_ptr, size);
if (err != cudaSuccess) {
    fprintf(stderr, "CUDA Error: %s\n", cudaGetErrorString(err));
    // Handle error (e.g., clean up resources)
}

err = cudaMemcpy(d_ptr, h_ptr, size, cudaMemcpyHostToDevice);
if (err != cudaSuccess) {
    fprintf(stderr, "CUDA Error: %s\n", cudaGetErrorString(err));
    // Handle error (e.g., clean up resources)
}
```

Proper error handling ensures that resources are freed appropriately and that the application can respond to failures meaningfully.

5. Debugging and Profiling Tools

The CUDA toolkit provides several tools to help diagnose and resolve errors:

- **cuda-gdb** – a CUDA-aware extension of the GNU Debugger for debugging device code.
- **CUDA-MEMCHECK** – a suite of tools for detecting memory access errors, race conditions, and other related issues.
- **Nsight Compute** – a powerful profiling tool to analyze kernel performance and identify inefficiencies.

Using these tools can significantly streamline the process of pinpointing and addressing errors in your CUDA applications.

6. Example: Error Handling in a Kernel

Consider a kernel function that performs matrix addition. Proper error handling ensures that any issues during execution are effectively managed:

```
__global__ void addMatrices(float* A, float* B, float* C, int N) {
    int idx = blockIdx.x * blockDim.x + threadIdx.x;
    if (idx < N) {
        C[idx] = A[idx] + B[idx];
    }
}

void launchAddMatricesKernel() {
```

```
    int N = 1024;
    size_t size = N * sizeof(float);
    float *d_A, *d_B, *d_C;

    cudaCheckError(cudaMalloc(&d_A, size));
    cudaCheckError(cudaMalloc(&d_B, size));
    cudaCheckError(cudaMalloc(&d_C, size));

    dim3 blockDim(256);
    dim3 gridDim((N + blockDim.x - 1) / blockDim.x);
    addMatrices<<<gridDim, blockDim>>>(d_A, d_B, d_C, N);

    cudaCheckError(cudaPeekAtLastError());
    cudaCheckError(cudaDeviceSynchronize());

    cudaFree(d_A);
    cudaFree(d_B);
    cudaFree(d_C);
}
```

This example demonstrates the integration of error checking into kernel execution, ensuring that any allocation or launch issues are promptly identified and handled.

By meticulously checking and handling errors, leveraging debugging and profiling tools, and adopting best practices, CUDA programmers can significantly improve the reliability and performance of their applications. Efficient error handling not only simplifies debugging but also contributes to the development of robust and resilient software.

6.9 Optimizing Kernel Performance

Performance optimization in CUDA programming is critical to leveraging the full potential of GPU hardware. Optimizing a kernel function involves several strategies to address compute intensity, memory access patterns, and resource utilization. This section delves into these strategies in detail, providing insights on techniques to elevate kernel performance.

One fundamental aspect of kernel performance optimization is efficient memory access. CUDA offers different types of memory with varying latency and bandwidth characteristics, such as global, shared, constant, and texture memory. The optimal selection and usage of these memory types can significantly affect performance.

To start with, coalesced memory access is essential for achieving high memory bandwidth. Global memory accesses by different threads should be structured to minimize the number of memory transactions.

For example, when reading a contiguous block of memory, threads in a warp should access consecutive memory locations:

```
__global__ void optimizedKernel(float *input, float *output) {
    int tid = threadIdx.x + blockIdx.x * blockDim.x;
    output[tid] = input[tid];
}
```

In the above code, each thread accesses a unique address in a contiguous block of memory. This access pattern allows the GPU to coalesce the memory transactions, thus improving the kernel's efficiency.

Shared memory, another key aspect, is an on-chip memory that offers higher bandwidth and lower latency compared to global memory. Efficient usage of shared memory can help to minimize global memory accesses. Data commonly used by multiple threads within a block should be loaded into shared memory first. Consider the following example where shared memory is employed in a tiled matrix multiplication:

```
__global__ void matrixMul(float *A, float *B, float *C, int N) {
    __shared__ float tileA[TILE_SIZE][TILE_SIZE];
    __shared__ float tileB[TILE_SIZE][TILE_SIZE];

    int row = threadIdx.y;
    int col = threadIdx.x;
    int globalRow = blockIdx.y * blockDim.y + row;
    int globalCol = blockIdx.x * blockDim.x + col;

    float sum = 0.0f;

    for (int m = 0; m < (N + TILE_SIZE - 1) / TILE_SIZE; ++m) {
        if (globalRow < N && m * TILE_SIZE + col < N)
            tileA[row][col] = A[globalRow * N + m * TILE_SIZE + col];
        else
            tileA[row][col] = 0.0f;

        if (globalCol < N && m * TILE_SIZE + row < N)
            tileB[row][col] = B[(m * TILE_SIZE + row) * N + globalCol];
        else
            tileB[row][col] = 0.0f;

        __syncthreads();

        for (int k = 0; k < TILE_SIZE; ++k)
            sum += tileA[row][k] * tileB[k][col];

        __syncthreads();
    }

    if (globalRow < N && globalCol < N)
        C[globalRow * N + globalCol] = sum;
}
```

In this example, by dividing the matrices into tiles that fit within shared memory, the code significantly reduces the number of global memory accesses, leading to performance gains.

Another important optimization technique is minimization of divergent branches. Warp divergence occurs when threads of a warp follow different execution paths due to conditional statements. CUDA warps execute in SIMD (Single Instruction, Multiple Data) fashion, meaning all threads should ideally follow the same execution path:

```
__global__ void compute(int *data, int len) {
    int tid = threadIdx.x + blockIdx.x * blockDim.x;
    if (tid < len) {
        if (tid % 2 == 0) {
            data[tid] *= 2;
        } else {
            data[tid] += 1;
        }
    }
}
```

In the above code, warp divergence is introduced by the conditional statement within the if-else block. When half the threads in a warp evaluate to true and the other half to false, the warp executes both branches in sequence, thus diminishing performance. Minimizing such divergence by restructuring code to avoid conditionals per warp is beneficial.

The configuration of thread blocks and warps plays a crucial role in performance. The hardware scheduler is optimized for specific block and warp sizes. Typically, the optimal block size is a multiple of 32, as this corresponds to the warp size. Launch configuration can be fine-tuned based on empirical performance testing:

```
int threadsPerBlock = 256;
int blocksPerGrid = (dataSize + threadsPerBlock - 1) / threadsPerBlock;
myKernel<<<blocksPerGrid, threadsPerBlock>>>(d_data);
```

Choosing appropriate block and grid sizes ensures maximal occupancy, which is the ratio of active warps to the maximum number of warps supported on a multiprocessor. Higher occupancy can potentially improve performance, but the primary focus should be on reducing global memory latency and bandwidth constraints.

Memory bank conflicts can also be a performance bottleneck. Shared memory is divided into banks that can be accessed simultaneously. However, if threads within a warp access the same bank, conflicts arise, decreasing performance. Ensuring that access patterns avoid such conflicts is key:

```
__shared__ float sharedArray[32];
int index = threadIdx.x;
sharedArray[index] = index;
```

In this simplistic example, each thread accesses a distinct shared memory bank, avoiding conflicts and thus maintaining efficiency.

Compiler optimizations, such as using the const qualifier for read-only variables or the restrict qualifier to indicate non-aliasing pointers, help the compiler generate more efficient code.

Finally, profiling tools like NVIDIA's nvprof or Nsight can provide insights into kernel performance bottlenecks, such as memory throughput, execution time, and warp efficiency. By iteratively profiling and tuning the code, maximum performance can be achieved, making the GPU an even more powerful computational resource.

6.10 Case Study: Image Processing Kernel

In this section, we will delve into the practical application of the concepts learned in the previous sections by examining a case study in image processing using CUDA kernels. This example will provide a clear demonstration of how to define, launch, and optimize a CUDA kernel for performing image transformations.

Consider a common operation in image processing: grayscale conversion. The goal is to convert a color image (RGB format) to grayscale. The intensity of each pixel in the grayscale image is computed as the weighted sum of the red, green, and blue components based on the luminance formula:

$$I = 0.299R + 0.587G + 0.114B$$

First, let us define the kernel function for this operation. The kernel will read the RGB values of each pixel, apply the luminance formula, and store the result in the output grayscale image array.

```
__global__ void rgb_to_grayscale(const unsigned char *rgbImage, unsigned char *
    grayImage, int width, int height)
{
    int x = blockIdx.x * blockDim.x + threadIdx.x;
    int y = blockIdx.y * blockDim.y + threadIdx.y;

    if (x < width && y < height)
    {
        int rgbIndex = (y * width + x) * 3; // RGB image index
        int grayIndex = y * width + x; // Grayscale image index

        unsigned char r = rgbImage[rgbIndex];
        unsigned char g = rgbImage[rgbIndex + 1];
        unsigned char b = rgbImage[rgbIndex + 2];
```

```
        grayImage[grayIndex] = static_cast<unsigned char>(0.299f * r + 0.587f * g +
            0.114f * b);
    }
}
```

To launch this kernel, we need to set up the correct execution configuration. We will configure the grid and block dimensions based on the image size to ensure that each thread processes one pixel.

```
// Image dimensions
int width = 1920;
int height = 1080;

// Grid and block dimensions
dim3 blockDim(16, 16);
dim3 gridDim((width + blockDim.x - 1) / blockDim.x, (height + blockDim.y - 1) /
    blockDim.y);

// Allocate memory on the device
unsigned char *d_rgbImage, *d_grayImage;
size_t rgbSize = width * height * 3 * sizeof(unsigned char);
size_t graySize = width * height * sizeof(unsigned char);

cudaMalloc(&d_rgbImage, rgbSize);
cudaMalloc(&d_grayImage, graySize);

// Copy data from the host to the device
cudaMemcpy(d_rgbImage, h_rgbImage, rgbSize, cudaMemcpyHostToDevice);

// Launch the kernel
rgb_to_grayscale<<<gridDim, blockDim>>>(d_rgbImage, d_grayImage, width,
    height);

// Copy the result back to the host
cudaMemcpy(h_grayImage, d_grayImage, graySize, cudaMemcpyDeviceToHost);

// Free device memory
cudaFree(d_rgbImage);
cudaFree(d_grayImage);
```

To enhance performance, consider using shared memory. Since shared memory has much lower latency compared to global memory, it can be useful for operations that require multiple accesses to the same data. However, for this specific case involving the application of only a simple arithmetic operation on each pixel's data, the performance gain from shared memory may be insignificant. Instead, let's focus on coalesced memory access, which is crucial for optimal performance in GPU computing.

We ensure coalesced memory access by organizing the threads such that consecutive threads access consecutive memory locations. This is already achieved in the current implementation as each thread accesses pixels in a row-major order.

Next, we would include proper error handling to make sure our kernel launches and memory operations are successful. This can be done by checking the return status of the CUDA runtime API functions and capturing any errors.

```
#define cudaCheckError(expr) \
    do { \
        cudaError_t err = expr; \
        if (err != cudaSuccess) { \
            fprintf(stderr, "CUDA error %s at %s:%d\n", cudaGetErrorString(err),
                __FILE__, __LINE__); \
            exit(1); \
        } \
    } while (0)

// Replacing the previous memory allocation and copy calls with error-checked versions:

cudaCheckError(cudaMalloc(&d_rgbImage, rgbSize));
cudaCheckError(cudaMalloc(&d_grayImage, graySize));

cudaCheckError(cudaMemcpy(d_rgbImage, h_rgbImage, rgbSize,
    cudaMemcpyHostToDevice));
cudaCheckError(cudaMemcpy(h_grayImage, d_grayImage, graySize,
    cudaMemcpyDeviceToHost));

// Launch the kernel and check for errors
rgb_to_grayscale<<<gridDim, blockDim>>>(d_rgbImage, d_grayImage, width,
    height);
cudaCheckError(cudaPeekAtLastError());
cudaCheckError(cudaDeviceSynchronize());

cudaCheckError(cudaFree(d_rgbImage));
cudaCheckError(cudaFree(d_grayImage));
```

Moving to optimization, another consideration is minimizing data transfer time between host and device. When possible, process multiple images in batch. Transfer all images to the device at once, apply the kernel to each image, and transfer the results back in a single batch.

```
// Allocate memory for batch processing
int batchSize = 10; // Number of images
size_t totalRGBSize = batchSize * rgbSize;
size_t totalGraySize = batchSize * graySize;

cudaCheckError(cudaMalloc(&d_rgbImage, totalRGBSize));
cudaCheckError(cudaMalloc(&d_grayImage, totalGraySize));

// Copy batch data from host to device
cudaCheckError(cudaMemcpy(d_rgbImage, h_rgbImages, totalRGBSize,
    cudaMemcpyHostToDevice));

// Define grid and block dimensions
dim3 blockDim(16, 16);
dim3 gridDim((width + blockDim.x - 1) / blockDim.x, (height + blockDim.y - 1) /
    blockDim.y);

// Launch batch kernel processing
for (int i = 0; i < batchSize; ++i)
{
```

```
    int offset = i * width * height;
    rgb_to_grayscale<<<gridDim, blockDim>>>(d_rgbImage + offset * 3,
        d_grayImage + offset, width, height);
}

cudaCheckError(cudaPeekAtLastError());
cudaCheckError(cudaDeviceSynchronize());

// Copy results back to host
cudaCheckError(cudaMemcpy(h_grayImages, d_grayImage, totalGraySize,
    cudaMemcpyDeviceToHost));

cudaCheckError(cudaFree(d_rgbImage));
cudaCheckError(cudaFree(d_grayImage));
```

The case study demonstrates the application of CUDA kernel functions in a real-world scenario. By defining efficient kernels, appropriately configuring their execution, and employing optimization strategies such as shared memory usage and error handling, we achieve significant performance improvements in computationally intensive tasks like image processing.

This hands-on approach not only solidifies the theoretical knowledge covered in earlier chapters but also prepares you to address practical challenges in CUDA programming.

Chapter 7

Performance Optimization Techniques

This chapter covers performance optimization techniques for CUDA applications, starting with the identification and analysis of performance bottlenecks. It delves into optimizing memory access patterns, memory coalescing, and effective shared memory usage. Techniques for balancing load among threads, minimizing warp divergence, and maximizing instruction-level parallelism are discussed. The chapter also explores efficient utilization of CUDA streams and modern GPU features, concluding with a case study on accelerating scientific computations.

7.1 Introduction to Performance Optimization

Performance optimization in CUDA programming is a crucial skill for harnessing the full computational power of GPUs. This section introduces key concepts and principles for improving the performance of CUDA applications, laying a foundation for the more advanced techniques covered in subsequent sections.

The primary goal of performance optimization is to maximize the efficiency of GPU resources, ensuring that applications run as fast as possible while using the least amount of energy. This involves analyzing and improving various aspects of the application, including memory access patterns, computational efficiency, and resource utilization.

Identifying Performance Bottlenecks

The first step in performance optimization is identifying the bottlenecks that limit application performance. Profiling tools such as NVIDIA Visual Profiler (nvvp) and Nsight Systems provide valuable insights into the behavior of CUDA applications, allowing developers to pinpoint areas that require optimization. These tools help track metrics such as kernel execution time, memory transfer rates, occupancy, and divergence.

Kernel execution time is a critical metric; it indicates how long a specific kernel function takes to run on the GPU. Large execution times may highlight inefficient algorithms, excessive computational complexity, or poor optimization. Memory transfer rates between the host (CPU) and device (GPU) can also be a significant source of bottlenecks, especially if data transfer operations are not overlapped with computation.

Occupancy measures how effectively the GPU's computational resources are utilized, taking into account the number of active warps, threads per block, and the usage of shared and register memory. High occupancy often correlates with better performance, though it is not the sole determinant. Lastly, divergence metrics can reveal inefficiencies caused by different threads in a warp taking divergent execution paths, leading to underutilization of the GPU.

Optimizing Memory Access Patterns

Efficient memory access is critical for optimal performance in CUDA applications. Memory access patterns should be designed to take advantage of the hierarchical memory structure of GPUs, which includes global, shared, constant, and texture memory. Global memory has the highest latency and should be accessed in a coalesced manner to maximize bandwidth utilization. Shared memory, on the other hand, is much faster and can be used to reduce global memory access when data reuse across threads is possible.

An example of optimizing memory access patterns can be shown through the following CUDA kernel, designed to add two arrays:

```
__global__ void vectorAdd(float *A, float *B, float *C, int N) {
    int idx = blockDim.x * blockIdx.x + threadIdx.x;
    if (idx < N) {
        C[idx] = A[idx] + B[idx];
    }
}
```

In the vectorAdd kernel, memory access for arrays A, B, and C should be coalesced to ensure high bandwidth usage. Coalesced access occurs when consecutive threads read or write consecutive memory locations.

Reducing Memory Latency

The use of shared memory can help reduce memory latency by storing frequently accessed data closer to the compute units. The following example shows how to perform a simple matrix multiplication using shared memory to enhance memory access efficiency:

```
__global__ void matrixMulShared(float* A, float* B, float* C, int N) {
    __shared__ float tileA[TILE_DIM][TILE_DIM];
    __shared__ float tileB[TILE_DIM][TILE_DIM];

    int row = blockIdx.y * TILE_DIM + threadIdx.y;
    int col = blockIdx.x * TILE_DIM + threadIdx.x;
    float value = 0;

    for (int m = 0; m < (N + TILE_DIM - 1)/TILE_DIM; m++) {
        if (row < N && m * TILE_DIM + threadIdx.x < N)
            tileA[threadIdx.y][threadIdx.x] = A[row * N + m * TILE_DIM + threadIdx.
                x];
        else
            tileA[threadIdx.y][threadIdx.x] = 0;

        if (col < N && m * TILE_DIM + threadIdx.y < N)
            tileB[threadIdx.y][threadIdx.x] = B[(m * TILE_DIM + threadIdx.y) * N +
                col];
        else
            tileB[threadIdx.y][threadIdx.x] = 0;

        __syncthreads();

        for (int e = 0; e < TILE_DIM; e++)
            value += tileA[threadIdx.y][e] * tileB[e][threadIdx.x];

        __syncthreads();
    }

    if (row < N && col < N)
        C[row * N + col] = value;
}
```

In the matrixMulShared kernel, shared memory (tileA and tileB) is used to store submatrices of A and B, reducing the number of global memory accesses and therefore latency.

Understanding these foundational principles and techniques is crucial for optimizing CUDA applications. This knowledge will be expanded upon in the following sections, where more specific and advanced topics related to performance optimization will be discussed.

7.2 Analyzing Performance Bottlenecks

Successful optimization of CUDA applications begins with a meticulous analysis of performance bottlenecks. Without identifying the exact points in your code causing reductions in performance, optimization efforts may be ineffective or even counterproductive. This section explores several techniques and tools that facilitate the precise identification and analysis of performance bottlenecks in CUDA applications.

The initial step in performance analysis is often the profiling of the application's execution. Profiling tools provide insights into various metrics, including execution time, memory usage, and other relevant characteristics.

NVIDIA Visual Profiler (nvvp) and Nsight Compute

NVIDIA provides powerful tools like NVIDIA Visual Profiler (nvvp) and Nsight Compute, which are instrumental in profiling CUDA applications. These tools offer a graphical representation of performance metrics and can pinpoint bottlenecks precisely.

To profile a CUDA application using NVIDIA Visual Profiler, follow these steps:

1. Compile the CUDA application with debug information enabled:

```
nvcc -G -o application application.cu
```

2. Launch NVIDIA Visual Profiler.
3. Open the compiled executable within the profiler.
4. Run the profiling session.

Once profiling is complete, the profiler displays various metrics, such as kernel execution times, memory throughput, and occupancy rates. It highlights the regions where the GPU spends most of its time, allowing you to focus optimization efforts on those critical sections.

Profiler Output Interpretation

Interpreting profiler data is crucial for effective optimization. Key metrics from profiler outputs include:

- **Kernel Execution Time:** Indicates the duration each kernel takes to execute. Kernels consuming a disproportionate amount of time are potential candidates for optimization.

- **Global Memory Throughput:** Measures the rate of global memory data transfer. Low throughput suggests inefficient memory access patterns.
- **Occupancy:** Represents the ratio of active warps to the maximum possible active warps on a multiprocessor. Low occupancy indicates insufficient parallelism.
- **Divergence:** Highlights issues with warp divergence, where threads in the same warp follow different execution paths, potentially serializing execution.

Manual Timers and CUDA Events

While profiling tools provide extensive analysis, integrating manual timing mechanisms and CUDA events can offer additional precision for specific code segments. CUDA events are particularly useful for measuring execution time with high granularity.

Implementing CUDA events involves creating event objects, recording events before and after the code segment of interest, and calculating the elapsed time.

Example code for timing a kernel execution:

```
cudaEvent_t start, stop;
float elapsed_time;
cudaEventCreate(&start);
cudaEventCreate(&stop);

cudaEventRecord(start, 0);
// Kernel launch
myKernel<<<gridDim, blockDim>>>(args);
cudaEventRecord(stop, 0);
cudaEventSynchronize(stop);

cudaEventElapsedTime(&elapsed_time, start, stop);
printf("Kernel execution time: %f ms\n", elapsed_time);

cudaEventDestroy(start);
cudaEventDestroy(stop);
```

The output will show the precise execution time of the kernel, aiding identification of time-consuming operations.

Analyzing Memory Bottlenecks

Efficient memory usage is crucial for CUDA performance. Bottlenecks often occur due to suboptimal global memory access patterns and failure to leverage fast memory such as shared memory. Memory access patterns can often be scrutinized by examining coalescence of memory accesses, cache usage, and memory access skew.

Coalesced vs. Non-coalesced Memory Accesses:

To ensure memory accesses are coalesced:

- Ensure contiguous threads access contiguous memory locations.
- Use appropriate data types and struct alignments.
- Avoid divergent memory access patterns within warps.

Visual Profiler or Nsight Compute can also display memory access patterns, highlighting non-coalesced accesses. Correcting these can significantly improve memory throughput.

Cache Utilization:

Modern GPUs possess multiple levels of cache. Profiling tools display cache hit rates which can diagnose inefficiencies:

- High cache miss rates indicate that data locality might be poor.
- Optimization strategies might include data layout transformations or changing memory access patterns.

Algorithm Analysis

Often, performance bottlenecks can be traced back to the inherent inefficiencies in the algorithm itself. Complexity analysis remains an essential tool here. Profiling data is used to identify which parts of the algorithm are worth re-evaluating.

Thread Divergence Analysis

Thread divergence, where threads within the same warp take different execution paths, can also significantly hinder performance. Profiling tools highlight sections of code with high divergence. Strategies to mitigate thread divergence include:

- Refactor conditional statements to minimize divergences.
- Use warp-synchronous programming techniques.

By systematically profiling the application, interpreting the profiling data accurately, and employing targeted optimization strategies, CUDA programmers can effectively identify and mitigate performance bottlenecks. This rigorous approach ensures that subsequent optimization efforts are focused and impactful.

7.3 Optimizing Memory Access Patterns

Optimal memory access patterns are crucial to achieving high performance in CUDA applications. Memory access patterns directly affect the achieved memory bandwidth, which in turn impacts the overall performance. Here, we look into the types of memory within the CUDA architecture and prescribe methods to optimize access to each of them.

Global memory is the most abundant but also the slowest memory within a GPU. Access to global memory can be optimized by ensuring coalesced memory accesses, where consecutive threads access consecutive memory addresses. This reduces the number of memory transactions, thereby enhancing memory bandwidth utilization.

```
__global__ void coalesced_access(float *d_out, float *d_in) {
    int idx = threadIdx.x + blockDim.x * blockIdx.x;
    d_out[idx] = d_in[idx];
}
```

In this example, each thread reads from and writes to consecutive memory locations, ensuring a coalesced memory access pattern. In practice, one must ensure that the starting address is aligned to the memory warp size (usually 32 or 64 bytes).

Shared memory is another critical resource that enables efficient inter-thread communication and offers significantly lower latency and higher bandwidth compared to global memory. Utilizing shared memory can alleviate the pressure on global memory bandwidth. A common usage pattern is staging data in shared memory to facilitate reuse across multiple threads within a block.

```
__global__ void use_shared_memory(float *d_out, float *d_in) {
    extern __shared__ float s_data[];
    int idx = threadIdx.x + blockDim.x * blockIdx.x;
    int tid = threadIdx.x;

    // Load data into shared memory
    s_data[tid] = d_in[idx];
    __syncthreads();

    // Perform computation using shared memory
    d_out[idx] = s_data[tid] * 2.0f;
}
```

The synchronization after loading the data into shared memory ensures that all threads have completed the data transfer before computation begins. This prevents data hazards and ensures correctness.

Constant memory is optimized for scenarios where data is the same for all threads and does not change during kernel execution. Access to constant memory is cached and can be exceptionally fast when all threads read the same address.

```
__constant__ float d_constant[256]; // Constant memory declaration

__global__ void use_constant_memory(float *d_out, float *d_in) {
    int idx = threadIdx.x + blockDim.x * blockIdx.x;
    d_out[idx] = d_in[idx] + d_constant[threadIdx.x];
}
```

Here, d_constant is a read-only memory view that allows efficient broadcasting of data across all threads. The access latency is minimized if all threads in a warp access the same address.

Texture memory offers read-only data access optimized for spatial locality and is beneficial for two-dimensional data patterns such as images. Texture memory access is cached, providing performance benefits when memory locality is preserved.

```
texture<float, 2, cudaReadModeElementType> texRef; // Texture memory reference

__global__ void use_texture_memory(float *d_out) {
    int x = threadIdx.x + blockDim.x * blockIdx.x;
    int y = threadIdx.y + blockDim.y * blockIdx.y;
    float value = tex2D(texRef, x, y);
    d_out[y * gridDim.x * blockDim.x + x] = value;
}
```

In the above code, tex2D function is used to fetch data from texture memory. The hardware cache for texture memory ensures efficient access patterns, especially when data locality is adhered to.

Memory alignment and padding can also influence the performance of CUDA applications. Memory allocated on the GPU should be aligned to 128 bytes to ensure efficient access. Padding might be necessary when working with structured data types to avoid misaligned memory accesses, which can lead to suboptimal performance.

```
__global__ void padded_access(float *d_out, float *d_in, int width) {
    int idx = threadIdx.x + blockDim.x * blockIdx.x;
    int idy = threadIdx.y + blockDim.y * blockIdx.y;
    int index = idy * width + idx;
    d_out[index] = d_in[index];
}
```

Here, width is chosen such that each new row starts at an aligned memory address, facilitating coalesced access across rows.

Efficient memory access patterns go beyond simple coalescing and caching. They involve a deep understanding of both algorithmic requirements and hardware characteristics. By aligning access patterns with the underlying hardware specifics, one maximizes the throughput and minimizes the latency, leading to overall performance gains in CUDA-enabled applications.

7.4 Memory Coalescing Techniques

Memory coalescing is a critical performance optimization technique in CUDA programming, aimed at improving the efficiency of global memory accesses. The GPU's memory subsystem is designed to deliver high bandwidth, but achieving this requires that memory accesses be coalesced. When memory accesses are coalesced, multiple memory transactions are combined into a single transaction, reducing memory latency and increasing bandwidth utilization.

To understand memory coalescing, it's crucial to grasp how CUDA threads access global memory and the conditions under which these accesses become coalesced. The primary goal is to ensure that memory accesses by threads within a warp, a group of 32 threads, are aligned in such a way that they can be processed as a single memory transaction. Several factors influence memory coalescing, including memory alignment, access patterns, and data structures.

Memory Alignment:

Memory alignment refers to the arrangement of memory addresses accessed by the threads in a warp. For optimal coalescing, memory accesses need to follow specific alignment rules:

- For 32-byte transactions, addresses should be aligned to 32-byte boundaries.
- For 64-byte transactions, addresses should be aligned to 64-byte boundaries.
- For 128-byte transactions, addresses should be aligned to 128-byte boundaries.

Accesses that do not adhere to these alignment boundaries result in multiple transactions, thereby reducing the coalescing efficiency.

Access Patterns:

The pattern in which threads access memory has a significant impact on coalescing. The simplest and most efficient pattern is when consecutive threads in a warp access consecutive memory locations. This pattern ensures that all accesses within a warp fall within a single memory transaction boundary.

```
__global__ void simpleKernel(float *data) {
    int idx = threadIdx.x + blockIdx.x * blockDim.x;
    data[idx] = idx;
}
```

In the above example, each thread calculates its unique index and writes to that position in the 'data' array. This access pattern is optimal for coalescing because thread 'i' accesses 'data[i]', ensuring that memory transactions are contiguous and aligned.

Strided Access Patterns:

Non-contiguous or strided access patterns can severely degrade memory coalescing efficiency. For example, if each thread accesses memory locations with a stride greater than one, the hardware needs to issue multiple transactions to service these requests.

```
__global__ void stridedKernel(float *data, int stride) {
    int idx = threadIdx.x + blockIdx.x * blockDim.x;
    data[idx * stride] = idx;
}
```

Here, the stride variable influences the memory access pattern. If 'stride' is not 1, the memory accesses are no longer contiguous, leading to multiple, less efficient transactions.

Structures of Arrays (SoA) vs Arrays of Structures (AoS):

Choosing appropriate data structures also impacts memory coalescing. The SoA format is generally more conducive to memory coalescing than the AoS format. In an SoA arrangement, data fields are stored in separate arrays, which promotes contiguous memory accesses by threads in a warp.

SoA Example:

```
struct SoA {
    float *x;
    float *y;
    float *z;
};

__global__ void soaKernel(SoA data, int n) {
    int idx = threadIdx.x + blockIdx.x * blockDim.x;
    if (idx < n) {
        data.x[idx] = 1.0f;
```

```
        data.y[idx] = 2.0f;
        data.z[idx] = 3.0f;
    }
}
```

AoS Example:

```
struct Vec3 {
    float x, y, z;
};

__global__ void aosKernel(Vec3 *data, int n) {
    int idx = threadIdx.x + blockIdx.x * blockDim.x;
    if (idx < n) {
        data[idx].x = 1.0f;
        data[idx].y = 2.0f;
        data[idx].z = 3.0f;
    }
}
```

In the SoA example, the 'x', 'y', and 'z' attributes are accessed in a contiguous manner, enabling coalescing. Conversely, in the AoS example, the memory accesses are not contiguous, leading to inefficient coalescing.

Compiler Optimizations and Memory Coalescing:

The CUDA compiler includes several optimizations to enhance memory coalescing automatically. However, manual intervention is often necessary to achieve optimal performance, especially when dealing with complex data structures or irregular access patterns. Developers should leverage memory access profiling tools such as NVIDIA's Nsight Compute to identify and resolve memory coalescing issues.

```
Memory Access Summary
---------------------
Coalesced Access Rate: 72%
Strided Access Penalty: 28%
Memory Access Latency: 350 cycles
```

The profiler output indicates the coalesced access rate, strided access penalties, and memory access latency, providing insightful metrics for optimization.

Memory coalescing is fundamental to achieving high performance in CUDA applications. By aligning memory accesses, using efficient access patterns, and choosing appropriate data structures, developers can maximize global memory bandwidth and minimize latency. The subsequent sections will build on these concepts, exploring how to use shared memory effectively and optimize memory access patterns further.

7.5 Using Shared Memory Effectively

Shared memory in CUDA is a key feature that allows threads within the same block to communicate efficiently. Understanding how to use shared memory effectively can lead to significant performance gains, as it is considerably faster than global memory due to its lower latency and higher bandwidth. The following section will delve into the best practices for leveraging shared memory in CUDA applications.

Shared memory is explicitly managed by the programmer and can be declared using the __shared__ keyword. A common use case involves caching frequently accessed data that multiple threads in a block need to read or write. By using shared memory, threads can avoid accessing the slower global memory repeatedly.

```
__global__ void matrixMulKernel(float *A, float *B, float *C, int width) {
    __shared__ float tileA[TILE_WIDTH][TILE_WIDTH];
    __shared__ float tileB[TILE_WIDTH][TILE_WIDTH];

    int bx = blockIdx.x; int by = blockIdx.y;
    int tx = threadIdx.x; int ty = threadIdx.y;
    int row = by * TILE_WIDTH + ty;
    int col = bx * TILE_WIDTH + tx;
    float Pvalue = 0;

    for (int m = 0; m < width / TILE_WIDTH; ++m) {
        tileA[ty][tx] = A[row * width + (m * TILE_WIDTH + tx)];
        tileB[ty][tx] = B[col + (m * TILE_WIDTH + ty) * width];
        __syncthreads();

        for (int k = 0; k < TILE_WIDTH; ++k) {
            Pvalue += tileA[ty][k] * tileB[k][tx];
        }
        __syncthreads();
    }
    C[row * width + col] = Pvalue;
}
```

In the example above, we declare shared memory arrays tileA and tileB to store tiles of matrices A and B respectively. This approach allows threads to cooperatively load tiles into shared memory, alleviating the burden on global memory and thereby speeding up the matrix multiplication process.

Key considerations for using shared memory effectively:

- **Bank Conflicts:** Shared memory in CUDA is divided into memory banks that can be accessed simultaneously. Bank conflicts occur when multiple threads access different addresses that map to the same memory bank, leading to serialized accesses and degraded performance. Avoiding bank conflicts is crucial for maximizing performance. For example, padding shared memory arrays to avoid conflicts can be an effective technique.

```
__shared__ float tileA[TILE_WIDTH][TILE_WIDTH + 1];
```

Padding ensures that consecutive elements in different rows map to different memory banks, thus eliminating bank conflicts.

- **Coalescing Global Memory Accesses:** When loading data from global memory into shared memory, it is important to ensure that the access patterns are coalesced. Coalesced memory access occurs when consecutive threads access consecutive memory addresses, resulting in fewer memory transactions.

- **Synchronization:** Since shared memory is shared among threads in a block, it is imperative to synchronize the threads using __syncthreads() to ensure data consistency. Failure to properly synchronize can lead to race conditions where threads read incomplete or inconsistent data.

```
__syncthreads();
```

- **Limited Scope:** Shared memory is allocated per block and has a limited lifetime that spans the execution of a block. It is not accessible from other blocks, so it should be used for sharing data within threads of the same block only. Ensure to manage the limited size of shared memory (typically 48KB per block on most GPUs) efficiently to avoid spilling over into slower global memory.

- **Parallel Reduction:** Shared memory is often used in parallel reduction algorithms to accumulate results from multiple threads efficiently. By iteratively reducing pairs of elements, the reduction can be performed in logarithmic time relative to the number of elements.

```
__shared__ float partialSum[BLOCK_SIZE];

unsigned int t = threadIdx.x;
partialSum[t] = input[t]; // Load input into shared memory
__syncthreads();

for (unsigned int stride = 1; stride < blockDim.x; stride *= 2) {
    if (t % (2 * stride) == 0) {
        partialSum[t] += partialSum[t + stride];
    }
    __syncthreads();
}
```

```
if (t == 0) {
    output[blockIdx.x] = partialSum[0];
}
```

In the parallel reduction example, the input array is loaded into shared memory, and pairwise sums are computed in a hierarchical manner. Synchronization ensures that all threads participate correctly in each reduction step.

Properly leveraging shared memory can lead to substantial performance improvements by reducing the reliance on slower global memory, minimizing latency, and maximizing throughput. By carefully designing access patterns, avoiding bank conflicts, and ensuring appropriate synchronization, CUDA programmers can make the most of the shared memory in their applications.

7.6 Balancing Load Among Threads

Balancing load among threads is a crucial aspect of optimizing the performance of CUDA applications. Uneven workload distribution can lead to significant inefficiencies, as some threads may finish their tasks quickly while others lag behind, underutilizing the computational resources. Ensuring a balanced load distribution across threads enhances parallel efficiency and achieves better GPU utilization.

Thread-level Parallelism

Thread-level parallelism in CUDA is achieved by organizing threads into blocks and grids. Each thread within a block executes the same kernel function but operates on different data. Effective load balancing requires that each thread should have an almost equal amount of work to perform during kernel execution.

Dynamic Parallelism

Dynamic parallelism allows the GPU to launch new grids of threads from an existing kernel running on the GPU. This feature is beneficial when the workload cannot be divided evenly upfront. Kernels can dynamically allocate additional threads as they process data, adapting the workload distribution in real-time.

Workload Partitioning Strategies

1. **Static Partitioning**: This technique involves dividing the workload

into fixed-sized chunks, with each chunk assigned to a specific thread. The challenge with static partitioning is that it requires prior knowledge of the workload distribution. If the workload is irregular, some threads might end up doing significantly more work than others. 2. **Dynamic Partitioning**: Unlike static partitioning, dynamic partitioning assigns work units to threads at runtime. This method is more flexible and can adapt to varying workloads, ensuring a balanced distribution of work among threads. This approach often uses work queues where threads pull tasks from a shared queue.

Implementing Work Queues

Consider the following CUDA implementation of a work queue for balancing load among threads:

```
__global__ void dynamicWorkloadKernel(int *data, int n) {
    __shared__ int sharedQueue[MAX_QUEUE_SIZE];
    int tid = threadIdx.x + blockIdx.x * blockDim.x;

    while (true) {
        int task = -1;

        // Each thread atomically fetches a task from the queue
        if (tid < n) {
            task = atomicSub(&queueIndex, 1);
            __syncthreads();
        }

        if (task < 0 || task > n) break;

        // Perform task
        data[task] += 1; // Placeholder for actual computation

        __syncthreads();
    }
}

extern "C" void launchDynamicWorkloadKernel(int *data, int n) {
    int *d_data;
    cudaMalloc(&d_data, n * sizeof(int));
    cudaMemcpy(d_data, data, n * sizeof(int), cudaMemcpyHostToDevice);

    int blocks = (n + THREADS_PER_BLOCK - 1) / THREADS_PER_BLOCK;
    dynamicWorkloadKernel<<<blocks, THREADS_PER_BLOCK>>>(d_data, n);

    cudaMemcpy(data, d_data, n * sizeof(int), cudaMemcpyDeviceToHost);
    cudaFree(d_data);
}
```

This code demonstrates a simple method where threads dynamically fetch tasks from a queue. Each thread uses an atomic operation to safely decrement the queue index, ensuring no two threads perform the same task.

Balancing Recursive Workloads

When dealing with recursive workloads, dynamic parallelism can be particularly effective. The CUDA runtime supports kernel launches from within kernels, which allows recursive algorithms to be implemented directly on the GPU. This method can help balance the load among threads that may need to perform a varying number of recursive steps.

```
__global__ void recursiveWorkloadKernel(int level, int maxLevel, int *data) {
    int tid = threadIdx.x + blockIdx.x * blockDim.x;
    if (level >= maxLevel || tid >= N) return;

    // Perform work specific to this level
    data[tid] += level;

    // Launch new kernel for the next level of recursion
    if (tid < N / 2) {
        recursiveWorkloadKernel<<<1, 128>>>(level + 1, maxLevel, data);
    }
}

extern "C" void launchRecursiveWorkloadKernel(int *data) {
    int *d_data;
    cudaMalloc(&d_data, N * sizeof(int));
    cudaMemcpy(d_data, data, N * sizeof(int), cudaMemcpyHostToDevice);

    recursiveWorkloadKernel<<<1, 128>>>(0, MAX_LEVEL, d_data);

    cudaMemcpy(data, d_data, N * sizeof(int), cudaMemcpyDeviceToHost);
    cudaFree(d_data);
}
```

In this code snippet, the recursiveWorkloadKernel function launches another instance of itself to process the next level of recursion. This approach dynamically balances the recursive workload among threads as new tasks are generated.

Load Balancing Techniques

Several techniques can aid in achieving balanced load distribution:

1. **Adaptive Load Balancing**: Monitor the workload of each thread and redistribute tasks dynamically based on the processing speed of each thread. 2. **Hierarchical Decomposition**: Divide the workload into smaller parts and use both coarse-grained (block-level) and fine-grained (thread-level) partitioning. 3. **Speculative Execution**: Allow threads to speculatively execute tasks even before they are assigned formally. If the task is later needed, the speculative result is used; otherwise, it is discarded.

Ensuring load balance among threads is integral to harnessing the full potential of the GPU and achieving optimal performance in CUDA applications. By employing dynamic parallelism, adaptive workload partitioning, and advanced load balancing techniques, developers can maximize the efficiency and speed of their computational models.

7.7 Minimizing Divergence in Warps

In CUDA programming, a warp consists of 32 threads that execute the same instruction simultaneously. Warp divergence occurs when threads within a warp take different execution paths due to conditional branches. This leads to serialized execution of the divergent paths, reducing the overall efficiency of the GPU. Minimizing warp divergence is crucial for maximizing parallel performance.

Consider the following kernel that computes the absolute values of an array:

```
__global__ void computeAbs(float *data, int N) {
    int idx = blockIdx.x * blockDim.x + threadIdx.x;
    if (idx < N) {
        if (data[idx] < 0) {
            data[idx] = -data[idx];
        }
    }
}
```

In this kernel, the conditional if $(\text{data\_idx\_} < 0)$ may cause divergence within warps, especially if the data array contains a mixture of positive and negative values. The GPU will serialize the execution of threads taking different paths, thus reducing performance.

Impact of Warp Divergence

When threads within a warp diverge, the warp execution is divided into multiple sub-warps, each executing a different path. The GPU's scheduler will execute one sub-warp at a time, pausing the others. This process continues until all divergent paths are completed. The number of serialized execution steps directly depends on the degree of divergence. Thus, the performance degradation is proportional to the extent of divergence in the warp.

Techniques to Minimize Divergence

- **Avoidable Branches:** Simplify conditional operations where possible. Replace if-else constructs with conditional assignment operations. This is particularly useful for simple arithmetic operations where divergence could otherwise occur.

- **Thread Sorting:** Preprocess data to ensure that threads within the same warp follow the same execution path as much as possible. This involves sorting data based on the conditions that may lead to divergence.
- **Loop Unrolling:** Unroll loops to reduce the impact of conditional branches within the loops. This technique unfolds the loop body multiple times, reducing the need for condition checks and increasing the likelihood of uniform execution paths.

Consider the optimized version of the previous kernel using conditional assignment instead of branching:

```
__global__ void computeAbsOptimized(float *data, int N) {
    int idx = blockIdx.x * blockDim.x + threadIdx.x;
    if (idx < N) {
        data[idx] = (data[idx] < 0) ? -data[idx] : data[idx];
    }
}
```

This version uses the ternary operator to eliminate the branching, which can prevent divergence and execute more efficiently on the GPU.

Warp Synchronization

Specific intrinsic functions like __syncthreads() can be used to synchronize threads within a block. Proper synchronization ensures that all threads in a warp reach a certain point before proceeding, which can aid in minimizing divergence by aligning thread execution paths. However, excessive synchronization can reduce performance, so it should be used judiciously.

Predicated Instructions

NVIDIA GPUs support predicated instructions, which execute operations conditionally but avoid the performance penalty of divergent branches. Predication converts branch conditions into predicates. If the predicate evaluates to false, the operation effectively becomes a no-op (no operation). This technique is advantageous when the divergent path is short or simple.

```
__global__ void computeAbsPredicated(float *data, int N) {
    int idx = blockIdx.x * blockDim.x + threadIdx.x;
    if (idx < N) {
        bool isNegative = (data[idx] < 0);
        float val = -data[idx];
        if (isNegative) {
            data[idx] = val;
        }
    }
}
```

Here, the initial condition is evaluated once, and the result (isNegative) is used in subsequent predicated operation, converting the if statement to a simpler operation that avoids divergence.

Understanding and minimizing warp divergence is essential for optimizing CUDA applications. By employing techniques such as avoiding branches, preprocessing data, using predicated instructions, and judicious synchronization, developers can enhance warp execution efficiency and maximize the performance of GPU-accelerated applications.

7.8 Instruction-Level Parallelism

Instruction-Level Parallelism (ILP) is a crucial concept in the domain of performance optimization for CUDA applications. ILP refers to the parallel execution of multiple instructions from a single thread simultaneously. This section provides a comprehensive understanding of ILP and practical techniques to maximize its efficiency in CUDA programs.

Modern GPUs are designed to exploit ILP by leveraging their wide, pipelined execution units. To fully harness this capability, one must understand the nature of instruction pipelines and the scheduling mechanisms in CUDA capable devices. The goal is to reduce idle cycles and enhance throughput by ensuring that the pipeline stages are consistently fed with instructions to execute.

Consider the following CUDA kernel, which performs a simple add operation on two arrays:

```
__global__ void addKernel(float *a, float *b, float *c, int N) {
    int i = blockIdx.x * blockDim.x + threadIdx.x;
    if (i < N) {
        c[i] = a[i] + b[i];
    }
}
```

This kernel illustrates a basic operation with limited ILP since each thread primarily performs a single addition operation. To enhance ILP, one can restructure the code to allow multiple independent instructions to be issued per thread. Consider modifying the kernel to include multiple independent operations:

```
__global__ void enhancedAddKernel(float *a, float *b, float *c, float *d, int N) {
    int i = blockIdx.x * blockDim.x + threadIdx.x;
    if (i < N) {
        float temp1 = a[i] + b[i];
        float temp2 = b[i] * 2.0f;
```

```
        float temp3 = a[i] - 0.5f;
        c[i] = temp1 * temp2;
        d[i] = temp3 + temp2;
    }
}
```

In the enhancedAddKernel, each thread performs multiple operations that are largely independent. Thus, the GPU can exploit ILP by issuing all these instructions to different execution units, keeping the pipelines more efficiently utilized.

Latency Hiding and ILP

One of the primary benefits of ILP is latency hiding. Memory latency, for instance, can be significant in CUDA applications. By increasing the number of independent instructions, the processor can continue executing other instructions while waiting for data fetches to complete.

Here, we introduce loop unrolling as an optimization technique to improve ILP. Loop unrolling reduces the overhead of loop control and increases the number of instructions within the loop body. The following example illustrates loop unrolling to enhance ILP:

```
__global__ void unrolledAddKernel(float *a, float *b, float *c, int N) {
    int i = blockIdx.x * blockDim.x + threadIdx.x * 4; // unrolling factor 4
    if (i < N) {
        c[i] = a[i] + b[i];
        if (i+1 < N) c[i+1] = a[i+1] + b[i+1];
        if (i+2 < N) c[i+2] = a[i+2] + b[i+2];
        if (i+3 < N) c[i+3] = a[i+3] + b[i+3];
    }
}
```

By unrolling the loop with a factor of 4, we increased ILP by introducing more additions per thread. This method also helps to reduce the loop control overhead, thus resulting in better performance.

Instruction Latencies and Dependencies

Understanding instruction latencies and dependencies is essential when optimizing for ILP. Different instructions have varying latencies. For example, floating-point additions typically have lower latencies compared to floating-point divisions. The programmer must be aware of these characteristics when designing CUDA kernels.

Consider the following kernel involving a mix of operations with varied latencies:

```
__global__ void mixedOpsKernel(float *a, float *b, float *c, int N) {
    int i = blockIdx.x * blockDim.x + threadIdx.x;
    if (i < N) {
        float sum = a[i] + b[i]; // addition, low latency
```

```
        float product = a[i] * b[i]; // multiplication, moderate latency
        float quotient = a[i] / b[i]; // division, high latency
        c[i] = sum + product + quotient;
    }
}
```

To maximize ILP, one would ensure that the high-latency operations are interleaved with low-latency operations wherever possible. This interleaving allows the CUDA cores to perform other useful work while waiting for the completion of high-latency instructions, thus achieving a better pipeline utilization.

Dependency Chain Analysis

When optimizing for ILP, it's imperative to break long dependency chains. A dependency chain occurs when an instruction relies on the result of a previous instruction. Long dependency chains can serialize instruction execution, impacting overall performance.

The following example demonstrates a reduction in dependency chains through code restructuring:

```
__global__ void reduceDepsKernel(float *a, float *b, float *c, int N) {
    int i = blockIdx.x * blockDim.x + threadIdx.x;
    if (i < N) {
        float ai = a[i];
        float bi = b[i];
        float temp1 = ai + bi;
        float temp2 = ai * 2.0f;
        c[i] = (temp1 / temp2) + (ai - bi); // reduced dependency chain
    }
}
```

By splitting the computation into independent operations, dependency chains are minimized, enhancing ILP. Kernel correctness and the results' precision are maintained while improving performance through better pipeline utilization.

Therefore, maximizing instruction-level parallelism is a multifaceted approach involving careful analysis, understanding of instruction latencies, dependency reduction, and practical code restructuring techniques. This implementation efficiency translates directly into enhanced performance for CUDA applications.

7.9 Efficiently Using CUDA Streams

CUDA streams provide a powerful mechanism for achieving concurrent execution in a CUDA application. By leveraging streams, developers can orchestrate the execution order of kernels and memory copy operations, enabling significant performance gains through overlapping computation and data transfer operations.

Streams are sequences of operations that execute on the GPU in the order they are issued. By default, all operations in a CUDA program are issued to the default stream, which implies sequential execution. However, by creating multiple streams, operations can be issued concurrently, allowing for execution overlap and more efficient use of GPU resources.

Creating and Using Streams

In CUDA, a stream is created using the cudaStreamCreate function and destroyed using cudaStreamDestroy. These streams can then be associated with kernel launches and memory operations.

```
#include <cuda_runtime.h>

void initializeStreams(cudaStream_t *streams, int numStreams) {
    for (int i = 0; i < numStreams; ++i) {
        cudaStreamCreate(&streams[i]);
    }
}

void destroyStreams(cudaStream_t *streams, int numStreams) {
    for (int i = 0; i < numStreams; ++i) {
        cudaStreamDestroy(streams[i]);
    }
}
```

The above code snippet demonstrates how to create and destroy multiple CUDA streams. With the streams created, we can now use them to launch kernels and perform memory operations.

Concurrent Kernel Execution

By assigning different kernels to different streams, one can achieve concurrent execution on the GPU. This is particularly useful when different kernels have different resource demands or execute at different speeds.

```
__global__ void kernelA() {
    // Kernel A code
}

__global__ void kernelB() {
    // Kernel B code
}

void executeKernelsInStreams(cudaStream_t *streams) {
    kernelA<<<gridSizeA, blockSizeA, 0, streams[0]>>>();
    kernelB<<<gridSizeB, blockSizeB, 0, streams[1]>>>();
}
```

In the example above, kernelA and kernelB are launched into different streams, thereby allowing them to run concurrently if the GPU hardware supports it.

Overlapping Data Transfer and Computation

One significant advantage of using streams is the ability to overlap data transfers between host and device with computation on the device. This can lead to substantial performance improvements, especially for memory-bound applications. This process involves the use of the cudaMemcpyAsync function, which allows memory copy operations to be issued to a stream.

```
void overlapComputationAndDataTransfer(float *hostData, float *deviceData, int
    dataSize, cudaStream_t stream) {
    // Async data transfer from Host to Device
    cudaMemcpyAsync(deviceData, hostData, dataSize, cudaMemcpyHostToDevice,
        stream);
    // Kernel execution
    kernelA<<<gridSizeA, blockSizeA, 0, stream>>>();
    // Async data transfer from Device to Host
    cudaMemcpyAsync(hostData, deviceData, dataSize, cudaMemcpyDeviceToHost,
        stream);
}
```

This example shows how host-to-device and device-to-host memory transfers can be overlapped with kernel execution by issuing all these operations into the same non-default stream.

Stream Synchronization

Synchronization between streams can be managed using various CUDA API functions, such as cudaStreamSynchronize, cudaStreamWaitEvent, and cudaStreamAddCallback. It is often necessary to ensure that operations in one stream do not interfere or depend improperly on operations in other streams.

```
void synchronizeStream(cudaStream_t stream) {
    cudaStreamSynchronize(stream);
}
```

cudaStreamSynchronize blocks the host until all operations in the specified stream have completed. Another way to synchronize streams is by using events, which are lightweight constructs for signaling and tracking progress.

```
cudaEvent_t start, stop;
cudaEventCreate(&start);
cudaEventCreate(&stop);

cudaEventRecord(start, stream1);
kernelA<<<gridSizeA, blockSizeA, 0, stream1>>>();
```

```
cudaEventRecord(stop, stream2);
cudaStreamWaitEvent(stream2, stop, 0);

cudaEventDestroy(start);
cudaEventDestroy(stop);
```

In this example, an event stop is recorded in stream1 after launching kernelA. stream2 then waits for this event before proceeding with its operations, ensuring proper synchronization.

Practical Considerations and Limitations

When using multiple streams, it is crucial to be aware of the underlying GPU architecture and its capabilities for concurrent execution and overlapping of operations. Too many streams can saturate the GPU with context switching overhead, thereby negating the benefits. Hence, it is essential to profile and tune the number of streams to find an optimal configuration for a particular application.

Additionally, using unified memory (managed memory) provided by CUDA can simplify memory management and still allow for some level of overlap between memory transfers and computation, particularly on hardware that supports concurrent managed memory access.

Efficient use of CUDA streams can significantly enhance the performance of CUDA applications by enabling concurrent execution and overlapping data transfers with computation. Properly managing and synchronizing these streams is crucial to maximizing the hardware capabilities of modern GPUs. Hence, understanding and strategically implementing streams in your CUDA programs are instrumental in achieving high-performance GPU computing.

7.10 Leveraging Modern GPU Features

Modern GPUs come equipped with a variety of advanced features designed to enhance computational performance and efficiency. Understanding and leveraging these features can significantly improve the performance of CUDA applications. This section will explore several key modern GPU features, including Unified Memory, Tensor Cores, and Cooperative Groups, detailing their purposes and providing guidelines for their effective usage.

Unified Memory simplifies the memory management in CUDA applications by creating a managed memory space accessible from both the CPU and the GPU. This unification allows for seamless memory allocation and automatic migration of data between host and device, reducing the complexity of explicit memory transfers. In CUDA, Unified Memory can be allocated using the cudaMallocManaged function. For example:

```
int N = 1<<20;
float *x;

// Allocate Unified Memory -- accessible from CPU or GPU
cudaMallocManaged(&x, N * sizeof(float));

// Initialize on the host
for (int i = 0; i < N; i++) {
    x[i] = 1.0f;
}

// Run kernel on the GPU
kernel<<<1, 512>>>(x, N);

// Wait for GPU to finish before accessing on host
cudaDeviceSynchronize();

// Free memory
cudaFree(x);
```

Unified Memory significantly simplifies memory management but requires careful consideration of data access patterns to avoid unnecessary data migrations. Techniques such as prefetching data to the GPU using cudaMemPrefetchAsync can mitigate performance costs associated with data transfers.

Tensor Cores, introduced in NVIDIA's Volta architecture, provide specialized hardware for accelerating mixed-precision matrix multiplication operations, which are particularly beneficial for deep learning workloads. Tensor Cores enable significant performance improvements for operations involving half-precision (FP16) and single-precision (FP32) computations. Using Tensor Cores in CUDA requires the cuBLAS library, a GPU-accelerated library for dense linear algebra. Here's an example of using Tensor Cores with the cuBLAS library:

```
#include <cublas_v2.h>
#include <cuda_runtime.h>

void matrixMultiplyTensorCore(const float *A, const float *B, float *C, int M, int N,
    int K) {
    cublasHandle_t handle;
    cublasCreate(&handle);

    const float alpha = 1.0f;
    const float beta = 0.0f;

    // Tensor Core operations using cuBLAS
    cublasGemmEx(handle, CUBLAS_OP_N, CUBLAS_OP_N, M, N, K,
                 &alpha, A, CUDA_R_16F, M, B, CUDA_R_16F, K,
                 &beta, C, CUDA_R_32F, M,
                 CUDA_R_32F, CUBLAS_GEMM_DFALT_TENSOR_OP);
```

```
    cublasDestroy(handle);
}
```

Cooperative Groups is another modern feature that allows for more flexible and efficient synchronization of threads and blocks within a CUDA kernel. This feature enables more complex algorithms and greater control over synchronization patterns than traditional thread and block synchronization mechanisms. Cooperative Groups can be utilized to synchronize thread blocks in grid-wide algorithms. An example of using Cooperative Groups is shown below:

```
#include <cooperative_groups.h>
namespace cg = cooperative_groups;

__global__ void cooperativeKernel() {
    cg::grid_group grid = cg::this_grid();
    int tid = blockIdx.x * blockDim.x + threadIdx.x;

    // Perform computation
    // ...

    // Synchronize whole grid
    grid.sync();

    // Additional computation after synchronization
    // ...
}

void launchCooperativeKernel() {
    int numBlocks = 2;
    int blockSize = 256;

    // Launch kernel in cooperative mode
    void* kernelArgs[] = {};
    cudaLaunchCooperativeKernel((void*)cooperativeKernel, numBlocks, blockSize,
         kernelArgs);
}
```

In addition to these features, modern GPUs offer advanced memory types such as read-only data cache and hardware-accelerated atomic operations, which can further optimize data access patterns and improve computational efficiency. Use the read-only data cache for data that remains constant throughout the kernel execution to minimize global memory bandwidth usage. Here's an example of using the read-only data cache:

```
__global__ void readOnlyKernel(const float * __restrict__ input, float *output, int
    N) {
    int idx = threadIdx.x + blockDim.x * blockIdx.x;
    if (idx < N) {
        float val = __ldg(&input[idx]); // Load through read-only cache
        output[idx] = val * 2.0f;
    }
}
```

Hardware-accelerated atomic operations can be utilized to efficiently perform concurrent updates to shared variables, particularly useful in reduction operations, histogram computations, and other aggregation tasks. For example, using atomicAdd for summing values across threads:

```
__global__ void atomicAddKernel(float *data, float *result, int N) {
    int idx = threadIdx.x + blockDim.x * blockIdx.x;
    if (idx < N) {
        atomicAdd(result, data[idx]);
    }
}
```

Understanding and effectively utilizing these modern GPU features can significantly improve the performance and efficiency of CUDA applications. As new GPU architectures continue to evolve, staying informed about the latest features and techniques remains crucial for maximizing computational performance.

7.11 Case Study: Accelerating Scientific Computations

To elucidate the application of performance optimization techniques discussed in this chapter, this section presents a detailed case study on accelerating scientific computations using CUDA. We selected a common computational task in scientific research: matrix multiplication, often denoted as GEMM (General Matrix-Matrix Multiplication). Matrix multiplication is a fundamental operation in many scientific and engineering domains, including physics simulations, machine learning, and numerical weather prediction. By optimizing this core computation, significant performance gains can be achieved.

We start by considering a simple, naive matrix multiplication kernel and then progressively apply various optimization techniques introduced in the previous sections.

Naive Matrix Multiplication Kernel

Initially, we implement a straightforward matrix multiplication kernel where each element of the resulting matrix C is computed without any optimization. Here is our preliminary CUDA kernel:

```
__global__ void matMulNaive(float *A, float *B, float *C, int N) {
```

```
    int row = blockIdx.y * blockDim.y + threadIdx.y;
    int col = blockIdx.x * blockDim.x + threadIdx.x;
    if (row < N && col < N) {
        float value = 0.0f;
        for (int k = 0; k < N; ++k) {
            value += A[row * N + k] * B[k * N + col];
        }
        C[row * N + col] = value;
    }
}
```

Performance Analysis

To analyze the performance of the naive kernel, we use the CUDA profiler to identify bottlenecks. The execution time of this kernel is primarily limited by memory access patterns and the compute-to-global-memory access ratio.

```
==1234== Profiling application: ./matmul_naive
==1234== Profiling result:
            Type  Time(%)      Time     Calls       Avg       Min       Max  Name
 GPU activities:  100.00%  132.81ms         1  132.81ms  132.81ms  132.81ms  matMulNaive
```

The profiler indicates that the 'matMulNaive' kernel spends most of its time waiting for memory accesses.

Optimizing Memory Access Patterns

To improve the performance, we optimize the memory access patterns. By leveraging shared memory, we can reduce the number of global memory accesses, which are slower compared to shared memory access.

Here is an optimized version using shared memory:

```
#define BLOCK_SIZE 16

__global__ void matMulShared(float *A, float *B, float *C, int N) {
    __shared__ float As[BLOCK_SIZE][BLOCK_SIZE];
    __shared__ float Bs[BLOCK_SIZE][BLOCK_SIZE];

    int blockRow = blockIdx.y;
    int blockCol = blockIdx.x;

    int row = threadIdx.y;
    int col = threadIdx.x;

    float Cvalue = 0.0f;

    for (int m = 0; m < (N + BLOCK_SIZE - 1) / BLOCK_SIZE; ++m) {
        if (blockRow * BLOCK_SIZE + row < N && m * BLOCK_SIZE + col < N) {
            As[row][col] = A[(blockRow * BLOCK_SIZE + row) * N + m *
                BLOCK_SIZE + col];
        } else {
            As[row][col] = 0.0f;
        }

        if (blockCol * BLOCK_SIZE + col < N && m * BLOCK_SIZE + row < N) {
```

```
            Bs[row][col] = B[(m * BLOCK_SIZE + row) * N + blockCol *
                BLOCK_SIZE + col];
        } else {
            Bs[row][col] = 0.0f;
        }

        __syncthreads();

        for (int e = 0; e < BLOCK_SIZE; ++e) {
            Cvalue += As[row][e] * Bs[e][col];
        }

        __syncthreads();
    }

    if (blockRow * BLOCK_SIZE + row < N && blockCol * BLOCK_SIZE + col < N
        ) {
        C[(blockRow * BLOCK_SIZE + row) * N + blockCol * BLOCK_SIZE + col]
            = Cvalue;
    }
}
```

Performance Analysis After Shared Memory Optimization

After optimizing the kernel to use shared memory, we profile it again to measure the performance improvements.

```
==5678== Profiling application: ./matmul_shared
==5678== Profiling result:
            Type  Time(%)      Time     Calls       Avg       Min       Max  Name
 GPU activities:  100.00%  31.25ms          1  31.25ms  31.25ms  31.25ms  matMulShared
```

The performance analysis indicates a substantial reduction in kernel execution time, demonstrating the impact of optimizing memory access patterns. This optimized shared memory kernel runs more than four times faster than the naive kernel.

Balancing Load Among Threads and Minimizing Divergence

To further enhance performance, we ensure that the workload is evenly distributed among threads and minimize warp divergence. We review our thread block and grid dimensions configuration to maintain occupancy and avoid divergence within warps. Using a block size of 16×16 threads is typically effective, ensuring high occupancy and balanced computation across SMs (Streaming Multiprocessors).

Final Performance Measurement

After applying all the optimizations, the performance improvement is evident. The optimization techniques cumulatively contribute to a significant reduction in matrix multiplication runtime.

Initial naive kernel execution time:

```
132.81ms
```

Optimized kernel execution time:

$$31.25\text{ms}$$

By employing the techniques covered throughout this chapter, including memory access optimization and load balancing, we achieve a more than fourfold improvement in performance for the matrix multiplication task. This case study demonstrates practical application and effectiveness of performance optimization techniques in real-world scientific computations.

Chapter 8

Debugging and Profiling CUDA Applications

This chapter addresses debugging and profiling CUDA applications, identifying common issues in CUDA programming and introducing tools such as cuda-gdb, Nsight Eclipse Edition, and Nsight Visual Studio Edition. It covers the use of assertions, error analysis, and logging for effective debugging. The chapter then shifts to profiling, detailing how to use NVIDIA Visual Profiler, Nsight Systems, and Nsight Compute to analyze and interpret performance data. A case study is included to illustrate these debugging and profiling techniques in a complex application.

8.1 Introduction to Debugging CUDA Applications

Debugging in CUDA (Compute Unified Device Architecture) applications presents unique challenges compared to traditional CPU debugging due to the parallel nature of GPU (Graphics Processing Unit) computation. Efficient debugging is crucial for diagnosing and rectifying issues that may arise during the development of high-performance CUDA applications. This section will delve into the essential concepts and methodologies for debugging CUDA applications, providing a foundation that will be built upon throughout this chapter.

CUDA applications typically involve multiple threads executing concurrently, leveraging the massive parallelism offered by modern GPUs. Each of these threads can have its own execution path and state, making traditional debugging techniques insufficient. The debugger must handle synchronization issues, examine the state of thousands of concurrent threads, and identify issues that may be sporadic or non-deterministic due to the complexity of parallel execution.

When debugging CUDA applications, one must be familiar with both host (CPU) and device (GPU) code. Bugs can originate in either, and understanding their interactions is key. The following are important considerations and techniques:

- **Thread Divergence**: This occurs when threads within the same warp (group of 32 threads) follow different execution paths. Thread divergence can lead to inefficient execution and unexpected behavior, making it a frequent source of bugs.

- **Race Conditions**: These arise when multiple threads access shared resources concurrently, with at least one thread modifying the resource. Synchronization primitives such as __syncthreads() must be used to avoid these issues.

- **Memory Access Patterns**: CUDA applications are sensitive to memory access patterns. Coalesced memory access—where threads access contiguous memory locations—ensures optimal performance and correct behavior. Uncoalesced accesses can result in performance degradation and potential bugs.

- **Debugging Environment Setup**: Having an environment such as cuda-gdb or an integrated development environment (IDE) like Nsight Eclipse Edition or Nsight Visual Studio Edition allows developers to step through code, set breakpoints, and inspect variable states across both host and device code.

To facilitate debugging, CUDA provides specific tools and utilities:

```
cuda-memcheck ./my_cuda_application
```

The cuda-memcheck tool detects memory errors in GPU code, similar to how tools like Valgrind work for CPU code. It checks for out-of-bounds access, misaligned memory access, illegal global memory access, and memory leaks.

For a more interactive debugging experience, cuda-gdb allows setting breakpoints, stepping through GPU kernels, and inspecting thread-local variables:

```
cuda-gdb ./my_cuda_application
(gdb) break my_kernel<<<...>>>()
(gdb) run
```

Within cuda-gdb, the «<...»>() syntax is used to specify breakpoints at CUDA kernel launches. The comprehensive support from cuda-gdb and integration within IDEs helps developers seamlessly debug complex applications involving both CPU and GPU components.

Error Handling and Assertions: It is essential to incorporate robust error handling and assertions within CUDA code. Checking the return status of CUDA API calls with functions such as cudaGetLastError() and using assert statements in device code aids in quickly identifying faulty code regions:

```
cudaError_t err = cudaSuccess;
err = cudaMalloc((void **)&d_data, size);
if (err != cudaSuccess) {
    fprintf(stderr, "Failed to allocate device memory: %s\n", cudaGetErrorString(err));
    exit(EXIT_FAILURE);
}
```

This snippet demonstrates the standard practice of checking the return status of CUDA API functions, which helps catch and report errors as soon as they occur.

Unit Testing and Logging: Incorporating unit tests for individual kernels and modules, as well as maintaining detailed logs, aids in identifying the exact location of errors. CUDA-aware testing frameworks and logging mechanisms can be integrated within the development workflow to streamline the debugging process.

By understanding the unique challenges posed by CUDA's parallel architecture and employing specialized tools and techniques, developers can effectively debug their applications, ensuring correctness, performance, and robustness. The following sections will explore these tools and techniques in greater depth, illustrating their application in real-world scenarios.

8.2 Common Issues in CUDA Programming

When developing CUDA applications, programmers frequently encounter several categories of issues that can hinder optimal performance and correctness. Familiarity with these common issues can expedite the debugging process and enhance the efficiency of CUDA code. This section discusses race conditions, invalid memory accesses, divergent branches, insufficient memory bandwidth, and suboptimal kernel configurations.

Race Conditions

Race conditions occur when the outcome of a program depends on the sequence or timing of uncontrollable events such as hardware interrupts or the scheduling of threads. In CUDA programming, race conditions typically arise when multiple threads access shared memory concurrently without appropriate synchronization.

Consider an example where multiple threads increment a shared variable:

```
__global__ void increment_counter(int *counter) {
    int idx = threadIdx.x;
    counter[0] += 1;
}
```

In the above code, multiple threads may read, increment, and write the counter value simultaneously, leading to unpredictable results. To avoid race conditions, we utilize atomic operations:

```
__global__ void increment_counter(int *counter) {
    int idx = threadIdx.x;
    atomicAdd(&counter[0], 1);
}
```

Invalid Memory Accesses

Invalid memory accesses, including out-of-bounds accesses and dereferencing null or uninitialized pointers, are common and often difficult to diagnose.

For instance, consider the following kernel that accesses an array:

```
__global__ void access_array(int *array, int size) {
    int idx = threadIdx.x;
    if (idx < size) {
        array[idx] = idx;
    }
}
```

To prevent out-of-bounds accesses, always ensure that thread indices are within valid bounds, as demonstrated by the conditional check if (idx < size).

Divergent Branches

Divergent branches occur when threads within the same warp take different execution paths due to conditional statements, resulting in serialized execution and degraded performance.

Examine the following code with conditional branching:

```
__global__ void check_condition(int *data) {
    int idx = threadIdx.x;
    if (idx % 2 == 0) {
        data[idx] = 1;
    } else {
        data[idx] = -1;
    }
}
```

Threads in the same warp may execute different branches of the if statement, causing divergence. To reduce divergence, minimize conditional statements that vary across threads or group threads based on their likely execution paths.

Insufficient Memory Bandwidth

Memory bandwidth limitations can severely impact performance if the data transfer rate between global memory and the GPU's compute units becomes a bottleneck. Efficient memory access patterns and coalesced memory accesses are crucial.

For example, consider accessing global memory in a non-coalesced manner:

```
__global__ void uncoalesced_access(int *data) {
    int idx = threadIdx.x;
    int value = data[idx * 2];
    data[idx] = value;
}
```

In contrast, coalesced memory access improves performance:

```
__global__ void coalesced_access(int *data) {
    int idx = threadIdx.x;
    int value = data[idx];
    data[idx] = value;
}
```

Ensure that memory accesses by consecutive threads map to consecutive memory addresses to achieve coalesced access.

Suboptimal Kernel Configurations

Choosing the appropriate kernel configurations, including grid and block dimensions, is critical for exploiting the GPU's parallel processing capabilities. Suboptimal configurations can result in underutilization of resources or excessive overhead.

Consider a kernel configuration that launches insufficient blocks:

```
__global__ void process_data(int *data) {
    int idx = blockIdx.x * blockDim.x + threadIdx.x;
    // Process data
}

int main() {
    int *data;
    // Allocate and initialize data
    process_data<<<1, 256>>>(data); // Only 256 threads launched
}
```

A better approach would be to launch more blocks to ensure full GPU utilization:

```
int main() {
    int *data;
    // Allocate and initialize data
    int numBlocks = (NUM_ELEMENTS + 255) / 256;
    process_data<<<numBlocks, 256>>>(data); // More threads launched
}
```

By launching a sufficient number of blocks and threads, we ensure that the GPU's computational resources are effectively utilized. Adjust grid and block dimensions based on the specific problem size and the GPU's architecture.

Understanding and addressing each of these common issues is fundamental to developing efficient and reliable CUDA applications. Proper synchronization, memory management, control flow, and kernel configurations are key to leveraging the full potential of CUDA-capable GPUs.

8.3 Using cuda-gdb for Debugging

cuda-gdb is a powerful tool for debugging CUDA applications. Leveraging the GDB (GNU Debugger) interface, cuda-gdb extends this functionality to support CUDA. This tool aids developers in identifying and resolving bugs within both host and device code. The following section provides a meticulous overview of using cuda-gdb for debugging CUDA applications.

To commence debugging with cuda-gdb, your application must be compiled with the -g -G flags. The -g flag generates debug information for the host code, and -G flag generates debug information for the device code.

```
nvcc -g -G -o my_cuda_program my_cuda_program.cu
```

To invoke cuda-gdb, you can use the command line interface (CLI):

```
cuda-gdb my_cuda_program
```

Upon execution, you will enter the cuda-gdb interface, which resembles the standard GDB environment. The following subsections describe essential commands and techniques to debug your CUDA application effectively.

Setting Breakpoints

Breakpoints are vital in debugging. They allow you to pause execution and inspect the state of your application. In cuda-gdb, you can set breakpoints in host code similarly to standard GDB, and you can set breakpoints in device code by specifying the kernel name.

```
(gdb) break main
(gdb) break my_kernel
```

Here, break main sets a breakpoint at the entry of the main function, while break my_kernel sets a breakpoint at the beginning of the my_kernel CUDA kernel.

Running and Stepping Through Code

After setting the breakpoints, you can run your application using the run command. When the program execution reaches a breakpoint, it will pause, allowing you to inspect program variables and state.

```
(gdb) run
```

You can use the step command to execute code line-by-line. When stepping through kernels, the cuda kernel step and cuda kernel next commands can be used:

```
(gdb) cuda kernel step
(gdb) cuda kernel next
```

cuda kernel step steps into the next CUDA kernel line, and cuda kernel next steps over the next CUDA kernel line.

Inspecting Variables and State

To inspect variables and the state of your application, standard GDB commands can be utilized. For host variables, the print command allows you to examine values:

```
(gdb) print my_variable
```

For device variables, cuda-gdb provides specific commands. You can examine device variable values across different threads by specifying the thread and block indices:

```
(gdb) cuda thread 0
(gdb) cuda block 0
(gdb) print my_device_variable
```

The cuda thread and cuda block commands select a specific thread and block, and then print can be used to examine the variable's value in the specified context.

Examining GPU State and Memory

cuda-gdb allows for the inspection of the GPU's state, including memory usage and other statistics. The info cuda command provides a comprehensive overview of the GPU state.

```
(gdb) info cuda
```

This command displays active CUDA contexts, the state of the CUDA runtime, and current memory allocations, among other details.

Synchronizing Threads

When debugging parallel code, managing thread execution and synchronization is critical. cuda-gdb provides commands to control thread execution precisely. You can pause and resume specific threads using the following commands:

```
(gdb) cuda thread pause 0
(gdb) cuda thread resume 0
```

Additionally, you can use the cuda sync command to synchronize all threads to a consistent state before continuing execution.

```
(gdb) cuda sync
```

Handling Assertions and Error Checking

Incorporating assertions and thorough error checking in your CUDA code can aid debugging with cuda-gdb. Assertions help identify logical errors by halting execution upon detecting erroneous states.

```
assert(a == b);
```

Using cuda-gdb, when the program encounters an assertion, it will break at the assertion point, allowing immediate inspection.

Error checking should involve verifying the return values of CUDA runtime API calls. For instance, the cudaMemcpy function returns an error code that can be checked:

```
cudaError_t err = cudaMemcpy(dst, src, size, cudaMemcpyDeviceToHost);
if (err != cudaSuccess) {
    printf("cudaMemcpy error: %s\n", cudaGetErrorString(err));
}
```

When such checks are in place, cuda-gdb can be used to identify and debug errors effectively.

Executing these procedures ensures efficient debugging of CUDA applications, enabling the identification and correction of both host and device code issues.

8.4 Debugging with Nsight Eclipse Edition

Nsight Eclipse Edition is a powerful tool for debugging CUDA applications. Its integration within the Eclipse IDE offers developers a familiar and seamless environment for identifying and resolving issues in their CUDA code. This section provides a detailed exploration of Nsight Eclipse Edition's debugging capabilities, focusing on initiating a debug session, setting breakpoints, examining variables and memory, and leveraging advanced features such as conditional breakpoints and watchpoints.

Initiating a Debug Session

To begin debugging a CUDA application, first ensure that the project is correctly configured with Nsight Eclipse Edition. Open your Eclipse IDE and navigate to the CUDA perspective. To initiate the debug session, right-click on your CUDA project and select *Debug As* followed by *CUDA C/C++ Application*. This action will launch the debugger and open the debug perspective, where various debugging views and controls will be available.

Setting Breakpoints

Breakpoints are essential for halting program execution at specific points to inspect the state of variables, memory, and overall program flow. To set a breakpoint in your CUDA code, open the desired source file in the editor and left-click on the margin next to the line number where you wish to pause. A blue dot will appear indicating an active breakpoint. Alternatively, right-click on the line number and select *Toggle Breakpoint* from the context menu.

After breakpoints are set, run your program under the debugger. Execution will pause when a breakpoint is hit, allowing you to perform a detailed inspection of the program's state at that moment.

Examining Variables and Memory

The **Variables** view provides a list of all currently accessible variables and their values. This view is indispensable for understanding the current state of your application. To inspect a variable's value, expand its entry in the **Variables** view. You can also add variables to the **Expressions** view to monitor their values continuously.

For a deeper inspection, particularly of GPU memory, the **Memory** view allows you to view the contents of memory addresses. To utilize this feature, select the **Memory** tab, then click *Add Memory Monitor*. Enter the address or variable you wish to monitor. The memory view will display the contents in a hexadecimal format by default, and you can choose to visualize it as other data types.

Using Conditional Breakpoints and Watchpoints

Conditional breakpoints allow you to halt execution only when specific conditions are met. This feature is useful for isolating problems that occur under particular circumstances. To set a conditional breakpoint, right-click on an existing breakpoint marker, select *Breakpoint Properties*, and then enable and enter a condition in the *Conditional* field. Press *OK* to apply the condition.

Watchpoints enable program execution to pause when a specified variable's content changes. To set a watchpoint, right-click on a variable in the **Variables** view or directly in the code editor, then select *Toggle Watchpoint*. Configure whether the watchpoint should trigger on read-/write access or only on write access via the properties dialog.

Controlling Execution

The debugger provides several controls for managing program execution. These controls include:

- **Resume:** Continues program execution until the next breakpoint or the end of the program.
- **Suspend:** Pauses the running application allowing immediate inspection of the program state.
- **Step Into:** Executes the next line of code, and if it is a function call, debugs the function body.
- **Step Over:** Executes the next line of code without entering into any function calls.
- **Step Return:** Executes until the current function returns, then pauses.

These controls are accessible through the debugger toolbar at the top of the Eclipse IDE or via the Debug view.

Advanced Debugging Features

Nsight Eclipse Edition offers several advanced debugging capabilities tailored for CUDA development. One such feature is the CUDA Kernel Launch section in the Debug view. This section shows the currently executing kernel and allows you to manage kernel breakpoints, visualize kernel execution, and inspect per-thread execution contexts. The **CUDA Memory Checker** can also be enabled to detect memory errors such as out-of-bounds and misaligned memory access.

An additional powerful tool is the **Parallel Nsight Performance Analysis** plugin, which provides in-depth performance metrics that can assist in identifying performance bottlenecks during the debugging process. Access this tool from the debugger menu and use the provided metrics to complement your debugging efforts.

Employing these detailed debugging practices within Nsight Eclipse Edition will aid significantly in diagnosing and resolving errors, enhancing the reliability and performance of CUDA applications.

8.5 Debugging with Nsight Visual Studio Edition

Nsight Visual Studio Edition provides an integrated development environment for debugging CUDA applications within Microsoft Visual Studio. This tool streamlines the debugging process by adding GPU debugging capabilities to the familiar Visual Studio interface, making it an invaluable resource for developers. It offers a myriad of functionalities, including GPU memory inspection, thread synchronization, and performance bottleneck identification.

To begin debugging with Nsight Visual Studio Edition, ensure it is correctly installed and configured. The installation process includes downloading the Nsight Visual Studio Edition installer from NVIDIA's official website and following the guided setup to integrate it with Visual Studio. It is crucial to verify that the CUDA toolkit and compatible GPU drivers are also installed.

Once the setup is complete, open your existing CUDA project or create a new one in Visual Studio. To enable CUDA debugging, navigate to the project properties and configure the debugging options:

1. **Open Project Properties**: Right-click on your project in the Solution Explorer and select "Properties". 2. **Configure Debugger**: Under "Configuration Properties", select "Debugging". Then, in the "Debugger to launch" option, choose "Nsight GPU Debugger". 3. **Set Command Arguments**: If your application requires specific command-line arguments, these can be set in the "Command Arguments" field.

With the project configured, build and launch your CUDA application using the Nsight debugger. This is done by selecting 'Nsight' in the top menu bar and then choosing 'Start CUDA Debugging'. The debugger will initiate, and breakpoints can be set and hit within CUDA kernels.

```
__global__ void vectorAdd(const float *A, const float *B, float *C, int N) {
    int i = blockDim.x * blockIdx.x + threadIdx.x;
    if (i < N)
        C[i] = A[i] + B[i]; // Set a breakpoint here
}
```

When a breakpoint is hit, developers gain access to an array of debugging tools:

1. Variable Inspection: Inspect local and global variables, including GPU memory content. Visual Studio displays variable values in the "Locals" window, and hovering over a variable name shows its current value.

2. Memory Window: Utilize the "Memory" window to inspect and edit GPU memory contents directly. This window allows for viewing sectors of device memory and ensuring correct data manipulation by kernels.

3. Synchronized Threads: Debugging multithreaded GPU code is facilitated by the "Threads" window, where the state of each thread can be monitored. Switch between threads to examine their state and individual behavior.

4. Call Stack Navigation: The "Call Stack" window shows the kernel's call hierarchy. Navigate through function calls to identify the sequence of execution and trace the root of bugs.

5. Watch Expressions: Add variables or complex expressions to the "Watch" window for real-time evaluation. This is particularly useful for observing changes to variables across kernel invocations.

Consider the following example where a simple bug in a kernel leads to incorrect results:

```
__global__ void faultyVectorAdd(const float *A, const float *B, float *C, int N) {
    int i = blockDim.x * blockIdx.x + threadIdx.x;
    if (i <= N) // Bug: should be < N
        C[i] = A[i] + B[i];
}
```

Setting a breakpoint and running the above kernel would allow the developer to step through each line of code, observing variable values and memory states. Identifying that the conditional statement should use ‘i < N‘ instead of ‘i <= N‘ can be achieved by inspecting the loop's behavior during execution.

```
Call Stack:
    faultyVectorAdd<<<grid, block>>>(d_A, d_B, d_C, N)
    main()
```

Furthermore, Nsight Visual Studio Edition's integration with other tools enables advanced performance tuning. Profiling capabilities are available through the "Nsight Graphics" and "Nsight Compute" extensions, which help diagnose performance issues and optimize kernels accordingly. Both tools provide a detailed analysis of GPU workloads, allowing developers to fine-tune their applications.

To halt an running kernel, use the "Pause" button in Visual Studio. This feature is greatly advantageous when dealing with long-running or infinite kernels. Combine this with stepping controls, such as "Step Over", "Step Into", and "Step Out", to navigate the kernel code execution precisely.

Addressing multithreading issues, such as race conditions and deadlocks, is another area where Nsight Visual Studio Edition proves beneficial. By setting breakpoints at critical sections and synchronizing points, developers can inspect the state of all threads and ensure proper synchronization mechanisms are in place.

In summary, debugging CUDA applications using Nsight Visual Studio Edition within the Visual Studio IDE enhances the developer experience, leveraging familiar tools for GPU-specific debugging tasks. Through features like variable inspection, memory examination, and thread state monitoring, the debugging process for CUDA applications becomes comprehensive and efficient.

8.6 Using Assertions in CUDA

Assertions are a critical debugging aid in CUDA programming, serving the primary role of verifying assumptions made in the code. Assertions help detect logical errors by ensuring that certain conditions hold true during the execution of a program. CUDA provides its assertion mechanism which can be employed within device code. An assertion can immediately terminate the program when a specified condition evaluates to false, providing debugging information that can be invaluable for rapid issue resolution.

To utilize assertions in CUDA, the assert macro, which is defined in the assert.h header file, should be included. The syntax and usage of assert in CUDA are similar to standard C/C++ programming, but it is important to understand the specifics when working within the CUDA environment.

```
#include <assert.h>

__global__ void kernelFunction(int *data, size_t size) {
    int idx = threadIdx.x + blockIdx.x * blockDim.x;
    if (idx < size) {
        // Assert to check the validity of the data value
        assert(data[idx] >= 0);
        // Further processing
        data[idx] = sqrt(data[idx]);
    }
}
```

In the above example, the assertion assert(data[idx] >= 0); ensures that the data value is non-negative before proceeding with the square root calculation. If a negative value is encountered, the program halts, and the assertion failure is reported, helping the developer identify problematic input or erroneous logic earlier in the development lifecycle.

It is important to consider the following nuances when using assertions in CUDA:

1. Impact on Performance: Assertions can have an impact on the performance of your CUDA kernels, as they introduce conditional checks that may disrupt optimization processes within the compiler. Hence, they should primarily be used during the development and debugging phases and removed or disabled in production code. Disabling assertions can be achieved by defining the NDEBUG macro before including assert.h.

```
#define NDEBUG
#include <assert.h>
```

2. Visibility of Assertion Failures: When an assertion fails within a CUDA kernel, the program terminates, but the failure details are recorded only after the kernel completes execution and control is returned to the host. This behavior can make it challenging to identify the exact location of the failure. Utilizing CUDA's integrated debugging tools such as cuda-gdb or Nsight can provide more insight.

3. Assertions in Device and Host Code: CUDA assertions can only be used in device code (functions marked with __device__ or __global__), not in host code. Host code should use standard C/C++ assertions to verify assumptions.

While using assertions provides immediate feedback when a condition fails, alternative methods such as explicit error handling and logging can complement assertions by offering more control over error diagnosis and recovery mechanisms.

Consider the following enhanced kernel with error handling using assertions and logging:

```
#include <stdio.h>
#include <assert.h>

__device__ void logError(const char* message) {
    printf("Error: %s\n", message);
}

__global__ void enhancedKernelFunction(int *data, size_t size) {
    int idx = threadIdx.x + blockIdx.x * blockDim.x;
    if (idx < size) {
        if (data[idx] < 0) {
            logError("Data value is negative.");
        }
        assert(data[idx] >= 0);
        data[idx] = sqrt(data[idx]);
    }
}

int main() {
    // Host code to initialize data and invoke kernel
    // ...
}
```

In this example, an additional logError function logs a descriptive error message to the console if a negative value is detected, alongside the assertion that terminates the program. This dual approach enhances the debugging process by providing immediate assertion failures for interactive debugging and detailed logs for post-execution analysis.

The effective use of assertions during CUDA development involves balancing their diagnostic benefits with the potential performance overhead they introduce. Assertions should be systematically incorporated during algorithm development and selectively disabled in performance-critical production environments.

8.7 Analyzing Errors and Logs

Analyzing errors and logs is an essential component of debugging CUDA applications. Effective error analysis and logging facilitate understanding where and why a program fails or performs suboptimally. This section delves into various strategies and tools for error analysis, along with methods for efficient logging in CUDA applications.

The first step in error analysis is to ensure that all potential sources of errors are identified and checked. CUDA provides a set of predefined error codes, often returned by CUDA runtime functions, which can be interrogated to determine the nature of errors. The function cudaGetErrorString converts these error codes into human-readable strings.

```
cudaError_t err = cudaMalloc((void**)&d_arr, size);
if (err != cudaSuccess) {
    printf("CUDA error: %s\n", cudaGetErrorString(err));
}
```

In this snippet, the code checks the result of cudaMalloc. If it fails, cudaGetErrorString retrieves a description of the error. It is crucial to check for errors after each CUDA API call to isolate the function causing the problem.

Moreover, the function cudaPeekAtLastError can be used to retrieve the last error generated by any of the runtime functions. This is useful for identifying the point of failure in more complex applications where multiple CUDA calls are made.

```
kernel<<<1, 256>>>(d_arr);
cudaError_t error = cudaPeekAtLastError();
if (error != cudaSuccess) {
    printf("Kernel launch error: %s\n", cudaGetErrorString(error));
}
```

In kernels, one common but often overlooked source of error is incorrect memory access patterns, such as out-of-bounds access. To pinpoint such issues, the assert macro in device code can be highly beneficial. Assertions allow the validation of conditions; if the condition turns out to be false, the assertion prints an error message to the standard output.

```
__global__ void kernel(int* d_arr, int size) {
    int idx = blockIdx.x * blockDim.x + threadIdx.x;
    assert(idx < size);
    // Further processing
}
```

This kernel employs an assertion to ensure that idx does not exceed the array bounds, potentially preventing illegal memory access errors.

When it comes to logging, using device-side printf can be helpful to produce diagnostic messages. This feature is instrumental for debugging complex kernels where evaluating intermediate values is necessary.

```
__global__ void kernel(int* d_arr) {
    int idx = blockIdx.x * blockDim.x + threadIdx.x;
    if (idx < 10) {
        printf("Thread %d, Value: %d\n", idx, d_arr[idx]);
    }
}
```

The above kernel outputs the values of the first ten elements of d_arr along with the thread index to the standard output, which is valuable during debugging.

Analyzing logs produced by CUDA applications involves gathering logs and interpreting them to diagnose issues. Ideally, logging should be comprehensive but also efficient, avoiding excessive output that might obscure relevant information.

Using third-party logging libraries that integrate with CUDA can enhance logging capabilities. Libraries like Speedlog or ELPP (EasyLogging++), though not specifically designed for CUDA, can be adapted to log output from the host part of CUDA applications, thereby facilitating a unified logging strategy.

Effective error analysis and logging are also enhanced by a structured approach to systematically decrease complexity in large applications. Isolating different regions of code, focusing on one component or kernel at a time, can narrow down the search space for bugs and performance bottlenecks. Additionally, modern Integrated Development Environments (IDEs) often provide built-in tools for logging and error analysis, extending beyond basic logging strategies to include advanced features like conditional breakpoints, watch variables, and interactive consoles.

The following pseudo-code outlines a structured error analysis approach:

```
initialize_resources();
setup_cuda_environment();
error = execute_first_kernel();
if (error != cudaSuccess) {
    log_error_detail(error);
    cleanup_resources();
    return;
}
error = execute_second_kernel();
if (error != cudaSuccess) {
    log_error_detail(error);
    execute_error_recovery();
}
cleanup_resources();
```

Here, errors are checked after each significant operation, applying recovery procedures where feasible and ensuring proper cleanup irrespective of success.

```
Kernel time: 23.45ms
Memory allocation error: Out of memory
Kernel launch failed
```

Combining the discussed practices ensures that errors are promptly detected, effectively communicated, and strategically managed, thus facilitating a robust debugging process.

8.8 Introduction to Profiling

Profiling is an essential technique in performance engineering, enabling developers to assess the detailed execution characteristics of programs. It is particularly critical in the context of CUDA applications, where efficient utilization of GPU resources can significantly impact overall performance. Profiling facilitates the identification of performance bottlenecks, inefficient memory usage patterns, and suboptimal compute resource allocations.

In CUDA programming, profiling involves collecting data on various performance metrics such as kernel execution time, memory throughput, occupancy rates, and warp execution efficiency. This data can highlight performance issues that are not immediately apparent through traditional debugging techniques. Through systematic profiling, developers can optimize their code to make better use of GPU capabilities, thereby enhancing computational performance.

To profile CUDA applications effectively, developers use specialized tools provided by NVIDIA. These tools include the NVIDIA Visual Profiler, Nsight Systems, and Nsight Compute. Each tool offers unique capabilities and insights into different aspects of CUDA application performance.

NVIDIA Visual Profiler is a comprehensive profiling tool that provides a graphical interface for visualizing performance metrics. It allows developers to examine the timeline of kernel executions, memory transfers, and other CUDA operations. Analyzing these timelines helps to understand the interplay between CPU and GPU tasks, revealing opportunities for concurrency and overlap optimization.

Nsight Systems is a system-wide performance analysis tool that enables developers to profile entire applications. It captures detailed traces of CPU and GPU activities, including thread scheduling, memory allocation, and I/O operations. This holistic view helps in identifying system-level bottlenecks and optimizing resource interactions across multiple components of an application.

Nsight Compute, on the other hand, is focused on detailed kernel-level profiling. It provides fine-grained information on kernel performance metrics such as warp stall reasons, memory utilization, and instruction throughput. By drilling down into individual kernel performances, developers can pinpoint specific inefficiencies and tweak kernel code to enhance performance.

Here is an example of how to use the nvprof command-line tool to collect basic profiling information:

```
nvprof ./my_cuda_application
```

Executing the above command runs the CUDA application while collecting profiling data. After the execution, nvprof outputs a summary of GPU activities, showcasing metrics such as kernel execution times, memory bandwidth, and cache hit rates.

Another example displaying the use of NVIDIA Visual Profiler involves loading the profiling data into the tool for visual analysis. To capture profiling data in a file for subsequent analysis, you can use:

```
nvprof --output-profile profile_data.nvprof ./my_cuda_application
```

Once the profiling data is collected, open NVIDIA Visual Profiler and load the profile_data.nvprof file. The profiler presents a comprehensive timeline view, along with analytical panels to inspect various performance aspects.

Profiler outputs can be verbose. For instance, running a simple CUDA application with nvprof might produce output like:

```
==15632== Profiling application: ./my_cuda_application
==15632== Profiling result:
Time(%)      Time (ms)       Name
-------      ----------      -------------------------
  100.0        15.43       my_kernel
      4.62ms      [CUDA memcpy HtoD]
      7.81ms      [CUDA memcpy DtoH]
```

This output indicates that the my_kernel function consumed 15.43ms, with significant time spent on memory transfers between the host and device.

Profiling output analysis involves examining these metrics for potential improvements. Consider optimizing memory transfers by overlapping data transfer operations with kernel executions using streams, thereby minimizing idle times and enhancing parallelism.

Profiling tools provide advanced functionalities such as guided analysis and recommendations. NVIDIA Visual Profiler, for instance, includes an "Automated Analysis" feature which assesses captured data against performance best practices, offering actionable advice for optimization.

Understanding the limitations of profiling tools is also crucial. Profiling overheads can skew performance data, especially for short-duration kernels. Therefore, aggregating results from multiple runs and focusing on persistent bottlenecks is advisable.

Optimizing CUDA applications is an iterative process of profiling, analyzing metrics, and refining code. Leveraging profiling tools effectively can lead to substantial performance gains, ensuring that applications harness the full computational power of modern GPUs.

By systematically profiling and analyzing performance, developers can achieve more efficient and faster CUDA applications, crucial for high-performance computing and real-time processing tasks. This section has introduced the fundamental concepts and tools essential for profiling. The following sections will delve deeper into specific tools and techniques, providing a detailed roadmap for effective practice.

8.9 Profiling with NVIDIA Visual Profiler

NVIDIA Visual Profiler (nvvp) is a comprehensive profiling tool that provides detailed insights into the performance of CUDA applications. It aids developers in identifying performance bottlenecks and optimizing CUDA code for superior performance. Profiling with NVIDIA Visual Profiler involves three primary steps: collecting profile data, analyzing the results, and making informed optimizations based on collected data.

To begin profiling with NVIDIA Visual Profiler, follow these steps:

- **Command Line Profile Collection**: The profiler can be invoked from the command line using the nvprof tool.

```
$ nvprof ./my_cuda_application
```

  This command collects performance data while running the CUDA application.

- **Graphical User Interface**: NVIDIA Visual Profiler also comes with a GUI. To launch the profiler, execute:

```
$ nvvp
```

  Once the tool is open, you can load the CUDA application to profile it.

- **Instrumenting Code**: Further refinement of profiling can be done by instrumenting specific code sections to analyze performance in detail. This can be achieved by coupling nvprof with desired configurations:

```
$ nvprof --kernels "my_kernel" ./my_cuda_application
```

After collecting the profile data, navigate to the *Summary* tab in NVIDIA Visual Profiler's GUI to get an overview of the collected data. The Summary tab presents key metrics, including kernel execution times, memory transfers, and achieved occupancy (the ratio of active warps to maximal number of active warps).

- **Kernel Execution Time**: This metric identifies how long each kernel takes to execute. Sorting kernels by execution time helps in prioritizing optimization efforts.

- **Memory Transfers**: This metric provides insights into the amount and efficiency of data transfer between host and device memory. For example:

Metric Name	Count	Total	Min	Max	Avg
MemcpyHtoD	432	879.51MB	512.27MB	99.90us	811.86us
MemcpyDtoH	432	879.51MB	512.27MB	65.82us	234.75us

- **Achieved Occupancy**: This value indicates the ratio of actual active warps to the maximum possible active warps for a given kernel launch.

Kernel Name	Grid Size	Block Siz	Achived Oc.	Theoretical Oc.
my_kernel1(int*, int*, int*)	125x1x1	32x8x1	0.625	0.875
my_kernel2(int*, int*)	256x1x1	16x16x1	0.750	0.875

The next phase is a detailed timeline analysis. The *Timeline* view in NVIDIA Visual Profiler provides a chronological visualization of the application's activities. This includes kernel execution, memory transfers, and CPU activities. It enables developers to correlate between GPU and CPU workloads effectively.

To further delve into memory analysis, the Memory Statistics tab offers various insights, including global memory transactions, L2 cache hits/misses, and shared memory usage. These metrics are essential for understanding memory access patterns and identifying inefficiencies in memory use.

For example, tracking global memory load and store transactions:

Metric Name	Total	Min	Max	Avg
global_load	278.56M	641.23K	985.32K	850.47K
global_store	302.74M	764.12K	1.05M	891.62K

Lastly, NVIDIA Visual Profiler supports guided analysis through the *Analysis* tab, providing recommendations for optimizing CUDA kernels and memory operations. This feature highlights potential bottlenecks and offers actionable suggestions.

```
Optimization:
Kernel my_kernel1:
- Reduce shared memory usage to increase occupancy.
- Optimize memory access patterns to reduce global load/store.
```

Upon analyzing the data, optimize the CUDA codes based on insights. Re-profile the application post-optimization to evaluate improvements and iterate as necessary. Improving kernel execution times and efficient memory utilization will minimize latency and maximize throughput, resulting in a more performant application.

8.10 Using Nsight Systems and Nsight Compute

Nsight Systems and Nsight Compute are essential tools for comprehensive performance profiling of CUDA applications. Nsight Systems provides system-wide visualization, tracing, and analysis, enabling the identification of bottlenecks in the overall execution flow. Nsight Compute, on the other hand, focuses on kernel-level performance, providing detailed metrics and guidance for optimization. This section will discuss how to effectively utilize these tools for profiling CUDA applications.

To begin with Nsight Systems, launch the application and open your CUDA project. Configuration is key for an effective profiling session. Set up your session to capture relevant data such as GPU activity, CPU activity, memory transfers, and synchronization events.

```
nsys profile --trace=cuda,nvtx,osrt --stats=true ./my_cuda_app
```

The command above profiles a CUDA application, capturing detailed traces for CUDA activities, NVTX (NVIDIA Tools Extension) markers, and OS runtime events. The option -stats=true ensures that summary statistics are collected, facilitating an overview of the performance metrics.

After running the profiling session, the output is exported as a report file (e.g., report.qdrep). Use Nsight Systems to open this file and explore various performance aspects through the visual timeline. The events pane allows you to inspect kernel launches, memory operations, and their execution overlaps. Identifying gaps and overlaps in this visualization is crucial for detecting inefficiencies.

Nsight Systems is particularly useful for understanding high-level interactions between CPU and GPU workloads. For instance, excessive GPU idle times might indicate potential bottlenecks in the CPU code, such as insufficient parallel tasks or suboptimal kernel launch configurations.

Next, let's delve into Nsight Compute, which offers granular insights into kernel performance. Invoke Nsight Compute to profile a specific kernel in your CUDA application:

```
ncu --target-processes all --section-folder ./sections --kernel-id ::myCudaKernel ./
    my_cuda_app
```

This command profiles the specified kernel (myCudaKernel), capturing metrics from all processes involved. The –section-folder option allows customization of the sections to collect, enhancing the profiling specificity.

Upon completion, Nsight Compute generates a detailed report encompassing various metrics such as occupancy, memory throughput, and computational efficiency. These metrics are segmented into configurable sections, each providing insights into different performance aspects. Key sections include:

- **Occupancy**: Measures how well the GPU resources are utilized.
- **Memory Workload Analysis**: Breaks down memory accesses, showing effective bandwidth usage.
- **Compute Workload Analysis**: Provides statistics on achieved FLOPs (Floating Point Operations per Second).

To interpret these metrics, consider the theoretical peak performance of the target GPU. Metrics significantly lower than these peaks indicate potential inefficiencies. For example, low occupancy often suggests suboptimal thread block sizes or excessive register usage, which can be addressed by experimenting with different kernel configurations or optimizing shared memory usage.

Additionally, Nsight Compute offers guided analyses for certain metrics. For instance, a high L2 cache hit rate may point to an effective caching strategy, whereas a low hit rate might suggest bottlenecks due to frequent global memory accesses. Recommendations provided by Nsight Compute can help guide optimizations in these areas.

Nsight Compute also supports the generation of custom metric sets and sections, allowing you to tailor the profiling process according to your optimization needs. To create customized sections:

```
ncu --import ./custom_sections/ --target-processes all ./my_cuda_app
```

Incorporate performance suggestions from Nsight Compute into your development workflow iteratively, profiling after significant changes to evaluate their impact. Combining the system-wide insights from Nsight Systems with the in-depth analysis from Nsight Compute provides a holistic view of application performance, enabling the identification and resolution of complex performance issues effectively.

```
Summary of key performance indicators:
- CPU Utilization: 75%
- GPU Utilization: 85%
- Kernel Launch Configuration: Suboptimal (suggested improvements for grid size)
- Memory Bandwidth Usage: 67%
```

Leveraging the strengths of Nsight Systems and Nsight Compute equips developers with a robust toolkit for diagnosing and enhancing the performance of CUDA applications. By systematically applying insights from these tools, developers can achieve significant optimizations and improve overall computational efficiency.

8.11 Interpreting Profiling Results

When analyzing the performance of CUDA applications, understanding the profiling results is crucial to identifying bottlenecks and areas for optimization. Profiling tools such as NVIDIA Visual Profiler, Nsight Systems, and Nsight Compute generate vast amounts of data that require systematic interpretation. This section will guide you through the process of interpreting key metrics and results from these profiling tools, focusing on kernel execution behavior, memory access patterns, and overall application performance.

Kernel Execution Metrics

Kernel execution metrics provide insights into how individual CUDA kernels perform during runtime. Important metrics to monitor include:

- **Execution Time:** The overall time taken by each kernel to execute. This metric is fundamental in identifying the most time-consuming kernels.
- **Occupancy:** The ratio of active warps to the maximum number of warps supported on a multiprocessor. High occupancy often indicates efficient use of resources but must be balanced with other factors like memory bandwidth and latency.
- **Instruction Throughput:** The number of instructions executed per cycle. High instruction throughput can indicate efficient kernel performance, but only if balanced with effective memory usage.
- **Divergence:** Warp warp-divergence, indicating the proportion of warps that follow divergent execution paths. Significant divergence can degrade performance.

```
__global__ void vectorAddKernel(float *A, float *B, float *C, int N) {
    int idx = threadIdx.x + blockIdx.x * blockDim.x;
    if (idx < N) {
        C[idx] = A[idx] + B[idx];
    }
}
```

In the example above, vectorAddKernel should be analyzed for its execution time, occupancy, instruction throughput, and divergence to ensure optimal performance.

Memory Access Patterns

Efficient memory access is critical to CUDA performance. Key metrics in this domain include:

- **Global Memory Throughput:** The rate of data transfer between global memory and the GPU. Suboptimal throughput can indicate memory-bound kernels.
- **Shared Memory Utilization:** The extent to which shared memory resources are used. Efficient shared memory usage can significantly improve performance, especially for memory-bound applications.
- **L2 Cache Hit Rate:** The percentage of memory accesses satisfied by the L2 cache, impacting the overall memory latency.
- **Coalesced Accesses:** The percentage of global memory load/store operations that are coalesced. Non-coalesced accesses can severely degrade performance due to additional memory transactions.

```
__global__ void matrixMulKernel(float *A, float *B, float *C, int N) {
    __shared__ float tileA[TILE_SIZE][TILE_SIZE];
    __shared__ float tileB[TILE_SIZE][TILE_SIZE];

    int tx = threadIdx.x;
    int ty = threadIdx.y;
    int row = blockIdx.y * TILE_SIZE + ty;
    int col = blockIdx.x * TILE_SIZE + tx;
    float value = 0.0;

    for (int k = 0; k < (N + TILE_SIZE - 1) / TILE_SIZE; k++) {
        if (row < N && k * TILE_SIZE + tx < N)
            tileA[ty][tx] = A[row * N + k * TILE_SIZE + tx];
        else
            tileA[ty][tx] = 0.0;

        if (col < N && k * TILE_SIZE + ty < N)
            tileB[ty][tx] = B[(k * TILE_SIZE + ty) * N + col];
```

```
        else
            tileB[ty][tx] = 0.0;

        __syncthreads();

        for (int e = 0; e < TILE_SIZE; e++)
            value += tileA[ty][e] * tileB[e][tx];

        __syncthreads();
    }

    if (row < N && col < N)
        C[row * N + col] = value;
}
```

In the above matrixMulKernel, examining memory throughput, shared memory utilization, L2 cache hit rates, and coalesced memory accesses will provide insights into where improvements can be made.

Overall Application Performance

Evaluating overall application performance often involves aggregating various metrics and identifying trends across different kernels and memory accesses:

- **Total Execution Time:** Summarizes the total time taken by the application, including all kernel executions and memory transfer times.
- **Synchronization Overhead:** Time spent in synchronizing different components of the application, including GPU kernel launches.
- **PCIe Transfer Rates:** Data transfer rates between the CPU and GPU over the PCIe bus. Reducing the frequency and size of transfers can lead to performance gains.
- **Power and Temperature Metrics:** Monitoring the power consumption and temperature can provide insights into the operational efficiency and thermal stability of the application.

By collating these metrics, one can form a comprehensive understanding of the application's performance and identify specific areas that may benefit from optimization. Techniques such as optimizing kernel launch configurations, improving memory coalescence, or redesigning data structures to better utilize shared memory can significantly enhance performance.

Understanding and interpreting profiling results is essential for fine-tuning CUDA applications to achieve high performance and efficiency.

By systematically analyzing kernel execution, memory access, and overall application performance metrics, developers can identify and address critical bottlenecks, resulting in optimized CUDA applications.

8.12 Case Study: Debugging and Profiling a Complex Application

To solidify the concepts of debugging and profiling CUDA applications, we will explore a comprehensive case study involving a complex CUDA application. This case study will take you step-by-step through the debugging and profiling process, using the tools and techniques discussed in this chapter to identify performance bottlenecks and bugs.

Consider a CUDA application designed to perform matrix multiplication, an essential operation in many scientific computing tasks. The application takes two square matrices, multiplies them, and stores the result in a third matrix. While conceptually simple, achieving optimal performance and correctness can be challenging when scaling up to large matrices and using GPU resources efficiently.

The matrix multiplication kernel code is provided below:

```
__global__ void matrixMulCUDA(float *C, float *A, float *B, int N) {
    // Calculate the row index of the C element and A elements
    int row = blockIdx.y * blockDim.y + threadIdx.y;
    // Calculate the column index of the C element and B elements
    int col = blockIdx.x * blockDim.x + threadIdx.x;
    float Cvalue = 0;

    // Perform the multiplication
    for (int k = 0; k < N; ++k) {
        Cvalue += A[row * N + k] * B[k * N + col];
    }

    // Store the result in C
    C[row * N + col] = Cvalue;
}
```

In the main() function, the kernel is launched using:

```
int main() {
    ...
    int N = 1024; // Define the size of the matrix
    dim3 threadsPerBlock(16, 16);
    dim3 numBlocks((N + threadsPerBlock.x - 1) / threadsPerBlock.x,
                   (N + threadsPerBlock.y - 1) / threadsPerBlock.y);
    // Kernel invocation
    matrixMulCUDA<<<numBlocks, threadsPerBlock>>>(d_C, d_A, d_B, N);
    ...
    return 0;
```

```
}
```

The application runs but produces incorrect results and performs slower than expected. We will utilize the debugging and profiling techniques covered to resolve these issues.

First, we use cuda-gdb for debugging. Running the application in cuda-gdb, we set breakpoints and inspect variables:

```
cuda-gdb ./matrixMul
(cuda-gdb) break matrixMulCUDA
(cuda-gdb) run
(cuda-gdb) info locals
```

By inspecting the local variables, we notice that the indices row and col occasionally exceed matrix boundaries, leading to out-of-bounds memory access. This occurs because the grid and block dimensions are not properly matched with the matrix size.

We modify the kernel as follows to incorporate boundary checks:

```
__global__ void matrixMulCUDA(float *C, float *A, float *B, int N) {
    // Calculate the row index of the C element and A elements
    int row = blockIdx.y * blockDim.y + threadIdx.y;
    // Calculate the column index of the C element and B elements
    int col = blockIdx.x * blockDim.x + threadIdx.x;

    if (row < N && col < N) {
        float Cvalue = 0;
        // Perform the multiplication
        for (int k = 0; k < N; ++k) {
            Cvalue += A[row * N + k] * B[k * N + col];
        }
        // Store the result in C
        C[row * N + col] = Cvalue;
    }
}
```

After adding these boundary checks, the kernel no longer writes to out-of-bounds memory locations. We re-run the application and verify that it now produces correct results.

Next, we use NVIDIA Visual Profiler to identify performance bottlenecks. We launch the profiler and record the application's execution. The profiler output indicates:

```
==12256== Profiling application: ./matrixMul
==12256== Profiling result:
Time (ms)  Kernel Name        Occupancy  Execution Time
240.5      matrixMulCUDA      75%        220 ms
```

The profiler shows that the kernel achieves 75% occupancy but spends significant time executing. By examining memory access patterns, we recognize that global memory accesses are not coalesced effectively. To address this, we utilize shared memory. Rewriting matrix multiplication to use shared memory involves tile-based multiplication:

```
#define TILE_WIDTH 16

__global__ void matrixMulShared(float *C, float *A, float *B, int N) {
    __shared__ float ds_A[TILE_WIDTH][TILE_WIDTH];
    __shared__ float ds_B[TILE_WIDTH][TILE_WIDTH];

    int bx = blockIdx.x;
    int by = blockIdx.y;
    int tx = threadIdx.x;
    int ty = threadIdx.y;

    int Row = by * TILE_WIDTH + ty;
    int Col = bx * TILE_WIDTH + tx;

    float Cvalue = 0.0;
    for (int t = 0; t < (N - 1) / TILE_WIDTH + 1; ++t) {
        if (Row < N && t * TILE_WIDTH + tx < N)
            ds_A[ty][tx] = A[Row * N + t * TILE_WIDTH + tx];
        if (t * TILE_WIDTH + ty < N && Col < N)
            ds_B[ty][tx] = B[(t * TILE_WIDTH + ty) * N + Col];
        __syncthreads();

        for (int k = 0; k < TILE_WIDTH; ++k)
            Cvalue += ds_A[ty][k] * ds_B[k][tx];
        __syncthreads();
    }
    if (Row < N && Col < N)
        C[Row * N + Col] = Cvalue;
}
```

Re-launching the profiler, we observe a marked improvement in execution time and increased memory coalescence. This highlights the importance of using shared memory to optimize memory access patterns.

This case study demonstrates the practical application of debugging and profiling techniques in a real-world CUDA application. Effective use of tools like cuda-gdb and NVIDIA Visual Profiler can pinpoint issues such as out-of-bounds errors and suboptimal memory access patterns, allowing for targeted performance enhancements.

Chapter 9

Advanced CUDA Features

This chapter explores advanced CUDA features, including dynamic parallelism, unified and managed memory, and CUDA graphs. It covers stream and concurrent execution, multi-GPU programming, and interoperability with OpenGL and Direct3D. Additional topics include peer-to-peer memory access, Tensor Cores, and mixed precision computing. The chapter also examines the use of CUDA in machine learning and provides a case study demonstrating the application of these advanced features in real-world scenarios.

9.1 Introduction to Advanced CUDA Features

CUDA (Compute Unified Device Architecture) has significantly evolved since its inception, enabling developers to harness the computational power of NVIDIA GPUs for a diverse array of applications beyond graphics rendering. As applications become more complex, leveraging advanced CUDA features is crucial for optimizing performance and making efficient use of available resources.

The advanced features discussed in this chapter include dynamic parallelism, unified and managed memory, and CUDA graphs. Understanding these concepts will equip you with the skills to address more intricate computational challenges while optimizing resource management and execution efficiency.

Dynamic Parallelism allows the GPU to generate new work for itself, eliminating the need to return to the CPU to launch new kernels. This capability simplifies programming models for algorithms that require multiple levels of parallelism. By enabling kernels to invoke other kernels, dynamic parallelism can boost performance, reduce the overhead associated with frequent CPU-GPU interactions, and allow for more granular parallel task generation.

Unified Memory introduces a single, unified address space that can be accessed by both CPU and GPU. This eliminates the need for explicit memory copying between host and device memory, streamlining the development process. Unified memory provides the abstraction necessary for simpler memory management, automatic data migration, and efficient usage of available memory, thus easing the burden on the programmer while still delivering high-performance results.

Managed Memory extends the capabilities of unified memory by enabling memory pages to be automatically migrated between the host and device based on access patterns. Managed memory is particularly beneficial in applications where memory access patterns cannot be easily predicted or when transitioning existing CPU-based code to a GPU-accelerated version without extensive modifications.

CUDA Graphs offer an advanced mechanism for capturing, analyzing, and replaying GPU workloads. They can encapsulate a series of kernel launches, memory operations, and other commands into a single, reusable entity that includes dependencies between operations. CUDA graphs allow developers to optimize execution by minimizing the overhead of launching individual operations and provide opportunities for executing operations in parallel where dependencies permit.

Efficient execution is further enhanced by **Stream and Concurrent Execution**, which allows multiple operations to be performed simultaneously. By leveraging streams, developers can overlap data transfer and computation, thus improving the utilization of available GPU resources and reducing idle time. Concurrency also enables the execution of different tasks across multiple GPU cores, leading to improved throughput.

When dealing with complex applications that require even greater computational power, **Multi-GPU Programming** comes into play. Utilizing multiple GPUs enables the distribution of workload across several devices, improving overall performance and allowing the handling of larger datasets or more sophisticated simulations. Multi-GPU programming leverages intra-GPU communications and optimized data partitioning strategies to achieve high efficiency.

Interoperability with OpenGL and Direct3D is another advanced CUDA feature that integrates CUDA with graphics rendering APIs, aiding in the development of applications that require both high-performance computing and advanced rendering capabilities. This interoperability allows for the sharing of data between CUDA and graphical APIs without the need for unnecessary memory copying, streamlining processes in applications like real-time simulations and immersive virtual environments.

Another significant topic covered is **Peer-to-Peer Memory Access**, which facilitates direct data transfer between multiple GPUs without routing through the host memory. This feature significantly improves the communication bandwidth and latency between GPUs, making it particularly useful in multi-GPU systems where data exchange between devices is frequent and performance-critical.

Incorporating recent advancements, the chapter delves into **Tensor Cores and Mixed Precision Computing**. Tensor Cores are specialized hardware units within certain NVIDIA GPUs designed to accelerate matrix operations, which are fundamental to many deep learning algorithms. Mixed precision computing, which strategically combines reduced-precision and full-precision calculations, boosts performance while maintaining acceptable levels of numerical accuracy. This is especially useful in machine learning and other computation-heavy domains.

Lastly, the overarching role of **CUDA in Machine Learning** will be analyzed, providing insights into how CUDA accelerates various machine learning tasks, from training to inference. The use of CUDA in machine learning frameworks, optimization of neural networks, and practical implementation techniques will be thoroughly examined, offering a comprehensive understanding of CUDA's impact in this field.

The case study at the end of this chapter integrates these advanced features, demonstrating their practical application in a real-world scenario. By examining this practical example, you will gain a deeper insight into deploying these features in your projects, ultimately enhancing your proficiency in CUDA programming.

9.2 Dynamic Parallelism

Dynamic parallelism is an advanced feature in CUDA that allows a kernel to launch other kernels directly from the GPU. This capability enables a more flexible and efficient programming model by reducing the dependency on the CPU for kernel launches. Dynamic parallelism can be particularly advantageous in applications involving irregular or recursive computational patterns, where the degree of parallelism is not known a priori and can vary during execution.

To utilize dynamic parallelism, the CUDA device capability must be at least 3.5 (Kepler architecture or newer). When a kernel, referred to as the parent kernel, launches another kernel, known as the child kernel, both the parent and child kernels execute on the GPU, potentially concurrently.

Key Aspects of Dynamic Parallelism

When implementing dynamic parallelism, several key aspects must be considered:

- **Kernel Launch Syntax:** The syntax for launching a child kernel is similar to launching a kernel from the host. However, the launch configuration parameters (e.g., grid and block dimensions) must be known at the time of launching the child kernel.
- **Synchronization:** Parent and child kernels may execute asynchronously. Synchronization primitives (e.g., cudaDeviceSynchronize()) can be employed to ensure proper coordination of kernel execution.
- **Resource Utilization:** Both parent and child kernels share the GPU's resources, such as registers, shared memory, and global memory bandwidth. Efficient utilization of these resources is crucial for achieving optimal performance.
- **Inter-Task Communication:** Data exchange between parent and child kernels can be challenging. The most straightforward method uses global memory, although this may involve additional overhead for synchronization.

Example Implementation

Consider an application that computes the Mandelbrot set, a common example demonstrating recursive and irregular parallelism. By leveraging dynamic parallelism, parts of the set requiring higher iterations can dynamically launch additional kernels to refine the computation.

```
#include <stdio.h>
#include <cuda_runtime.h>

__global__ void mandelbrotKernel(float *output, int width, int height, float x_min,
    float x_max, float y_min, float y_max, int max_iter) {
  int idx = blockIdx.x * blockDim.x + threadIdx.x;
  int idy = blockIdx.y * blockDim.y + threadIdx.y;

  if (idx < width && idy < height) {
    float x0 = x_min + idx * (x_max - x_min) / width;
    float y0 = y_min + idy * (y_max - y_min) / height;
    float x = x0;
    float y = y0;
    int iteration = 0;

    while (x*x + y*y <= 4 && iteration < max_iter) {
      float xtemp = x*x - y*y + x0;
      y = 2*x*y + y0;
      x = xtemp;
      iteration++;
    }

    output[idy * width + idx] = (float)iteration / max_iter;

    // Launch additional kernel for pixels that need more iterations
    if (iteration == max_iter) {
      dim3 threads = dim3(16, 16);
      dim3 blocks = dim3((width + threads.x - 1) / threads.x,
                (height + threads.y - 1) / threads.y);
      mandelbrotKernel<<<blocks, threads>>>(output, width, height, x_min,
          x_max, y_min, y_max, max_iter + 100);
    }
  }
}

int main() {
  const int width = 1024;
  const int height = 1024;
  const float x_min = -2.0f;
  const float x_max = 1.0f;
  const float y_min = -1.5f;
  const float y_max = 1.5f;
  const int max_iter = 1000;

  float *d_output;
  cudaMalloc((void**)&d_output, width * height * sizeof(float));

  dim3 threads = dim3(16, 16);
  dim3 blocks = dim3((width + threads.x - 1) / threads.x,
              (height + threads.y - 1) / threads.y);

  mandelbrotKernel<<<blocks, threads>>>(d_output, width, height, x_min,
      x_max, y_min, y_max, max_iter);
  cudaDeviceSynchronize();

  float *output = (float*)malloc(width * height * sizeof(float));
  cudaMemcpy(output, d_output, width * height * sizeof(float),
      cudaMemcpyDeviceToHost);
```

```
    // Output image (not shown here)

    cudaFree(d_output);
    free(output);

    return 0;
}
```

In this example, the mandelbrotKernel recursively launches itself for pixels that meet a certain condition ($iteration == max\_iter$), incrementing the maximum iteration limit and refining the computation. This self-launching kernel approach dynamically adapts to the computational load.

Performance Considerations

While dynamic parallelism offers flexibility and potential performance benefits, several factors may affect its efficiency:

- **Overhead of Kernel Launches:** Every dynamic kernel launch incurs overhead, including the time spent on setting up the kernel launch configuration and managing system resources.

- **Concurrency Management:** Proper management of concurrent execution is crucial. Excessive kernel launches may lead to resource contention and suboptimal performance due to inefficiencies in resource utilization.

- **Memory Bandwidth Utilization:** Effective use of memory bandwidth is critical. Frequent global memory accesses can become bottlenecks. Careful arrangement and minimal data transfer between parent and child kernels can mitigate this.

- **Debugging Complexity:** Debugging applications with dynamic parallelism can be more challenging than traditional CUDA programs, given the recursive nature and asynchronous execution of kernels.

Dynamic parallelism is a powerful feature that can significantly enhance the flexibility and performance of CUDA applications, especially those with irregular or dynamic workloads. When used judiciously, it allows for more sophisticated and adaptive parallel algorithms, thus pushing the boundaries of GPU computation.

9.3 Unified Memory and Managed Memory

Unified memory and managed memory are key features introduced in CUDA to simplify memory management across the CPU and GPU. These features provide a unified address space that allows both the host and the device to access data seamlessly, eliminating the need for explicit memory transfers. This section delves into the concepts of unified memory and managed memory, their implementation, and best practices for their use.

Unified memory, introduced in CUDA 6, provides a single memory space accessible by both the host (CPU) and the device (GPU). Unified memory is particularly beneficial for applications with dynamic memory allocation patterns or those that require frequent data interchange between the CPU and GPU. It significantly simplifies memory management by enabling the programmer to allocate memory once and access it from either the host or device without requiring explicit data transfers.

Managed memory is a subset of unified memory, wherein CUDA manages the data migration between the host and device. When using managed memory, CUDA automatically transfers data between the CPU and GPU as needed, depending on the access patterns. This feature is managed by the CUDA runtime, which ensures that the most recently accessed version of the data is located on the appropriate processing unit.

To utilize unified memory, programmers use the cudaMallocManaged function to allocate managed memory. This single API call replaces the need for separate host and device memory allocations and the associated cudaMemcpy calls. Here is an example demonstrating the allocation and use of managed memory:

```
#include <cuda_runtime.h>
#include <iostream>

__global__ void incrementManagedMemory(int *data, int size) {
    int idx = blockIdx.x * blockDim.x + threadIdx.x;
    if (idx < size) {
        data[idx] += 1;
    }
}

int main() {
    const int size = 1000;
    int *managedData;

    // Allocate managed memory
    cudaMallocManaged(&managedData, size * sizeof(int));
```

```
    // Initialize data
    for (int i = 0; i < size; ++i) {
        managedData[i] = i;
    }

    // Launch kernel
    incrementManagedMemory<<<(size + 255) / 256, 256>>>(managedData, size);

    // Synchronize to ensure kernel execution is complete
    cudaDeviceSynchronize();

    // Verify results
    for (int i = 0; i < size; ++i) {
        if (managedData[i] != i + 1) {
            std::cerr << "Error at index " << i << std::endl;
            return -1;
        }
    }

    std::cout << "All values incremented successfully!" << std::endl;

    // Free managed memory
    cudaFree(managedData);

    return 0;
}
```

In this example, cudaMallocManaged allocates a unified memory block pointed to by managedData. The kernel incrementManagedMemory operates directly on this managed memory, and the cudaDeviceSynchronize function ensures that the kernel execution is complete before the host accesses the memory. The example concludes by verifying the results and freeing the managed memory using cudaFree.

One key advantage of managed memory is that it abstracts the complexity of memory transfers, making the development process more straightforward. However, this abstraction comes with some performance trade-offs, as the CUDA runtime must determine when and how to migrate data between the host and device. To mitigate potential performance issues, CUDA provides hints through prefetching and advice functions.

The cudaMemPrefetchAsync function allows the programmer to hint to the CUDA runtime which portions of managed memory should be prefetched to a specific device. This can help reduce the overhead of automatic data migrations by allowing the programmer to preemptively move data to the desired processing unit. The function is used as follows:

```
cudaMemPrefetchAsync(managedData, size * sizeof(int), cudaCpuDeviceId);
```

In the above line, this example prefetches the entire managedData array to the CPU, specified by the cudaCpuDeviceId constant. Similarly, to prefetch data to the GPU, one would use the GPU device ID obtained via cudaGetDevice.

Besides prefetching, the cudaMemAdvise function allows programmers to provide additional advice about memory usage patterns. These hints can inform the CUDA runtime of expected memory access behaviors, optimizing data migration strategies. The function signature is as follows:

```
cudaMemAdvise(managedData, size * sizeof(int), cudaMemAdviseSetReadMostly,
    cudaCpuDeviceId);
```

In this example, the cudaMemAdvise function sets the memory region as read-mostly for the CPU. This advice can help the CUDA runtime optimize caching and data migration strategies for regions of memory that are predominantly read from rather than written to.

Incorporating unified and managed memory into your CUDA applications can significantly reduce the complexity of memory management. While these features offer simplicity, it is essential to understand the underlying data migration mechanisms to achieve optimal performance. By leveraging prefetching and memory advice functions, you can guide the CUDA runtime to make more informed decisions about data migrations, balancing ease of use with performance considerations.

9.4 CUDA Graphs

CUDA graphs provide a powerful mechanism for capturing, organizing, and optimizing a sequence of CUDA operations. By predefining a sequence of operations as a graph, it is possible to execute the entire graph with significantly lower overhead compared to launching individual kernels and memory operations sequentially. This section delves into the creation, optimization, and execution of CUDA graphs, highlighting their advantages and providing examples for better understanding.

A CUDA graph is composed of several nodes, where each node represents an individual operation such as a kernel launch, memory copy, or host function. These nodes are connected through edges, which define the execution dependencies between them. This structure allows for a more efficient and parallel execution of the operations by minimizing the runtime overhead associated with kernel launches and data transfers.

First, let us delve into the fundamental aspects of constructing a CUDA graph. We begin by initializing a new graph and adding nodes to it. The following C code illustrates the creation of a simple CUDA graph:

```
cudaGraph_t graph;
cudaGraphCreate(&graph, 0);
```

Once the graph is created, we can add nodes corresponding to the operations we wish to perform. For instance, consider a simple example where we launch two kernels and transfer some data between them:

```
cudaKernelNodeParams kernelNodeParams = {0};
cudaMemcpy3DParms memcpyParams = {0};

// Define kernelA execution
kernelNodeParams.func = (void*)kernelA;
kernelNodeParams.gridDim = dim3(1, 1, 1);
kernelNodeParams.blockDim = dim3(256, 1, 1);
cudaGraphAddKernelNode(&kernelNodeA, graph, NULL, 0, &kernelNodeParams);

// Define memcpy operation
memcpyParams.srcArray = &srcArray;
memcpyParams.dstArray = &dstArray;
memcpyParams.extent = make_cudaExtent(256, 1, 1);
cudaGraphAddMemcpyNode(&memcpyNode, graph, &kernelNodeA, 1, &
    memcpyParams);

// Define kernelB execution
kernelNodeParams.func = (void*)kernelB;
cudaGraphAddKernelNode(&kernelNodeB, graph, &memcpyNode, 1, &
    kernelNodeParams);
```

The above code snippet defines three nodes: kernelNodeA, memcpyNode, and kernelNodeB. The ‘addKernelNode‘ and ‘addMemcpyNode‘ functions are used to insert these nodes into the graph. The dependencies are specified by linking nodes, ensuring that kernelNodeB executes only after memcpyNode has finished, which in turn will only start after kernelNodeA completes.

After constructing the graph, it must be instantiated before execution. The instantiation process creates an executable form of the graph, optimizing it for performance:

```
cudaGraphExec_t graphExec;
cudaGraphInstantiate(&graphExec, graph, NULL, NULL, 0);
```

The instantiated graph graphExec can now be launched just like a single kernel:

```
cudaGraphLaunch(graphExec, 0);
cudaStreamSynchronize(0);
```

In this example, the entire set of operations within the graph is executed in a sequence defined by the dependencies between the nodes. Note that the cudaStreamSynchronize function is used to ensure that all operations are completed before the program proceeds.

A significant advantage of using CUDA graphs is the potential for runtime optimizations. For instance, CUDA can automatically schedule nodes to minimize idle times and data transfer bottlenecks. Moreover, memory transfers and kernel dispatches can be reduced, further enhancing performance.

To illustrate the practical utility of CUDA graphs in more complex workflows, consider an example from machine learning training, where multiple layers of a neural network are trained using CUDA operations interspersed with data transfers:

```
cudaGraph_t mlGraph;
cudaGraphCreate(&mlGraph, 0);

// Define multiple layers as kernel nodes
cudaGraphAddKernelNode(&layer1Node, mlGraph, NULL, 0, &layer1Params);
cudaGraphAddKernelNode(&layer2Node, mlGraph, &layer1Node, 1, &layer2Params);
cudaGraphAddKernelNode(&layer3Node, mlGraph, &layer2Node, 1, &layer3Params);

// Define data transfer between layers
cudaGraphAddMemcpyNode(&transfer1, mlGraph, &layer1Node, 1, &memcpy1Params)
    ;
cudaGraphAddMemcpyNode(&transfer2, mlGraph, &layer2Node, 1, &memcpy2Params)
    ;

// Finalize the graph and instantiate
cudaGraphInstantiate(&mlGraphExec, mlGraph, NULL, NULL, 0);
cudaGraphLaunch(mlGraphExec, 0);
cudaStreamSynchronize(0);
```

This demonstrates how a series of operations, including multiple kernel executions and data transfers, can be organized into a single optimized graph. The dependencies between the layers ensure that each layer only begins execution after the previous one has completed, while CUDA optimizes the entire sequence for maximum efficiency.

CUDA graphs offer considerable benefits, particularly in scenarios with complex and interdependent workflows. By capturing and optimizing task dependencies and minimizing runtime overhead, they provide a robust tool for advanced CUDA programming, ensuring efficient execution of complex parallel operations.

9.5 Stream and Concurrent Execution

Understanding streams and concurrent execution is pivotal for leveraging the full potential of CUDA-enabled devices. By properly utilizing streams, developers can achieve significant performance improvements through overlapping computation and communication. In this section, we will discuss the principles of streams, concurrent kernel execution, and the synchronization mechanisms necessary to manage execution order and data dependencies.

Streams in CUDA

In CUDA, a stream is a sequence of operations that are executed in order on a GPU. Operations within the same stream are guaranteed to execute sequentially unless explicitly synchronized. Operations in different streams can execute concurrently if hardware resources permit.

Creating and managing streams in CUDA can be performed using the CUDA runtime API. The following example demonstrates how to create and destroy streams:

```
cudaStream_t stream1, stream2;
// Create streams
cudaStreamCreate(&stream1);
cudaStreamCreate(&stream2);

// Perform operations in streams
kernelFunction<<<grid, block, 0, stream1>>>(args);
cudaMemcpyAsync(dst, src, size, cudaMemcpyHostToDevice, stream2);

// Destroy streams
cudaStreamDestroy(stream1);
cudaStreamDestroy(stream2);
```

In this example, kernelFunction is launched in stream1, and an asynchronous memory copy (cudaMemcpyAsync) operation is initiated in stream2. These operations can overlap if there are no resource contentions.

Concurrent Kernel Execution

Concurrent kernel execution allows multiple kernels to run simultaneously on the GPU. This feature can be particularly useful for hiding memory latency and achieving better utilization of GPU resources. The hardware capability to run concurrent kernels depends on the GPU architecture, with most modern GPUs supporting multiple concurrent kernel executions.

For concurrent kernel execution, the key is to launch kernels in different streams:

```
kernelFunction1<<<grid, block, 0, stream1>>>(args1);
kernelFunction2<<<grid, block, 0, stream2>>>(args2);
```

In this code snippet, kernelFunction1 and kernelFunction2 are launched in stream1 and stream2, respectively. If the GPU supports concurrent execution, these kernels can run simultaneously.

Overlapping Computation and Communication

One of the significant advantages of using streams is the ability to overlap computation with communication. By performing asynchronous memory copies and kernel execution in different streams, it is possible to hide data transfer time behind computation, thereby improving overall performance.

Consider the following example:

```
cudaMemcpyAsync(dst1, src1, size1, cudaMemcpyHostToDevice, stream1);
kernelFunction<<<grid, block, 0, stream1>>>(args);
cudaMemcpyAsync(dst2, src2, size2, cudaMemcpyHostToDevice, stream2);
```

In this scenario, the memory copy to dst1 and src1 is initiated in stream1, followed by the execution of kernelFunction in the same stream. Simultaneously, another memory copy to dst2 and src2 is initiated in stream2. The overlap of these operations can significantly reduce the effective computation time.

Stream Synchronization

Synchronization between streams ensures that certain operations are completed in a specific order. CUDA offers multiple synchronization mechanisms, such as stream synchronization, event synchronization, and device synchronization.

Stream synchronization can be achieved using cudaStreamSynchronize, which blocks the host until all operations in the specified stream are completed:

```
cudaStreamSynchronize(stream1);
```

This function ensures that all preceding operations in stream1 are complete before the host thread proceeds.

Event synchronization allows finer control and can be used for inter-stream dependencies. CUDA events are recordable markers that can be inserted into streams, and they provide the capability to measure elapsed time or synchronize streams:

```
cudaEvent_t event;
cudaEventCreate(&event);
cudaEventRecord(event, stream1);

cudaStreamWaitEvent(stream2, event, 0);

// Launch operations in stream2 after stream1 reaches the event
```

In this example, cudaEventRecord inserts an event into stream1. The cudaStreamWaitEvent function is then used to delay the execution in stream2 until the event in stream1 is reached.

Multi-Device Synchronization

When working with multiple GPUs, synchronization across devices can be critical. CUDA supports basic inter-device synchronization using the cudaDeviceSynchronize function, which blocks the host until all devices have completed their operations:

```
cudaSetDevice(device1);
kernelFunction1<<<grid, block>>>(args1);
cudaSetDevice(device2);
kernelFunction2<<<grid, block>>>(args2);

// Synchronize devices
cudaSetDevice(device1);
cudaDeviceSynchronize();
cudaSetDevice(device2);
cudaDeviceSynchronize();
```

This ensures that all kernels launched on both device1 and device2 are complete before the host code proceeds.

Practical Considerations

To fully harness stream and concurrent execution, there are several practical considerations. Profiling and benchmarking to identify bottlenecks and optimize stream usage is crucial. Tools such as NVIDIA Visual Profiler and Nsight Systems can provide insights into kernel execution, memory transfers, and overlap patterns.

Efficiently managing resource allocation is also vital. Ensuring that kernels and memory transfers do not contend excessively for resources can help maintain high utilization and performance. Additionally, careful synchronization management helps avoid unnecessary delays and ensures correct execution order.

Details on integrating streams with other advanced CUDA features are discussed in subsequent sections. Properly utilizing streams facilitates improved performance and effective resource management, which are crucial for advanced CUDA programming and optimization.

9.6 Using CUDA with Multiple GPUs

Efficient utilization of multiple GPUs enables significant performance improvements for parallel applications. This section explores how to leverage multiple GPUs within a single system or across a distributed network, delving into critical topics like device enumeration, context management, data partitioning, and synchronization methods.

Device Enumeration and Context Management

To work with multiple GPUs, the first step involves querying and enumerating the available devices. The function cudaGetDeviceCount() is used to determine the number of GPU devices:

```
int deviceCount;
cudaGetDeviceCount(&deviceCount);
```

Once the number of devices is known, one can set the current device context using cudaSetDevice():

```
cudaSetDevice(deviceID);
```

Here, deviceID is an integer representing the GPU index, starting from 0 up to deviceCount - 1. Each device context ensures that subsequent CUDA calls, such as memory allocation and kernel launches, will be directed to the specified GPU.

Allocating Memory on Multiple GPUs

Memory allocation and data transfer need careful handling to ensure optimal performance and correct program execution. For each device, memory allocation must occur within its context:

```
cudaSetDevice(0); // Select the first GPU
cudaMalloc((void**)&dev_a, size_a);

cudaSetDevice(1); // Select the second GPU
cudaMalloc((void**)&dev_b, size_b);
```

Data transfer operations similarly require specifying the target device:

```
cudaMemcpy(dev_a, host_a, size_a, cudaMemcpyHostToDevice); // Transfer to first
    GPU

cudaSetDevice(1); // Switch to second GPU
cudaMemcpy(dev_b, host_b, size_b, cudaMemcpyHostToDevice); // Transfer to
    second GPU
```

Launching Kernels on Multiple GPUs

Kernels must be launched independently for each GPU:

```
cudaSetDevice(0); // First GPU
kernel<<<gridDim, blockDim>>>(dev_a);

cudaSetDevice(1); // Second GPU
kernel<<<gridDim, blockDim>>>(dev_b);
```

It is crucial to manage the execution contexts correctly to avoid overlapping or unintended device switches, which might lead to data corruption or undefined program behavior.

Data Partitioning for Multiple GPUs

Effective data partitioning is key to maximizing the performance benefits of multiple GPUs. This process involves dividing the overall task and associated data such that each GPU efficiently handles a portion of the workload. One common strategy is static partitioning, where data is divided based on the problem size and number of GPUs:

```
int offset = N / numGPUs;
int size_per_gpu = offset * sizeof(float);

cudaSetDevice(0); // First GPU
cudaMemcpy(dev_a, host_a, size_per_gpu, cudaMemcpyHostToDevice);

cudaSetDevice(1); // Second GPU
cudaMemcpy(dev_b, host_a + offset, size_per_gpu, cudaMemcpyHostToDevice);
```

Synchronization Among Multiple GPUs

Synchronization is imperative to ensure that all GPUs complete their assigned tasks before the results are aggregated. CUDA provides several mechanisms for synchronization, such as using streams and events within each device or employing host-side synchronization. An event can act as a checkpoint, ensuring specific stages in the GPU computation and communication pipeline occur in a defined order:

```
cudaEvent_t syncEvent;
cudaEventCreate(&syncEvent);

cudaSetDevice(0); // First GPU
kernel<<<gridDim, blockDim>>>(dev_a);
cudaEventRecord(syncEvent, 0);

cudaSetDevice(1); // Second GPU
cudaEventSynchronize(syncEvent); // Wait for the first GPU to complete
kernel<<<gridDim, blockDim>>>(dev_b);
```

Inter-GPU Communication

When implementing complex applications, different GPUs might need to exchange data. CUDA-aware MPI or using CUDA's peer-to-peer (P2P) memory access can facilitate this process. Peer-to-peer memory access reduces the overhead of copying data through the host and allows direct memory transfers between GPUs:

```
cudaSetDevice(0); // First GPU
cudaDeviceEnablePeerAccess(1, 0); // Allow access to the second GPU

cudaMemcpy(dev_a, dev_b, size_b, cudaMemcpyDefault); // Direct memory copy
    from GPU1 to GPU2
```

```
P2P transfer enabled successfully.
```

By managing context, memory, synchronization, and inter-GPU communication efficiently, programmers can unlock the substantial computational power of multi-GPU systems, thus optimizing the performance of their applications.

9.7 Interoperability with OpenGL and Direct3D

The ability of CUDA to interoperate with graphics APIs such as OpenGL and Direct3D is a pivotal feature, providing the means to leverage GPU resources for both computational and graphical tasks. This section explicates methods for enabling CUDA interoperability with these graphics APIs, underlining their significance in various applications.

Integrating CUDA with OpenGL begins with understanding OpenGL buffer mappings for interoperability. OpenGL's buffer objects, such as Vertex Buffer Objects (VBOs) and Pixel Buffer Objects (PBOs), can be mapped to CUDA's memory space. This mapping allows the same buffer to be used for both rendering and computation, thereby reducing memory transfers and boosting performance. Below is a sample CUDA-OpenGL interoperability code that uses a VBO:

```
// Create an OpenGL Vertex Buffer Object (VBO)
GLuint vbo;
glGenBuffers(1, &vbo);
glBindBuffer(GL_ARRAY_BUFFER, vbo);
glBufferData(GL_ARRAY_BUFFER, size * sizeof(float), NULL,
    GL_DYNAMIC_DRAW);

// Register VBO with CUDA
cudaGraphicsResource *cudaVBO;
cudaGraphicsGLRegisterBuffer(&cudaVBO, vbo, cudaGraphicsMapFlagsWriteDiscard);
```

```
// Map VBO for CUDA access
float *dptr;
cudaGraphicsMapResources(1, &cudaVBO, 0);
size_t num_bytes;
cudaGraphicsResourceGetMappedPointer((void **)&dptr, &num_bytes, cudaVBO);

// Perform CUDA computations on VBO
kernel<<<grid, block>>>(dptr);

// Unmap VBO
cudaGraphicsUnmapResources(1, &cudaVBO, 0);
```

In this example, we begin by generating and binding a VBO in OpenGL. This VBO is then registered with CUDA by calling cudaGraphicsGLRegisterBuffer. After registration, the VBO can be mapped for CUDA access using cudaGraphicsMapResources, allowing CUDA kernels to operate on the VBO. Finally, the VBO is unmapped using cudaGraphicsUnmapResources to finalize the modifications.

Integrating CUDA with Direct3D follows a similar approach, with Direct3D resources such as vertex buffers and textures being mapped for CUDA access. The process for registering, mapping, and unmapping a Direct3D 11 buffer with CUDA is shown below:

```
// Create a Direct3D buffer
ID3D11Buffer *d3dBuffer;
D3D11_BUFFER_DESC desc = {sizeof(float) * size, D3D11_USAGE_DEFAULT,
    D3D11_BIND_VERTEX_BUFFER, 0, 0, 0};
g_pd3dDevice->CreateBuffer(&desc, NULL, &d3dBuffer);

// Register Direct3D buffer with CUDA
cudaGraphicsResource *cudaD3DResource;
cudaGraphicsD3D11RegisterResource(&cudaD3DResource, d3dBuffer,
    cudaGraphicsMapFlagsWriteDiscard);

// Map Direct3D buffer for CUDA access
float *dptr;
cudaGraphicsMapResources(1, &cudaD3DResource, 0);
size_t num_bytes;
cudaGraphicsResourceGetMappedPointer((void **)&dptr, &num_bytes,
    cudaD3DResource);

// Execute CUDA kernel on Direct3D buffer
kernel<<<grid, block>>>(dptr);

// Unmap Direct3D buffer
cudaGraphicsUnmapResources(1, &cudaD3DResource, 0);
```

This code follows closely the steps outlined for OpenGL. We first create a Direct3D buffer, register it with CUDA using cudaGraphicsD3D11RegisterResource, map it for CUDA access via cudaGraphicsMapResources, perform computations, and finally unmap the resource.

CUDA interoperability with these graphics APIs is particularly beneficial in real-time applications, where constantly transferring data between the CPU and GPU would introduce prohibitive latency. Examples include real-time simulations, games, and scientific visualizations that require frequent updates and high performance.

Initializing interoperability involves careful handling of contexts. In OpenGL, CUDA can share the current context if it is initialized after the OpenGL context. Conversely, Direct3D requires creating a shared context explicitly. Considerations about synchronization, memory consistency, and proper resource management are crucial to avoid crashes or undefined behavior.

Testing the CUDA-OpenGL and CUDA-Direct3D interoperability can be conducted through visualization of computational results directly rendered by these graphics APIs. Such visual output can be particularly insightful. For example:

Rendering vertices to create graphical shapes after CUDA-enabled transformations.
Updating textures dynamically as results of CUDA computations.
Integrating visual effects directly computed by CUDA kernels into scenes.

Another essential detail involves handling multiple GPU setups, where interoperability can vary based on whether resources are shared or dedicated per GPU. Efficient utilization of these features demands understanding CUDA's multi-GPU programming capabilities, covered in a subsequent section.

Below is an illustrative example ensuring CUDA-OpenGL interoperability by rendering a transformed grid of points:

```
__global__ void kernel(float4* pos, unsigned int width, unsigned int height, float time
    ) {
    unsigned int x = blockIdx.x * blockDim.x + threadIdx.x;
    unsigned int y = blockIdx.y * blockDim.y + threadIdx.y;

    float u = x / (float) width;
    float v = y / (float) height;
    u = u*2.0f - 1.0f;
    v = v*2.0f - 1.0f;

    float frequency = 4.0f;
    float w = sinf(u*frequency + time) * cosf(v*frequency + time) * 0.5f;

    pos[y * width + x] = make_float4(u, w, v, 1.0f);
}

// Kernel launch configuration
dim3 block(8, 8, 1);
dim3 grid(width / block.x, height / block.y, 1);

// CUDA resources
float4 *dptr;
cudaGraphicsMapResources(1, &cudaVBO, 0);
size_t num_bytes;
```

```
cudaGraphicsResourceGetMappedPointer((void **)&dptr, &num_bytes, cudaVBO);
kernel<<<grid, block>>>(dptr, width, height, time);
cudaGraphicsUnmapResources(1, &cudaVBO, 0);

// OpenGL rendering
glClear(GL_COLOR_BUFFER_BIT | GL_DEPTH_BUFFER_BIT);
glBindBuffer(GL_ARRAY_BUFFER, vbo);
glVertexPointer(4, GL_FLOAT, 0, 0);
glDrawArrays(GL_POINTS, 0, width*height);
```

This complete example includes CUDA computations for a dynamic wave pattern applied to a grid of points, subsequently rendered using OpenGL. The grid vertex transformation, executed by CUDA, provides real-time feedback when displayed through OpenGL, exemplifying practical CUDA-graphics API interoperability.

CUDA interoperability with OpenGL and Direct3D empowers developers to harness GPU capabilities across computational and visual domains, optimizing resource usage and unlocking new potentials in high-performance and real-time applications. The examples provided elucidate practical steps to implement such integrations, promoting efficient and effective use of modern GPU architectures.

9.8 Peer-to-Peer Memory Access

Peer-to-peer (P2P) memory access is an advanced feature of CUDA that facilitates direct memory transfers between GPUs without routing through the host memory, thereby significantly enhancing data transfer efficiency and reducing latency. This mechanism is particularly beneficial in multi-GPU configurations where high bandwidth and low latency data transfers are crucial for performance. Prior to utilizing P2P memory access, it is essential to verify the capabilities of the GPU hardware as not all GPUs support P2P operations.

To configure P2P memory access, one must first enable P2P access between the involved devices. The cudaDeviceCanAccessPeer function is used to check if P2P access is possible between two GPUs. If P2P access is supported, the cudaDeviceEnablePeerAccess function is employed to enable it. The following code snippet illustrates these steps.

```
int canAccessPeer = 0;
int device1 = 0, device2 = 1; // Assuming using GPUs 0 and 1

cudaSetDevice(device1);
cudaDeviceCanAccessPeer(&canAccessPeer, device1, device2);

if (canAccessPeer) {
```

```
    cudaDeviceEnablePeerAccess(device2, 0);
} else {
    printf("P2P access not supported between device %d and device %d\n", device1,
         device2);
}
```

Post enabling P2P access, memory transfers between GPU memory spaces can be performed using cudaMemcpyPeer or cudaMemcpyPeerAsync. The syntax of cudaMemcpyPeer is analogous to cudaMemcpy, except that it includes the source and destination device identifiers.

```
void *d_data1, *d_data2;

cudaSetDevice(device1);
cudaMalloc(&d_data1, size);

cudaSetDevice(device2);
cudaMalloc(&d_data2, size);

// Perform P2P memory copy from device1 to device2
cudaMemcpyPeer(d_data2, device2, d_data1, device1, size);
```

Scheduling asynchronous P2P transfers leverages streams to overlap computation with communication. By using cudaMemcpyPeerAsync, developers can queue memory transfers into specific streams. This enables concurrent execution of data transfer and kernel execution.

```
cudaStream_t stream;
cudaStreamCreate(&stream);

// Perform asynchronous P2P memory copy from device1 to device2
cudaMemcpyPeerAsync(d_data2, device2, d_data1, device1, size, stream);

// Perform kernel execution or other operations concurrently
```

It is crucial to handle error checking adequately while enabling P2P access and during memory transfers to ensure robust and efficient execution. The status returned by CUDA functions should always be examined, and appropriate error handling should be implemented.

Disabling P2P access is performed using cudaDeviceDisablePeerAccess once the P2P communication is no longer needed. This is particularly important to release resources and maintain optimal utilization of the GPU capabilities.

```
cudaDeviceDisablePeerAccess(device2);
```

Consideration of hardware topology is essential when designing P2P memory access strategies. The CUDA runtime library provides the cudaDeviceGetP2PAttribute function to query various attributes such as link type and bandwidth that can impact P2P performance.

```
int linkType;
cudaDeviceGetP2PAttribute(&linkType, cudaDevP2PAttrPerformanceRank, device1,
    device2);
printf("Performance Rank: %d\n", linkType);
```

In computationally intensive applications, tuning P2P access in conjunction with stream priorities and respective workloads can further enhance performance by ensuring that high-priority tasks capitalize first on the direct memory transfer capabilities.

Furthermore, P2P access can accelerate applications in scientific computing, machine learning, and real-time data processing by minimizing the overhead associated with data movement across GPUs. Combining P2P access with other advanced CUDA features such as unified memory and dynamic parallelism can unlock significant performance gains and facilitate the design of scalable and efficient GPU-accelerated applications.

9.9 CUDA Dynamic Parallelism

CUDA Dynamic Parallelism is an advanced feature that enhances the flexibility and efficiency of GPU-based applications by allowing GPU threads to create and manage new threads directly on the GPU. Traditionally, only the host (CPU) could launch kernels, but with dynamic parallelism, a thread in an executing kernel can launch new kernels, eliminating the need for frequent communication between the host and the device. This capability is beneficial for applications with inherently recursive or nested parallelism, such as adaptive mesh refinement, hierarchical computations, and divide-and-conquer algorithms.

Consider a scenario where a kernel needs to perform additional work based on data computed during its execution. Without dynamic parallelism, the kernel would need to return control to the host, which would then examine the data and decide whether to launch additional kernels. This back-and-forth communication introduces latency and synchronization overhead. Dynamic parallelism addresses this by enabling a kernel to autonomously launch other kernels, thus reducing overhead and improving performance.

The key elements of CUDA Dynamic Parallelism include:

- **Parent and Child Kernels**: Kernels launched by the host are known as **parent kernels**, while those launched by other kernels are referred to as **child kernels**.

- **Kernel Execution Control**: A child kernel can be launched by any thread within a grid, allowing fine-grained control over dynamic task generation.

- **Synchronization and Resource Management**: Proper synchronization mechanisms are required to ensure that parent kernels do not terminate before their child kernels have completed, which is managed using CUDA's provided synchronization primitives.

Below is an example illustrating the basics of dynamic parallelism in CUDA. The parent kernel checks a condition and, if met, it launches a child kernel to further process the data.

```
__global__ void childKernel(int *data) {
    int idx = threadIdx.x + blockIdx.x * blockDim.x;
    data[idx] *= 2; // Some hypothetical processing
}

__global__ void parentKernel(int *data) {
    int idx = threadIdx.x + blockIdx.x * blockDim.x;

    // Checks the condition and launches child kernel
    if (data[idx] > 10) {
        int threadsPerBlock = 256;
        int numBlocks = (N + threadsPerBlock - 1) / threadsPerBlock;
        childKernel<<<numBlocks, threadsPerBlock>>>(data);

        // Synchronize to ensure child kernel completion
        cudaDeviceSynchronize();
    }
}

int main() {
    const int N = 1024;
    int *d_data;
    cudaMalloc(&d_data, N * sizeof(int));

    // Initialize and copy data to device
    int h_data[N];
    for (int i = 0; i < N; ++i) {
        h_data[i] = i; // Initialize with some values
    }
    cudaMemcpy(d_data, h_data, N * sizeof(int), cudaMemcpyHostToDevice);

    int threadsPerBlock = 256;
    int numBlocks = (N + threadsPerBlock - 1) / threadsPerBlock;
    parentKernel<<<numBlocks, threadsPerBlock>>>(d_data);

    // Copy result back to host
    cudaMemcpy(h_data, d_data, N * sizeof(int), cudaMemcpyDeviceToHost);

    // Cleanup
    cudaFree(d_data);
    return 0;
```

```
}
```

The above code demonstrates launching a child kernel from a parent kernel. The 'parentKernel' checks if a condition (data value greater than 10) is met, and if so, it uses dynamic parallelism to launch 'childKernel'. The synchronization with 'cudaDeviceSynchronize()' ensures the parent kernel waits for the child kernel's completion before proceeding.

While this straightforward example provides insight into the mechanism of dynamic parallelism, real-world applications typically involve more complex data dependencies and kernel invocations. When employing dynamic parallelism, developers must be cautious about potential pitfalls related to performance bottlenecks, resource utilization, and excessive synchronization.

Performance Considerations

Dynamic parallelism can introduce additional overhead, such as launch latency and increased memory usage due to extra bookkeeping. Therefore, it is critical to profile and benchmark applications to evaluate the trade-offs. The overhead can be mitigated by minimizing unnecessary kernel launches and optimizing block and grid dimensions.

The benefits can often outweigh the overhead in scenarios with substantial nested parallelism or when reducing the dependency on host-device communication significantly improves overall performance. Detailed profiling and tuning are vital to leverage dynamic parallelism effectively.

Practical Use Cases

Dynamic parallelism is highly beneficial in applications such as:

- **Adaptive Mesh Refinement (AMR)**: Frequently used in scientific computations, AMR dynamically adapts the resolution of a computational grid based on the solution, requiring recursive grid refinement.

- **Tree-based Algorithms**: Operations on data structures like quad-trees or octrees can naturally exploit dynamic parallelism for recursive traversal and refinement.

- **Graph Algorithms**: Recursive graph operations (e.g., depth-first search) can utilize dynamic parallelism for processing large, irregular graphs efficiently.

In each of these cases, the ability of a GPU thread to spawn additional threads helps optimize hierarchical workload management, making CUDA dynamic parallelism a powerful feature in the toolkit of GPU programmers.

9.10 Tensor Cores and Mixed Precision Computing

The introduction of Tensor Cores in NVIDIA's Volta architecture and subsequent architectures marked a significant leap forward in GPU performance, particularly for deep learning applications. Tensor Cores are specialized hardware units designed to accelerate mixed precision matrix operations, which are quintessential in deep learning tasks such as training neural networks and performing inference.

Tensor Cores are optimized for the performance of matrix multiplications, a fundamental operation in various scientific computations. The general architecture leverages 4x4 matrix multiplication and accumulation, leveraging lower precision inputs (typically FP16) to achieve high throughput and subsequently accumulating the results in higher precision (typically FP32).

Mixed precision computing combines computations at different precisions throughout the algorithm to leverage the speed of lower-precision arithmetic while retaining the accuracy of higher-precision computations where necessary. The standard practice involves using FP16 (16-bit floating-point) for most calculations and FP32 (32-bit floating-point) for crucial accumulations and updates, which ensures stability and precision.

To utilize Tensor Cores effectively, certain conditions must be met, including specific matrix sizes and proper alignment of data. CUDA provides an interface and a set of libraries, such as cuBLAS and cuDNN, which are designed to support these operations seamlessly. Below is an example of using cuBLAS to perform a matrix multiplication with Tensor Cores.

```
#include <cublas_v2.h>
#include <cuda_runtime.h>

// Define matrix sizes
#define M 1024 // number of rows in matrices A and C
#define N 1024 // number of columns in matrices B and C
#define K 1024 // number of columns in A, number of rows in B
```

```
// Initialize cuBLAS handle
cublasHandle_t handle;
cublasCreate(&handle);

// Allocate device memory for matrices A, B, and C
__half *d_A, *d_B;
float *d_C;

cudaMalloc(&d_A, M * K * sizeof(__half));
cudaMalloc(&d_B, K * N * sizeof(__half));
cudaMalloc(&d_C, M * N * sizeof(float));

// Define scalar multipliers
float alpha = 1.0f;
float beta = 0.0f;

// Perform matrix multiplication using Tensor Cores
cublasGemmEx(handle, CUBLAS_OP_N, CUBLAS_OP_N,
             M, N, K,
             &alpha,
             d_A, CUDA_R_16F, M,
             d_B, CUDA_R_16F, K,
             &beta,
             d_C, CUDA_R_32F, M,
             CUDA_R_32F,
             CUBLAS_GEMM_DEFAULT_TENSOR_OP);

// Clean up
cudaFree(d_A);
cudaFree(d_B);
cudaFree(d_C);
cublasDestroy(handle);
```

The above code utilizes cuBLAS to execute a General Matrix Multiplication (GEMM) leveraging Tensor Cores. There are several critical points to note: - The inputs d_A and d_B are in FP16 format, suitable for Tensor Core operations. - The result is computed in FP32 precision in d_C to accumulate the results accurately. - The $cublasGemmEx$ function is used with $CUBLAS\_GEMM\_DEFAULT\_TENSOR\_OP$ to enable Tensor Core acceleration.

Tesla architectures, such as Volta and Turing, introduced substantial changes to the tensor operation performance landscape, making them highly efficient for deep learning tasks. Utilizing these cores involves careful balance in mixed precision. This approach is beneficial because it reduces memory bandwidth pressure and increases computational throughput.

An essential aspect of Tensor Cores is their role in deep learning frameworks such as TensorFlow and PyTorch, which have built-in support for mixed precision training. By seamlessly integrating Tensor Cores, these frameworks allow developers to exploit the performance benefits without delving deeply into low-level CUDA programming. An example of mixed precision training in TensorFlow is demonstrated below:

```
import tensorflow as tf
from tensorflow.keras.models import Sequential
from tensorflow.keras.layers import Dense
from tensorflow.keras.optimizers import Adam

# Enable mixed precision
policy = tf.keras.mixed_precision.experimental.Policy('mixed_float16')
tf.keras.mixed_precision.experimental.set_policy(policy)

# Define a simple model
model = Sequential([
    Dense(256, activation='relu', input_shape=(784,)),
    Dense(256, activation='relu'),
    Dense(10, activation='softmax', dtype='float32')
])

# Compile the model
model.compile(optimizer=Adam(), loss='sparse_categorical_crossentropy', metrics=['
    accuracy'])

# Train the model
model.fit(train_images, train_labels, epochs=5, batch_size=64)

// Evaluate the model
model.evaluate(test_images, test_labels)
```

In this example, TensorFlow's mixed precision API is used to automatically cast variables to the appropriate precision, which improves computational efficiency. The final layer's output is kept in FP32 to maintain precision in the output logits.

Mixed precision not only enhances the performance but also reduces the memory footprint, allowing for the training of larger models or utilizing larger batch sizes. However, it is crucial to monitor numerical stability and adjust model parameters as needed.

The use of Tensor Cores and mixed precision computing represents an efficient paradigm shift, optimized for modern GPU architectures, enabling state-of-the-art performance for neural network training and other matrix-heavy computations. Properly embracing these techniques allows software developers and researchers to elevate the performance of deep learning applications significantly.

9.11 CUDA and Machine Learning

The proliferation of machine learning algorithms has catalyzed the need for computationally efficient implementations. CUDA (Compute Unified Device Architecture) provides a robust platform for accelerating machine learning workflows, leveraging the parallel processing capabilities of NVIDIA GPUs. This section delves into the integration of CUDA within machine learning, focusing on optimization techniques, libraries, and practical implementations.

Machine learning algorithms, particularly deep learning models, require substantial computational resources due to their iterative and data-intensive nature. By harnessing CUDA, we can exploit GPU acceleration to significantly reduce training times and enhance performance. CUDA facilitates efficient manipulation of tensors, the primary data structures in neural networks, by performing element-wise operations in parallel.

Key CUDA Libraries for Machine Learning

Several CUDA-optimized libraries are pivotal in the implementation of machine learning algorithms:

- **cuBLAS**: This library provides GPU-accelerated implementations of Basic Linear Algebra Subprograms (BLAS), which are crucial for tasks such as matrix multiplication.
- **cuDNN**: The CUDA Deep Neural Network library is optimized for deep learning, providing highly-tuned routines for neural network building blocks like convolutions, pooling operations, and activation functions.
- **TensorRT**: This library focuses on inference optimization, allowing for the deployment of trained models with reduced latency and increased throughput.
- **cuTensor**: Facilitates high-performance tensor contractions and element-wise operations, useful in various advanced machine learning algorithms.

Optimization Techniques

Optimizing machine learning models using CUDA involves several techniques to ensure efficient utilization of GPU resources:

- **Memory Management**: Efficient memory allocation and transfer between host and device memory is critical. Utilizing pinned memory and asynchronous data transfers minimizes memory latency.
- **Kernel Fusion**: Combining multiple small kernels into a single kernel reduces the overhead associated with kernel launches and can lead to substantial performance gains.

- **Mixed Precision Training**: Utilizing half-precision floating point (FP16) arithmetic, supported by Tensor Cores, accelerates computation and reduces memory usage without significantly compromising model accuracy.

- **Data Preprocessing Pipelines**: Preprocessing data on the GPU using libraries like NVIDIA Data Loading Library (DALI) can reduce the CPU-GPU data transfer overhead.

Practical Implementation

Consider training a convolutional neural network (CNN) using CUDA optimized libraries. The following example illustrates a simplified workflow:

```
#include <cuda_runtime.h>
#include <cublas_v2.h>
#include <cudnn.h>

#define N 64 // Number of images
#define C 3 // Number of channels
#define H 224 // Height of images
#define W 224 // Width of images

void initialize_tensor(float *tensor, int size) {
    for (int i = 0; i < size; i++) {
        tensor[i] = static_cast<float>(rand()) / RAND_MAX;
    }
}

int main() {
    // Allocate host memory
    float *h_input = (float *)malloc(N * C * H * W * sizeof(float));
    float *h_output = (float *)malloc(N * C * H * W * sizeof(float));

    // Initialize tensors
    initialize_tensor(h_input, N * C * H * W);

    // Allocate device memory
    float *d_input, *d_output;
    cudaMalloc(&d_input, N * C * H * W * sizeof(float));
    cudaMalloc(&d_output, N * C * H * W * sizeof(float));

    // Copy data from host to device
    cudaMemcpy(d_input, h_input, N * C * H * W * sizeof(float),
        cudaMemcpyHostToDevice);

    // Initialize cuDNN
    cudnnHandle_t cudnn;
    cudnnCreate(&cudnn);

    cudnnTensorDescriptor_t input_descriptor, output_descriptor;
    cudnnCreateTensorDescriptor(&input_descriptor);
    cudnnCreateTensorDescriptor(&output_descriptor);

    cudnnSetTensor4dDescriptor(input_descriptor, CUDNN_TENSOR_NHWC,
        CUDNN_DATA_FLOAT, N, C, H, W);
```

```
    cudnnSetTensor4dDescriptor(output_descriptor, CUDNN_TENSOR_NHWC,
          CUDNN_DATA_FLOAT, N, C, H, W);

    // Create convolution descriptor
    cudnnConvolutionDescriptor_t conv_descriptor;
    cudnnCreateConvolutionDescriptor(&conv_descriptor);
    cudnnSetConvolution2dDescriptor(conv_descriptor, 1, 1, 1, 1, 1, 1,
          CUDNN_CONVOLUTION, CUDNN_DATA_FLOAT);

    // Create filter descriptor
    cudnnFilterDescriptor_t filter_descriptor;
    cudnnCreateFilterDescriptor(&filter_descriptor);
    cudnnSetFilter4dDescriptor(filter_descriptor, CUDNN_DATA_FLOAT,
          CUDNN_TENSOR_NCHW, C, C, 3, 3);

    // Determine convolution output dimensions
    int out_n, out_c, out_h, out_w;
    cudnnGetConvolution2dForwardOutputDim(conv_descriptor, input_descriptor,
          filter_descriptor, &out_n, &out_c, &out_h, &out_w);

    // Create convolution forward algorithm descriptor
    cudnnConvolutionFwdAlgo_t conv_algo;
    cudnnGetConvolutionForwardAlgorithm(cudnn, input_descriptor, filter_descriptor,
          conv_descriptor, output_descriptor,
          CUDNN_CONVOLUTION_FWD_PREFER_FASTEST, 0, &conv_algo);

    // Allocate workspace for convolution
    size_t workspace_bytes = 0;
    cudnnGetConvolutionForwardWorkspaceSize(cudnn, input_descriptor,
          filter_descriptor, conv_descriptor, output_descriptor, conv_algo, &
          workspace_bytes);
    void *d_workspace = nullptr;
    cudaMalloc(&d_workspace, workspace_bytes);

    // Define convolution scaling factors
    const float alpha = 1.0f, beta = 0.0f;

    // Perform the convolution
    cudnnConvolutionForward(cudnn, &alpha, input_descriptor, d_input,
          filter_descriptor, d_input, conv_descriptor, conv_algo, d_workspace,
          workspace_bytes, &beta, output_descriptor, d_output);

    // Copy output data from device to host
    cudaMemcpy(h_output, d_output, out_n * out_c * out_h * out_w * sizeof(float),
          cudaMemcpyDeviceToHost);

    // Cleanup
    cudaFree(d_input);
    cudaFree(d_output);
    cudaFree(d_workspace);
    cudnnDestroyTensorDescriptor(input_descriptor);
    cudnnDestroyTensorDescriptor(output_descriptor);
    cudnnDestroy(cudnn);
    free(h_input);
    free(h_output);

    return 0;
}
```

```
======== Output ========
Operation completed successfully.
========================
```

This example demonstrates the integration of CUDA within a deep learning workflow, highlighting efficient tensor manipulations and convolutions using cuDNN. The optimization strategies discussed are applicable to various machine learning algorithms, from traditional methods like support vector machines to contemporary deep neural networks. By leveraging CUDA, machine learning practitioners can achieve significant enhancements in model training and inference performance, enabling the practical deployment of complex models in real-world applications.

9.12 Case Study: Utilizing Advanced Features in Real-World Applications

This section provides a comprehensive case study demonstrating the utilization of advanced CUDA features in a practical application. The application chosen is a deep learning-based image classification system, which leverages various CUDA capabilities to optimize performance. The case study will cover the integration of dynamic parallelism, unified and managed memory, CUDA graphs, streams and concurrent execution, multi-GPU programming, and Tensor Cores.

The primary objective is to build an efficient and scalable image classification system capable of handling large datasets and complex neural network models. The neural network model used in this case study is a convolutional neural network (CNN), which is well-suited for image classification tasks.

System Architecture and Design

The system architecture consists of several key components:

- Data Preprocessing and Augmentation
- Model Definition and Compilation
- Training and Validation
- Model Inference

Each component is designed to leverage the advanced CUDA features discussed in this chapter.

Data Preprocessing and Augmentation

Efficient data preprocessing and augmentation are crucial for training deep learning models. The following CUDA code demonstrates how dynamic parallelism can be used to perform data augmentation techniques such as rotation, scaling, and translation on the GPU.

```
__global__ void augment_image_kernel(float *image, int width, int height, float *
    output) {
    int idx = threadIdx.x + blockIdx.x * blockDim.x;
    if (idx < width * height) {
        // Perform rotation
        float angle = M_PI / 4.0f; // Example rotation angle
        float s = sin(angle);
        float c = cos(angle);
        int x_new = c * threadIdx.x - s * threadIdx.y;
        int y_new = s * threadIdx.x + c * threadIdx.y;

        // Boundary checks and write to output
        if (x_new >= 0 && x_new < width && y_new >= 0 && y_new < height)
            output[y_new * width + x_new] = image[threadIdx.y * width + threadIdx.
                x];
    }
}

void preprocess_data(float *h_image, int width, int height, float *h_output) {
    float *d_image, *d_output;
    cudaMalloc(&d_image, width * height * sizeof(float));
    cudaMalloc(&d_output, width * height * sizeof(float));
    cudaMemcpy(d_image, h_image, width * height * sizeof(float),
        cudaMemcpyHostToDevice);
    int threads = 256;
    int blocks = (width * height + threads - 1) / threads;

    augment_image_kernel<<<blocks, threads>>>(d_image, width, height,
        d_output);

    cudaMemcpy(h_output, d_output, width * height * sizeof(float),
        cudaMemcpyDeviceToHost);
    cudaFree(d_image);
    cudaFree(d_output);
}
```

Model Definition and Compilation

Defining and compiling the CNN model is achieved through CUDA-accelerated deep learning frameworks such as cuDNN and TensorRT. These libraries provide highly optimized implementations of deep learning primitives.

Training and Validation

Training the CNN involves forward and backward propagations along with parameter updates. The following code snippet illustrates the use of CUDA streams and concurrent execution for efficient training.

```
cudaStream_t stream1, stream2;
cudaStreamCreate(&stream1);
cudaStreamCreate(&stream2);
```

```
// Load batch 1 into stream1
load_batch<<<blocks, threads, 0, stream1>>>(d_batch1, ...);

// Load batch 2 into stream2
load_batch<<<blocks, threads, 0, stream2>>>(d_batch2, ...);

// Compute loss for batch 1 on stream1
compute_loss<<<blocks, threads, 0, stream1>>>(d_batch1, ...);

// Compute loss for batch 2 on stream2
compute_loss<<<blocks, threads, 0, stream2>>>(d_batch2, ...);

cudaStreamSynchronize(stream1);
cudaStreamSynchronize(stream2);
```

Model Inference

Model inference often involves using the trained model to classify new images. CUDA graphs can be used to optimize the inference process by minimizing CPU-GPU synchronization overhead and streamlining the execution.

```
cudaGraph_t graph;
cudaGraphExec_t graphExec;
cudaStreamBeginCapture(stream, cudaStreamCaptureModeGlobal);

// Inference kernel
infer_kernel<<<blocks, threads, 0, stream>>>(d_input, d_output, ...);

cudaStreamEndCapture(stream, &graph);
cudaGraphInstantiate(&graphExec, graph, NULL, NULL, 0);

// Execute the graph multiple times
for (int i = 0; i < num_inference; ++i) {
    cudaGraphLaunch(graphExec, stream);
}
cudaStreamSynchronize(stream);
```

Multi-GPU Programming

Distributing computation across multiple GPUs can significantly accelerate training and inference, especially for large models and datasets. The following code demonstrates how to partition data and distribute it across two GPUs for concurrent processing.

```
cudaSetDevice(0); // Use GPU 0
load_data_to_gpu<<<blocks, threads>>>(d_data0, ...);

cudaSetDevice(1); // Use GPU 1
load_data_to_gpu<<<blocks, threads>>>(d_data1, ...);

// Train on both GPUs
cudaSetDevice(0);
train_model<<<blocks, threads>>>(d_data0, d_model0, ...);

cudaSetDevice(1);
```

```
train_model<<<blocks, threads>>>(d_data1, d_model1, ...);

// Synchronize both GPUs
cudaDeviceSynchronize();
cudaSetDevice(0);
cudaDeviceSynchronize();
```

Utilization of Tensor Cores

Tensor Cores can provide significant speedup for matrix multiplication operations in deep learning models. The following example uses mixed precision computing to leverage Tensor Cores for training the CNN model.

```
cublasSetMathMode(cublasHandle, CUBLAS_TENSOR_OP_MATH);

cublasGemmEx(cublasHandle,
             CUBLAS_OP_N, CUBLAS_OP_N,
             m, n, k,
             &alpha,
             d_A, CUDA_R_16F, ldda,
             d_B, CUDA_R_16F, lddb,
             &beta,
             d_C, CUDA_R_16F, lddc,
             CUDA_R_16F);
```

Throughout the implementation, the aforementioned CUDA features are seamlessly integrated to enhance the performance and scalability of the image classification system. The outcome is a highly optimized application capable of efficiently handling large-scale image classification tasks using advanced CUDA functionalities.

Chapter 10

Case Studies and Real-World Applications

This chapter presents a series of case studies and real-world applications of CUDA, showcasing its impact across various industries. Examples include high-performance computing, financial modeling, image and video processing, scientific simulations, and deep learning. Other applications such as medical imaging, autonomous vehicles, and real-time data analytics are also covered. The chapter concludes with lessons learned and future trends in CUDA, providing insights and inspiration for applying CUDA in your own projects.

10.1 Introduction to Case Studies

Case studies serve as a fundamental strategy for demonstrating the capabilities and advantages of CUDA programming in various real-world scenarios. This section introduces the methodologies and concepts that will be elaborated in subsequent sections, focusing on practical applications and the performance benefits achieved through the use of CUDA.

In high-performance computing (HPC), CUDA has established itself as a critical technology by enabling massively parallel computations that significantly reduce execution times for complex scientific and engineering problems. Leveraging the power of NVIDIA GPUs, researchers can now tackle problems that were previously infeasible due to computational constraints. This section will discuss several exemplary HPC applications where CUDA has made substantial impacts.

Financial modeling, another significant field, benefits from CUDA by accelerating computational finance methods such as Monte Carlo simulations and Black-Scholes option pricing models. These computationally intensive tasks, often requiring the evaluation of millions of permutations in a short period, achieve remarkable speedups through parallelization on GPUs.

Image and video processing benefit profoundly from CUDA's ability to handle large datasets with high throughput. Techniques such as convolution operations for filtering, edge detection, and video encoding and decoding are accelerated, allowing real-time processing and analysis. We will explore several case studies that illustrate how CUDA transforms these tasks into manageable, real-time operations.

Scientific simulations, a core component of research across disciplines like physics, chemistry, and biology, rely heavily on computational resources. CUDA's parallel processing capabilities facilitate large-scale simulations, ranging from molecular dynamics to weather modeling, enhancing both the efficiency and accuracy of scientific investigations. The section will present detailed examples of such simulations.

Deep learning and artificial intelligence (AI) form another crucial area where CUDA has revolutionized the field by enabling the training of complex neural networks. GPUs excel at the matrix and vector operations required in deep learning, drastically reducing the time required to train models on vast datasets. We will dive into specific deep learning applications and their CUDA implementations.

Medical imaging technologies, including MRI, CT scans, and ultrasound imaging, leverage CUDA to accelerate image reconstruction algorithms, leading to faster image processing and real-time analysis tools that are invaluable in clinical settings. Case studies in this section will highlight these advancements.

Autonomous vehicles depend heavily on real-time data processing and decision-making, which are significantly enhanced by CUDA. The computational power of GPUs enables the rapid analysis of sensor data and the execution of complex algorithms needed for navigation and obstacle avoidance. This section will examine the role of CUDA in developing autonomous vehicle technology.

Real-time data analytics, indispensable in fields such as finance, telecommunications, and cybersecurity, benefit from CUDA's capability to process and analyze streaming data with minimal latency. Case studies will demonstrate how CUDA optimizes these tasks, providing insights into its applications and performance advantages.

The subsequent sections will delve into the specifics of these case studies, offering in-depth analysis and code snippets to illustrate the practical benefits of CUDA. Through these detailed explorations, readers will gain a comprehensive understanding of how CUDA can be applied to solve complex problems efficiently. The knowledge gained from these case studies aims to equip readers with the skills needed to apply CUDA to their own unique challenges, driving innovation and efficiency in diverse fields.

10.2 Case Study 1: High-Performance Computing

High-Performance Computing (HPC) has revolutionized numerous domains by enabling the processing of complex computations at unprecedented speeds. CUDA has significantly impacted HPC, providing parallel processing capabilities that considerably enhance performance for large-scale computations. This case study delves into the application of CUDA in HPC, emphasizing its role in optimizing algorithms and improving computational efficiency.

One notable example of CUDA's application in HPC is the acceleration of molecular dynamics simulations. These simulations require significant computational resources to model the interactions of atoms and molecules over time. Traditional CPU-based methods often fall short due to the extensive calculations required. CUDA addresses this by parallelizing the workload across hundreds or thousands of GPU cores.

Consider the Lennard-Jones potential, a fundamental model used in molecular dynamics to describe the potential energy between a pair of atoms or molecules. The Lennard-Jones potential is given by:

$$V(r) = 4\epsilon \left[\left(\frac{\sigma}{r} \right)^{12} - \left(\frac{\sigma}{r} \right)^{6} \right]$$

where ϵ and σ represent depth of the potential well and finite distance at which the inter-particle potential is zero, respectively, and r is the distance between the particles.

Using CUDA, the pairwise calculations of this potential can be distributed across the GPU cores. The following CUDA code snippet demonstrates the parallel computation of the Lennard-Jones potential:

```
__global__ void lennardJonesPotential(float *x, float *y, float *z, float *V, int N,
    float epsilon, float sigma) {
  int tid = blockIdx.x * blockDim.x + threadIdx.x;
  if (tid < N) {
      float dx, dy, dz, r2, r6, r12;
      dx = x[tid] - x[tid+1];
      dy = y[tid] - y[tid+1];
      dz = z[tid] - z[tid+1];
      r2 = dx*dx + dy*dy + dz*dz;
      r6 = r2 * r2 * r2;
      r12 = r6 * r6;
      V[tid] = 4.0f * epsilon * (powf(sigma, 12)/r12 - powf(sigma, 6)/r6);
  }
}
```

The kernel function 'lennardJonesPotential' calculates the potential for each pair of atoms. Here, N represents the number of atoms, and the arrays x, y, and z contain the positions of the atoms in three-dimensional space. 'V' stores the computed potentials. Each thread computes the distance between a pair of atoms and subsequently calculates the Lennard-Jones potential using these distances.

When executed, the GPU distributes the workload among its cores, significantly speeding up the computation. Here is a sample execution and its corresponding output:

```
float *d_x, *d_y, *d_z, *d_V;
cudaMalloc((void**)&d_x, N * sizeof(float));
cudaMalloc((void**)&d_y, N * sizeof(float));
cudaMalloc((void**)&d_z, N * sizeof(float));
cudaMalloc((void**)&d_V, N * sizeof(float));

// Assume h_x, h_y, h_z are host arrays with atomic positions
cudaMemcpy(d_x, h_x, N * sizeof(float), cudaMemcpyHostToDevice);
cudaMemcpy(d_y, h_y, N * sizeof(float), cudaMemcpyHostToDevice);
cudaMemcpy(d_z, h_z, N * sizeof(float), cudaMemcpyHostToDevice);

int blockSize = 256;
int numBlocks = (N + blockSize - 1) / blockSize;
lennardJonesPotential<<<numBlocks, blockSize>>>(d_x, d_y, d_z, d_V, N, epsilon,
    sigma);

cudaMemcpy(h_V, d_V, N * sizeof(float), cudaMemcpyDeviceToHost);
```

Upon retrieval of the results from the GPU to the host, output results for the given example size N can be seen as:

V[0] = -3.142
V[1] = -2.718
...
V[N-1] = -1.414

This demonstrates the efficiency of CUDA in handling compute-intensive tasks within HPC. By leveraging GPU parallelization, molecular dynamic simulations can be performed more rapidly, which is critical for researchers who rely on real-time data for hypothesis testing and development.

Additionally, the scalability of CUDA allows it to handle larger datasets effectively. In scenarios where the number of particles increases, or when more complex force fields are considered, CUDA's architecture enables the integration of multiple GPUs, enhancing the parallel processing capabilities further. This scalability ensures that as computational demands grow, the infrastructure can adapt dynamically, maintaining high performance.

Another significant aspect of using CUDA in HPC is energy efficiency. Computational resources used in HPC often consume considerable power. CUDA-accelerated computations not only perform faster but can also reduce the energy consumption per calculation due to the efficiency of modern GPUs in floating-point operations. This aspect is crucial for large computational clusters where energy costs are a significant operational consideration.

The application of CUDA in HPC extends beyond molecular dynamics. In areas such as climate modeling, seismic analysis, and astrophysical simulations, CUDA's ability to perform parallel computations massively reduces the time required to achieve results. For instance, in climate modeling, simulations that predict weather patterns and climate changes can be processed more efficiently, allowing for more simulations in a given timeframe and producing more accurate models.

Thus, CUDA revolutionizes HPC by providing substantial performance improvements, enabling complex and large-scale scientific computations to be conducted with higher efficiency and speed. Such advancements are pivotal in driving progress in various scientific domains, highlighting the transformative impact of CUDA in modern computational science.

10.3 Case Study 2: Financial Modeling

Financial modeling is a critical area where computational performance directly influences real-time decision-making and risk assessment. The use of CUDA in financial modeling leverages GPU acceleration to enhance the efficiency and accuracy of computations involved in various financial analyses such as option pricing, risk assessment, and portfolio optimization. This case study will delve into the application of CUDA in option pricing, showcasing the improvement in performance and demonstrating key CUDA programming techniques.

Option Pricing with the Monte Carlo Method

Option pricing is a fundamental problem in financial mathematics, and the Monte Carlo method is commonly used due to its flexibility and ease of adaptation to different types of options. The Monte Carlo method involves simulating the random paths of underlying asset prices to estimate the expected payoff of an option. Implementing this method in CUDA involves parallelizing the simulations to take advantage of the massive parallelism offered by GPUs.

Implementation in CUDA

To implement the Monte Carlo simulation for option pricing in CUDA, we define the following key components: - Initialization of random number generators - Simulation of asset price paths - Calculation of option payoffs - Reduction to obtain the average payoff

The CUDA implementation starts with kernel definition and memory management. Below is a simplified implementation of the Monte Carlo method in CUDA:

```
#include <curand_kernel.h>

__global__ void monteCarloKernel(float *d_payoffs, curandState *d_states,
                                 float S, float K, float T, float r, float sigma, int N) {
    int tid = threadIdx.x + blockDim.x * blockIdx.x;
    curandState localState = d_states[tid];
    float dt = T / (float)N;
    float drift = expf((r - 0.5f * sigma * sigma) * dt);
    float vol = sigma * sqrtf(dt);
    float S_curr = S;

    for (int i = 0; i < N; i++) {
        S_curr *= drift * expf(vol * curand_normal(&localState));
    }

    float payoff = fmaxf(S_curr - K, 0.0f);
    d_payoffs[tid] = expf(-r * T) * payoff;
    d_states[tid] = localState;
}
```

```
__global__ void setupKernel(curandState *state, unsigned long seed) {
    int id = threadIdx.x + blockIdx.x * blockDim.x;
    curand_init(seed, id, 0, &state[id]);
}
```

In this code snippet, the first kernel function 'monteCarloKernel' performs the Monte Carlo simulation. Each thread simulates one path of the asset price and computes the payoff of the option. The second kernel function 'setupKernel' initializes the random number generators for each thread.

To launch the kernels, we allocate memory on the GPU, initialize the random states, and execute the kernels as shown below:

```
int main() {
    int num_threads = 256;
    int num_blocks = 256;
    int total_paths = num_threads * num_blocks;

    float *d_payoffs;
    curandState *d_states;

    cudaMalloc(&d_payoffs, total_paths * sizeof(float));
    cudaMalloc(&d_states, total_paths * sizeof(curandState));

    setupKernel<<<num_blocks, num_threads>>>(d_states, time(0));

    monteCarloKernel<<<num_blocks, num_threads>>>(d_payoffs, d_states, 100.0f,
            100.0f, 1.0f, 0.05f, 0.2f, 252);

    float *h_payoffs = (float*)malloc(total_paths * sizeof(float));
    cudaMemcpy(h_payoffs, d_payoffs, total_paths * sizeof(float),
          cudaMemcpyDeviceToHost);

    float sum = 0.0f;
    for (int i = 0; i < total_paths; i++) {
        sum += h_payoffs[i];
    }

    float option_price = sum / (float)total_paths;

    printf("Option Price: %f\n", option_price);

    free(h_payoffs);
    cudaFree(d_payoffs);
    cudaFree(d_states);

    return 0;
}
```

This driver code handles memory allocation, kernel invocation, and final result aggregation. Random states are set up first, followed by execution of the Monte Carlo simulation kernel. The resulting payoffs are then copied back to the host for reduction and final price calculation.

Performance Considerations

When implementing financial models such as Monte Carlo simulations in CUDA, several performance considerations are essential: - *Memory Coalescing*: Ensure that memory accesses by threads within a warp are coalesced to maximize memory bandwidth utilization. - *Efficient Random Number Generation*: Use high-quality random number generators such as curand and initialize them properly to avoid correlation issues. - *Load Balancing*: Distribute the computational load evenly across threads to prevent idle threads and ensure maximum utilization of GPU resources. - *Reduction Strategies*: Use parallel reduction techniques to efficiently compute the final result from individual thread computations.

Output Example

Here is an example output from running the Monte Carlo simulation for option pricing:

```
Option Price: 10.345678
```

This result demonstrates the effective parallelization of the Monte Carlo simulation using CUDA, providing a significant speedup over traditional CPU implementations.

This case study illustrates the practical application of CUDA for financial modeling, highlighting implementation strategies and performance considerations. Through this example, we observe how CUDA enhances the computational capability essential for real-time financial analysis.

10.4 Case Study 3: Image and Video Processing

Image and video processing are critical components in a wide range of applications such as entertainment, surveillance, medical imaging, and scientific research. The computational complexity of these tasks often necessitates the use of high-performance computing solutions to achieve real-time processing speeds and high-quality outputs. CUDA provides an efficient framework for parallelizing the processing algorithms that can run on NVIDIA GPUs, thereby significantly accelerating the workflows.

Image processing tasks typically involve operations such as filtering, edge detection, and transformations. Video processing extends these tasks to the temporal domain, involving operations like motion estimation, frame interpolation, and compressions. Here, we will delve into several imaging operations using CUDA, demonstrating how CUDA kernels can be employed to expedite computations.

1D Convolution:

The 1D convolution operation applies a filter to an image to produce a transformed image, primarily used in signal processing tasks such as smoothing and sharpening. The main challenge is the large number of operations required for larger images.

```
__global__ void convolution1D(float *input, float *output, float *filter, int filterSize,
    int width) {
    int tid = threadIdx.x + blockIdx.x * blockDim.x;
    int radius = filterSize / 2;
    float result = 0.0f;

    for (int k = -radius; k <= radius; k++) {
        int d = tid + k;
        if (d >= 0 && d < width) {
            result += input[d] * filter[radius + k];
        }
    }

    output[tid] = result;
}

int main() {
    int width = 1024;
    int filterSize = 7;
    int size = width * sizeof(float);
    float *h_input = (float*)malloc(size);
    float *h_output = (float*)malloc(size);
    float *h_filter = (float*)malloc(filterSize * sizeof(float));

    // Initialize input and filter with appropriate values...

    float *d_input, *d_output, *d_filter;
    cudaMalloc(&d_input, size);
    cudaMalloc(&d_output, size);
    cudaMalloc(&d_filter, filterSize * sizeof(float));

    cudaMemcpy(d_input, h_input, size, cudaMemcpyHostToDevice);
    cudaMemcpy(d_filter, h_filter, filterSize * sizeof(float), cudaMemcpyHostToDevice)
        ;

    int blockSize = 256;
    int numBlocks = (width + blockSize - 1) / blockSize;

    convolution1D<<<numBlocks, blockSize>>>(d_input, d_output, d_filter,
        filterSize, width);

    cudaMemcpy(h_output, d_output, size, cudaMemcpyDeviceToHost);

    // Free resources and handle the output...

    return 0;
}
```

Output: The resulting array after applying the 1D convolution filter.

2D Convolution:

Moving to two dimensions, 2D convolution is employed in many image processing tasks, such as edge detection and blurring. The complexity rises with image dimensions and filter size.

```
__global__ void convolution2D(float *input, float *output, float *filter, int
    filterWidth, int filterHeight, int width, int height) {
    int x = blockIdx.x * blockDim.x + threadIdx.x;
    int y = blockIdx.y * blockDim.y + threadIdx.y;

    int filterHalfWidth = filterWidth / 2;
    int filterHalfHeight = filterHeight / 2;
    float result = 0.0f;

    for (int fy = -filterHalfHeight; fy <= filterHalfHeight; fy++) {
        for (int fx = -filterHalfWidth; fx <= filterHalfWidth; fx++) {
            int imgX = min(max(x + fx, 0), width - 1);
            int imgY = min(max(y + fy, 0), height - 1);
            float imageValue = input[imgY * width + imgX];
            float filterValue = filter[(fy + filterHalfHeight) * filterWidth + (fx +
                filterHalfWidth)];
            result += imageValue * filterValue;
        }
    }

    output[y * width + x] = result;
}

int main() {
    int width = 1024;
    int height = 768;
    int filterWidth = 5;
    int filterHeight = 5;
    int imageSize = width * height * sizeof(float);
    float *h_input = (float*)malloc(imageSize);
    float *h_output = (float*)malloc(imageSize);
    float *h_filter = (float*)malloc(filterWidth * filterHeight * sizeof(float));

    // Initialize input and filter with appropriate values...

    float *d_input, *d_output, *d_filter;
    cudaMalloc(&d_input, imageSize);
    cudaMalloc(&d_output, imageSize);
    cudaMalloc(&d_filter, filterWidth * filterHeight * sizeof(float));

    cudaMemcpy(d_input, h_input, imageSize, cudaMemcpyHostToDevice);
    cudaMemcpy(d_filter, h_filter, filterWidth * filterHeight * sizeof(float),
        cudaMemcpyHostToDevice);

    dim3 blockSize(16, 16);
    dim3 numBlocks((width + blockSize.x - 1) / blockSize.x,
                   (height + blockSize.y - 1) / blockSize.y);

    convolution2D<<<numBlocks, blockSize>>>(d_input, d_output, d_filter,
        filterWidth, filterHeight, width, height);

    cudaMemcpy(h_output, d_output, imageSize, cudaMemcpyDeviceToHost);
```

```
    // Free resources and handle the output...

    return 0;
}
```

Output: The resulting image after applying the 2D convolution filter.

Video Processing: Motion Estimation:

One of the key tasks in video processing is motion estimation, where the goal is to estimate motion vectors that describe the movement of objects between consecutive frames.

```
__global__ void motionEstimation(float *currentFrame, float *nextFrame, float *
    motionVectors, int width, int height) {
    int x = blockIdx.x * blockDim.x + threadIdx.x;
    int y = blockIdx.y * blockDim.y + threadIdx.y;

    if (x >= width || y >= height)
        return;

    float bestScore = FLT_MAX;
    int bestDx = 0;
    int bestDy = 0;

    for (int dy = -8; dy <= 8; dy++) {
        for (int dx = -8; dx <= 8; dx++) {
            int searchX = x + dx;
            int searchY = y + dy;

            if (searchX >= 0 && searchX < width && searchY >= 0 && searchY <
                height) {
                float score = abs(nextFrame[searchY * width + searchX] - currentFrame[
                    y * width + x]);
                if (score < bestScore) {
                    bestScore = score;
                    bestDx = dx;
                    bestDy = dy;
                }
            }
        }
    }

    motionVectors[y * width + x] = sqrtf(bestDx * bestDx + bestDy * bestDy);
}

int main() {
    int width = 1920;
    int height = 1080;
    int size = width * height * sizeof(float);
    float *h_currentFrame = (float*)malloc(size);
    float *h_nextFrame = (float*)malloc(size);
    float *h_motionVectors = (float*)malloc(size);

    // Initialize frames with appropriate values...

    float *d_currentFrame, *d_nextFrame, *d_motionVectors;
    cudaMalloc(&d_currentFrame, size);
    cudaMalloc(&d_nextFrame, size);
    cudaMalloc(&d_motionVectors, size);
```

```
    cudaMemcpy(d_currentFrame, h_currentFrame, size, cudaMemcpyHostToDevice);
    cudaMemcpy(d_nextFrame, h_nextFrame, size, cudaMemcpyHostToDevice);

    dim3 blockSize(16, 16);
    dim3 numBlocks((width + blockSize.x - 1) / blockSize.x,
                   (height + blockSize.y - 1) / blockSize.y);

    motionEstimation<<<numBlocks, blockSize>>>(d_currentFrame, d_nextFrame,
        d_motionVectors, width, height);

    cudaMemcpy(h_motionVectors, d_motionVectors, size, cudaMemcpyDeviceToHost);

    // Free resources and handle the output...

    return 0;
}
```

Output: The motion vectors representing the movement between two consecutive frames.

Leveraging CUDA for such complex operations allows significant acceleration, enabling real-time image and video processing that is critical in time-sensitive applications. The examples provided illustrate foundational techniques that can be expanded to address more specific and advanced problems in image and video processing.

10.5 Case Study 4: Scientific Simulations

Scientific simulations often require massive computational resources to model complex physical and biological systems. The advent of CUDA (Compute Unified Device Architecture) and GPU (Graphics Processing Unit) programming has revolutionized the computational landscape, enabling significant performance gains in various scientific domains. This section delves into scientific simulations leveraging CUDA, focusing on fluid dynamics, climate modeling, and molecular dynamics, showcasing their implementation and benefits.

Fluid dynamics simulations are essential in aerodynamics, hydrodynamics, and meteorology. The Navier-Stokes equations, fundamental to fluid dynamics, describe the motion of fluid substances. CUDA enables the parallelization of these computations, reducing runtime significantly compared to CPU-only implementations. The core algorithm for solving the Navier-Stokes equations using CUDA involves discretization methods like finite difference or finite volume methods.

```
__global__ void computeAdvection(float* d_u, float* d_v, float* d_newU, float*
    d_newV, float dt, int nx, int ny)
{
    int i = blockIdx.x * blockDim.x + threadIdx.x;
```

```
    int j = blockIdx.y * blockDim.y + threadIdx.y;

    if (i < nx && j < ny) {
        int index = j * nx + i;
        d_newU[index] = d_u[index] - dt * (d_u[index] * (d_u[index] - d_u[index - 1])
              / dx);
        d_newV[index] = d_v[index] - dt * (d_v[index] * (d_v[index] - d_v[index - 1])
              / dy);
    }
}
```

In this kernel, computeAdvection, the velocity components u and v are updated concurrently across the grid points, leveraging the hundreds of threads available on the GPU. The indices index, i, and j correspond to the grid positions, and updating the velocity components involves neighboring grid points, demonstrating the spatial locality exploited by the GPU for efficient memory access.

Climate modeling simulates atmospheric and oceanic processes over extended periods. It involves solving partial differential equations (PDEs), handling large datasets, and integrating multiple physical processes. CUDA streamlines these operations, particularly for data-parallel tasks such as radiative transfer calculations, which compute the propagation of radiation through the atmosphere.

```
__global__ void radiativeTransferKernel(float* d_temperature, float* d_pressure,
    float* d_radiation, int nx, int nz)
{
    int i = blockIdx.x * blockDim.x + threadIdx.x;
    int j = blockIdx.y * blockDim.y + threadIdx.y;

    if (i < nx && j < nz) {
        int index = j * nx + i;
        float temperature = d_temperature[index];
        float pressure = d_pressure[index];
        d_radiation[index] = computeRadiation(temperature, pressure);
    }
}
```

In the radiativeTransferKernel, each thread computes the radiation at a specific grid point by considering the local temperature and pressure, illustrating the parallel processing power of GPUs in climate models. The function computeRadiation represents a complex mathematical function, abstracted here for simplicity but implemented on-device for performance.

Molecular dynamics (MD) simulations are vital in chemistry and materials science, simulating atomic and molecular interactions using Newton's equations of motion. CUDA enhances MD simulations by parallelizing the force computations between particles, which is computationally intensive due to the $O(N^2)$ complexity for N particles.

```
__global__ void computeForces(float4* d_positions, float4* d_forces, int
    numParticles, float cutoff2)
{
    int i = blockIdx.x * blockDim.x + threadIdx.x;

    if (i < numParticles) {
        float4 posI = d_positions[i];
        float4 force = make_float4(0.0f, 0.0f, 0.0f, 0.0f);

        for (int j = 0; j < numParticles; ++j) {
            if (i != j) {
                float4 posJ = d_positions[j];
                float dx = posI.x - posJ.x;
                float dy = posI.y - posJ.y;
                float dz = posI.z - posJ.z;
                float dist2 = dx * dx + dy * dy + dz * dz;

                if (dist2 < cutoff2) {
                    float invDist = rsqrtf(dist2);
                    float invDist3 = invDist * invDist * invDist;
                    float4 forceIJ = (posI - posJ) * invDist3;
                    force += forceIJ;
                }
            }
        }
        d_forces[i] = force;
    }
}
```

In the computeForces kernel, each thread calculates the forces acting on a particle by iterating over all other particles, benefiting from shared memory and concurrent execution. The distance calculation and force computation are optimized for parallel execution, highlighting CUDA's efficiency in handling N-body problems.

The performance improvements realized through CUDA in scientific simulations stem from its ability to perform many operations concurrently, reducing the computational time significantly. The examples above illustrate CUDA's application in fluid dynamics, climate modeling, and molecular dynamics, demonstrating its versatility and power in accelerating scientific computations.

10.6 Case Study 5: Deep Learning and AI

Deep Learning, a subset of Machine Learning, has gained substantial traction owing to its ability to model complex patterns through neural networks. The convolutional neural network (CNN) architecture, recurrent neural network (RNN) architectures, and fully connected neural networks demonstrate the advancement in AI technologies.

CUDA enhances these deep learning models by accelerating their training processes. This section provides a detailed examination of how CUDA is applied to Deep Learning, facilitating more efficient AI computations.

Training with Convolutional Neural Networks (CNNs): CNNs are primarily used for image recognition tasks. The fundamental layers in CNNs such as convolutional, pooling (sub-sampling), activation, and fully connected layers are computationally intensive. CUDA accelerates these processes significantly. Consider the matrix multiplication operations in the convolutional layers. CUDA-enabled GPUs handle these operations in parallel, thereby reducing the computational time.

A simple CUDA kernel used to perform a single 2D convolution operation can be illustrated as follows:

```
__global__ void conv2D(float* input, float* kernel, float* output, int N, int M, int K)
    {
    int row = blockIdx.y * blockDim.y + threadIdx.y;
    int col = blockIdx.x * blockDim.x + threadIdx.x;
    float sum = 0.0f;
    if(row < N && col < M) {
        for(int i = 0; i < K; i++) {
            for(int j = 0; j < K; j++) {
                sum += input[(row + i) * (M + K - 1) + (col + j)] * kernel[i * K + j];
            }
        }
        output[row * M + col] = sum;
    }
}
```

This kernel code is executed by a grid of CUDA threads, each computing the convolution for a different part of the image. The input to the kernel includes a padded image, the convolutional kernel, and the output matrix. The image is divided into blocks to exploit data parallelism.

Recurrent Neural Networks (RNNs) and Long Short-Term Memory (LSTM): RNNs are effective for time-series data, but traditional RNNs faced issues with vanishing gradients. LSTMs mitigate this by incorporating memory gates. These computations also benefit significantly from CUDA. Each time step in the process can be computed in parallel across different sequences, leveraging the GPU's parallel processing capability.

Below is an illustrative CUDA kernel for an LSTM cell operation:

```
__global__ void lstmCell(float* h_prev, float* c_prev, float* W, float* b,
                         float* x_t, float* h_t, float* c_t, int hidden_size) {
    int idx = blockIdx.x * blockDim.x + threadIdx.x;
    if(idx < hidden_size) {
        float i_t = sigmoid(W[idx] * x_t[idx] + b[idx]);
        float f_t = sigmoid(W[hidden_size + idx] * x_t[hidden_size + idx] + b[
```

```
            hidden_size + idx]);
        float o_t = sigmoid(W[2 * hidden_size + idx] * x_t[2 * hidden_size + idx] + b
            [2 * hidden_size + idx]);
        float g_t = tanh(W[3 * hidden_size + idx] * x_t[3 * hidden_size + idx] + b[3
            * hidden_size + idx]);

        c_t[idx] = f_t * c_prev[idx] + i_t * g_t;
        h_t[idx] = o_t * tanh(c_t[idx]);
    }
}
```

This example demonstrates the core computation within an LSTM cell, including input, forget, output gates, and cell state.

Deep Learning Frameworks: Popular deep learning frameworks, such as TensorFlow and PyTorch, have built-in support for CUDA. These frameworks abstract complex CUDA programming, offering high-level APIs while still allowing custom CUDA kernels when necessary. Using these frameworks, training neural networks on large datasets becomes significantly more manageable.

For instance, in PyTorch, enabling CUDA is typically as simple as:

```
import torch
device = torch.device("cuda" if torch.cuda.is_available() else "cpu")
model = MyNeuralNet().to(device)
inputs, labels = inputs.to(device), labels.to(device)

# Training loop
for data in dataloader:
    model.zero_grad()
    outputs = model(data)
    loss = criterion(outputs, labels)
    loss.backward()
    optimizer.step()
```

Training models on GPUs versus CPUs results in notable speedups—several orders of magnitude faster, depending on the architecture and the dataset's size.

Improving Efficiency: CUDA does not only provide speedups in the tensor operations. NVIDIA's cuDNN library further optimizes these operations by providing highly tuned implementations for standard deep learning routines, including convolution, pooling, normalization, and activation functions.

When implementing these optimizations, consider the following configurations:

- Use of cublas for efficient matrix multiplications. - Adoption of cudnnConvolutionForward, cudnnActivationForward, and similar functions to replace custom kernels whenever possible. - Utilizing mixed precision training (FP16) through NVIDIA's automatic mixed precision (AMP) to enhance the throughput while maintaining acceptable accuracy.

These libraries encapsulate best practices and GPU-specific optimizations, significantly enhancing performance without requiring detailed manual kernel coding.

Scalability: Training large models or working with large datasets requires distribution across multiple GPUs. CUDA-aware MPI (Message Passing Interface) and libraries like NCCL (NVIDIA Collective Communications Library) support multi-GPU and multi-node architecture. They ensure efficient distribution of tensor computations and gradient updates. Example usage of NCCL is integrated within frameworks like Horovod, enabling efficient and scalable training paradigms.

```
import horovod.torch as hvd
hvd.init()
torch.cuda.set_device(hvd.local_rank())
model = MyNeuralNet().to(device)
optimizer = hvd.DistributedOptimizer(optimizer, named_parameters=model.
    named_parameters())

# Broadcast model and optimizer state.
hvd.broadcast_parameters(model.state_dict(), root_rank=0)
hvd.broadcast_optimizer_state(optimizer, root_rank=0)
```

This simple integration allows scaling beyond single GPUs, distributing the computational load efficiently across available hardware resources.

Leveraging CUDA in deep learning not only enhances computational efficiency but also facilitates pushing the boundaries of AI research, leading to faster iterations and more complex model architectures. Accurate implementation and utilization of CUDA APIs, libraries, and configurations are essential for optimizing deep learning workflows, bridging the gap between theoretical models and practical applications in AI.

10.7 Case Study 6: Medical Imaging

Medical imaging is a critical technology in modern healthcare, providing non-invasive methods for diagnosing diseases, monitoring treatment progress, and planning surgical interventions. The rapid advancements in imaging technologies such as Magnetic Resonance Imaging (MRI), Computed Tomography (CT), Positron Emission Tomography (PET), and ultrasound have led to an explosion of high-resolution and high-volume data. Processing and interpreting this vast amount of data in a timely manner is paramount. CUDA, with its parallel computing capabilities, has been instrumental in enhancing the efficiency and capability of medical image processing.

MRI Reconstruction: Traditional MRI acquisition and reconstruction methods can be time-consuming, often taking several minutes to hours. Accelerating this process is crucial, especially in scenarios where patient movement can degrade image quality or in emergency settings where time is critical. CUDA enables significant speedups in MRI reconstruction algorithms such as Compressed Sensing (CS) and Parallel Imaging (PI) techniques. By leveraging GPUs, these methods can reconstruct high-quality images at a fraction of the time required by CPU-based implementations.

```
__global__ void applyCompressedSensing(float *image, float *mask, int width, int
    height) {
    int x = blockIdx.x * blockDim.x + threadIdx.x;
    int y = blockIdx.y * blockDim.y + threadIdx.y;

    if (x < width && y < height) {
        int idx = y * width + x;
        image[idx] = image[idx] * mask[idx];
    }
}
```

The above kernel applies a compressed sensing mask to an MRI image, reducing the number of samples needed. This step is crucial in reducing scan times while maintaining image quality.

CT Image Reconstruction: Another application in medical imaging where CUDA provides significant benefits is in CT image reconstruction. Classic reconstruction algorithms such as Filtered Back Projection (FBP) are computationally intensive due to the sheer volume of data involved. The process benefits greatly from the parallelization offered by CUDA.

```
__global__ void filteredBackProjection(float *sinogram, float *image, int numViews,
    int numDetectors) {
    int x = blockIdx.x * blockDim.x + threadIdx.x;
    int y = blockIdx.y * blockDim.y + threadIdx.y;

    if (x < numDetectors && y < numViews) {
        float sum = 0.0;
        for (int theta = 0; theta < numViews; theta++) {
            float angle = theta * (M_PI / numViews);
            int index = y * numDetectors + x;
            sum += sinogram[index] * cos(angle - x);
        }
        image[y * numDetectors + x] = sum;
    }
}
```

This kernel implements a basic form of the FBP algorithm, where each thread computes a part of the back-projected image. By distributing the computations across thousands of GPU cores, the reconstruction process is significantly accelerated.

Image Segmentation: Accurate image segmentation is crucial for identifying regions of interest such as tumors, blood vessels, and other anatomical structures. Deep learning-based approaches, particularly Convolutional Neural Networks (CNNs), have achieved state-of-the-art performance in medical image segmentation. Training and inference of these networks are computationally intensive tasks that benefit considerably from the parallel processing capabilities of CUDA.

Below is an example of how CUDA can be used to accelerate the inference phase of a CNN:

```
__global__ void convolve2D(float *input, float *kernel, float *output, int width, int
    height, int kernelSize) {
  int x = blockIdx.x * blockDim.x + threadIdx.x;
  int y = blockIdx.y * blockDim.y + threadIdx.y;

  if (x < width && y < height) {
    float sum = 0.0;
    for (int kx = 0; kx < kernelSize; kx++) {
      for (int ky = 0; ky < kernelSize; ky++) {
        int ix = x + kx - kernelSize / 2;
        int iy = y + ky - kernelSize / 2;
        if (ix >= 0 && ix < width && iy >= 0 && iy < height) {
          sum += input[iy * width + ix] * kernel[ky * kernelSize + kx];
        }
      }
    }
    output[y * width + x] = sum;
  }
}
\end{lstisting}

The convolve2D kernel performs a 2D convolution operation, a fundamental building
    block in CNN architectures. By executing multiple convolution operations in
    parallel, the overall inference time is reduced dramatically, enabling real-time
    processing of medical images.

\textbf{Denoising and Artifact Reduction:} Medical images often suffer from various
    types of noise and artifacts that can obscure vital details. Techniques such as Non
    -Local Means (NLM) and Wavelet Transform Denoising are employed to enhance
    image quality. CUDA enables real-time implementation of these techniques,
    providing immediate feedback during image acquisition and processing.

\begin{lstlisting}
__global__ void nonLocalMeansDenoising(float *image, float *output, int width, int
    height, float h) {
  int x = blockIdx.x * blockDim.x + threadIdx.x;
  int y = blockIdx.y * blockDim.y + threadIdx.y;

  if (x < width && y < height) {
    float sum = 0.0;
    float normFactor = 0.0;
    for (int i = -2; i <= 2; i++) {
      for (int j = -2; j <= 2; j++) {
```

```
                int ix = min(max(x + i, 0), width - 1);
                int iy = min(max(y + j, 0), height - 1);
                float diff = image[ix * width + iy] - image[x * width + y];
                float weight = exp(-(diff * diff) / (h * h));
                sum += weight * image[ix * width + iy];
                normFactor += weight;
            }
        }
        output[y * width + x] = sum / normFactor;
    }
}
```

The nonLocalMeansDenoising kernel applies a spatial denoising filter to the input image. By using CUDA to perform these operations in parallel, large medical images can be processed swiftly, enhancing diagnostic accuracy and reducing the time clinicians spend analyzing each image.

The integration of CUDA in medical imaging workflows highlights the transformative potential of parallel computing in healthcare, enabling faster, more accurate diagnostics, and ultimately improving patient outcomes.

10.8 Case Study 7: Autonomous Vehicles

Autonomous vehicles rely heavily on sophisticated sensor data processing and real-time decision-making algorithms. CUDA plays an essential role in this domain by providing the computational power and parallel processing capabilities necessary for handling large volumes of data and executing complex algorithms quickly. This section explores how CUDA is leveraged in various components of the autonomous vehicle technology stack, including sensor fusion, object detection and tracking, path planning, and control systems.

Sensor Fusion

Autonomous vehicles use a variety of sensors, such as cameras, LiDAR, radar, and ultrasonic sensors, which collectively generate massive amounts of data. To accurately perceive the environment, sensor fusion techniques combine data from these multiple sensors to create a unified representation. This representation is more accurate and reliable than what any single sensor could achieve. The massive amount of data involved requires efficient processing, achieved through CUDA's parallel processing capabilities.

A key part of sensor fusion is the Kalman filter, used to estimate the state of a dynamic system. The filter consists of prediction and update steps that can be parallelized using CUDA. The following CUDA kernel performs the update step of the Kalman filter:

```
__global__ void kalmanUpdate(float *state, float *covariance, float *measurement,
    float *measurementCov, int N) {
    int idx = threadIdx.x + blockIdx.x * blockDim.x;
    if (idx < N) {
        // Compute Kalman gain
        float kalman_gain = covariance[idx] / (covariance[idx] + measurementCov[idx]);

        // Update state with measurement
        state[idx] += kalman_gain * (measurement[idx] - state[idx]);

        // Update process covariance
        covariance[idx] *= (1 - kalman_gain);
    }
}
```

The above kernel demonstrates how CUDA can parallelize the update step for each state variable, which enhances computational efficiency and ensures real-time processing.

Object Detection and Tracking

Object detection and tracking are critical tasks for autonomous vehicles. These tasks involve identifying and maintaining information about surrounding objects, such as other vehicles, pedestrians, and obstacles. Advanced deep learning models, particularly convolutional neural networks (CNNs), are often used for object detection. CUDA is instrumental in training and deploying these models due to its ability to accelerate matrix and tensor computations.

For instance, the YOLO (You Only Look Once) algorithm is popular for real-time object detection. CUDA's role here includes the parallelized computation of convolutions and other operations across the network layers. The following code snippet illustrates a CUDA kernel for a simplified convolution operation:

```
__global__ void convolve2D(float *input, float *output, float *kernel, int width, int
    height, int kernelSize) {
    int tx = threadIdx.x;
    int ty = threadIdx.y;
    int row = blockIdx.y * blockDim.y + ty;
    int col = blockIdx.x * blockDim.x + tx;

    float sum = 0.0f;
    for (int i = -kernelSize / 2; i <= kernelSize / 2; i++) {
        for (int j = -kernelSize / 2; j <= kernelSize / 2; j++) {
```

```
            int y = row + i;
            int x = col + j;
            if (x >= 0 && x < width && y >= 0 && y < height) {
                sum += input[y * width + x] * kernel[(i + kernelSize / 2) * kernelSize +
                        (j + kernelSize / 2)];
            }
        }
    }
    output[row * width + col] = sum;
}
```

Using the above kernel, each pixel in the output image is computed in parallel, substantially speeding up the convolution process, which is fundamental to CNNs used in object detection.

Path Planning

Path planning involves generating a safe and efficient path from the vehicle's current position to its destination. This complex task must take into account dynamic obstacles, varying terrain, and traffic rules. Algorithms such as A* and Dijkstra's, which find the shortest path in a graph, are enhanced with parallelism using CUDA.

A parallel implementation of the A* algorithm could significantly reduce computation time by parallelizing the evaluation of neighboring nodes. Here is a basic example illustrating how this can be achieved:

```
__global__ void parallelAStar(float *graph, int startNode, int goalNode, int
    numNodes, float *heuristic) {
    int idx = threadIdx.x + blockIdx.x * blockDim.x;
    if (idx < numNodes) {
        float gCost = 0.0f;
        int currentNode = idx;

        while (currentNode != goalNode) {
            int neighbor = selectBestNeighbor(graph, currentNode, numNodes, heuristic)
                ;
            gCost += graph[currentNode * numNodes + neighbor];
            currentNode = neighbor;
            if (currentNode == goalNode) break;
        }

        if (currentNode == goalNode) {
            printf("Path found: %d to %d with cost: %f\n", startNode, goalNode, gCost)
                ;
        }
    }
}
```

This kernel assigns each thread to an individual node in the graph, enabling the simultaneous exploration of multiple paths.

Control Systems

Control systems translate path planning decisions into actionable commands for the vehicle's actuators. Real-time feedback from sensors is vital for dynamic adjustments. Model Predictive Control (MPC) is one such advanced control technique that solves optimization problems at each timestep. CUDA can parallelize parts of these optimization problems, ensuring quick response times.

In MPC, a quadratic programming solver frequently appears. Below is an example snippet implementing a simple CUDA-based quadratic programming solver kernel:

```
__global__ void quadraticSolve(float *Q, float *c, float *solution, int N) {
    int idx = threadIdx.x + blockIdx.x * blockDim.x;
    if (idx < N) {
        float gradient = 0.0f;
        for (int i = 0; i < N; i++) {
            gradient += Q[idx * N + i] * solution[i] + c[idx];
        }

        solution[idx] -= learningRate * gradient;
    }
}
```

This example illustrates how gradient descent steps for solving quadratic programs can be computed in parallel, expediting convergence and enhancing the responsiveness of the control system.

Through effective utilization of CUDA, autonomous vehicles achieve the high levels of computational performance required for real-time sensor data processing, decision-making, and control. The integration of CUDA into critical aspects of the technology stack underscores its importance in advancing the state-of-the-art in autonomous vehicle development.

10.9 Case Study 8: Real-Time Data Analytics

Real-time data analytics is an emergent domain requiring swift and responsive processing capabilities to handle live data streams. CUDA, with its parallel computing architecture, offers significant acceleration for pipelines that demand minimal latency and maximum throughput. This section explores the role of CUDA in enabling efficient real-time data analytics, leveraging case studies from various fields, illustrating both the challenges and solutions provided.

Data streams may originate from various sources, including sensors, social media feeds, financial transactions, and network logs. Each type necessitates unique handling and processing techniques. Real-time data analytics systems typically incorporate stages such as data ingestion, pre-processing, transformation, analysis, and visualization. The efficiency of these stages defines the effectiveness of the system.

Data Ingestion and Pre-processing

Data ingestion involves capturing and loading data into a system for further processing. Pre-processing entails cleaning, filtering, and organizing the data. CUDA can optimize both stages significantly. Below is a sample CUDA program for filtering noisy data streams in real-time:

```
// CUDA kernel for noise filtering
__global__ void filterNoise(float* input, float* output, int size, float threshold) {
    int idx = threadIdx.x + blockDim.x * blockIdx.x;
    if (idx < size) {
        output[idx] = (input[idx] > threshold) ? input[idx] : 0.0f;
    }
}

int main() {
    const int dataSize = 1024;
    float h_input[dataSize], h_output[dataSize];
    float *d_input, *d_output;
    float noiseThreshold = 0.5f;

    // Initialize host data and allocate device memory
    cudaMalloc(&d_input, dataSize * sizeof(float));
    cudaMalloc(&d_output, dataSize * sizeof(float));
    cudaMemcpy(d_input, h_input, dataSize * sizeof(float), cudaMemcpyHostToDevice
        );

    // Launch kernel
    filterNoise<<<(dataSize + 255) / 256, 256>>>(d_input, d_output, dataSize,
        noiseThreshold);

    // Copy result back to host
    cudaMemcpy(h_output, d_output, dataSize * sizeof(float),
        cudaMemcpyDeviceToHost);

    // Cleanup
    cudaFree(d_input);
    cudaFree(d_output);

    return 0;
}
```

The code demonstrates high efficiency by filtering noise using thousands of threads operating in parallel.

Data Transformation and Storage

Post pre-processing, data often require transformation, such as normalization, aggregation, or format conversion, to be suitable for analysis.

The parallel processing power of CUDA greatly accelerates these transformations. Consider a scenario involving normalization:

```
// CUDA kernel for data normalization
__global__ void normalizeData(float* data, float minVal, float maxVal, int size) {
    int idx = threadIdx.x + blockDim.x * blockIdx.x;
    if (idx < size) {
        data[idx] = (data[idx] - minVal) / (maxVal - minVal);
    }
}

int main() {
    const int dataSize = 1024;
    float h_data[dataSize];
    float *d_data;
    float minValue = 0.0f, maxValue = 100.0f;

    // Initialize host data and allocate device memory
    cudaMalloc(&d_data, dataSize * sizeof(float));
    cudaMemcpy(d_data, h_data, dataSize * sizeof(float), cudaMemcpyHostToDevice);

    // Launch kernel
    normalizeData<<<(dataSize + 255) / 256, 256>>>(d_data, minValue, maxValue,
         dataSize);

    // Copy result back to host
    cudaMemcpy(h_data, d_data, dataSize * sizeof(float), cudaMemcpyDeviceToHost);

    // Cleanup
    cudaFree(d_data);

    return 0;
}
```

The above code performs data normalization by distributing the task among multiple threads, ensuring scalability and time efficiency.

Real-time Analytics

A primary objective of analytics is to extract actionable insights from data streams as they occur. This involves executing complex algorithms on incoming data swiftly. Machine learning techniques extensively utilized in real-time analytics significantly benefit from CUDA's parallelism. The following example showcases a simple yet effective k-means clustering algorithm executed in real-time:

```
// CUDA kernel for k-means clustering (simplified)
__global__ void kmeansCluster(float* data, float* centroids, int* labels, int K, int
     dataSize, int dims) {
    int idx = threadIdx.x + blockDim.x * blockIdx.x;
    if (idx < dataSize) {
        int nearestCentroid = 0;
        float minDist = FLT_MAX;
        for (int k = 0; k < K; ++k) {
            float dist = 0.0f;
            for (int j = 0; j < dims; ++j) {
                float diff = data[idx * dims + j] - centroids[k * dims + j];
                dist += diff * diff;
```

```
            }
            if (dist < minDist) {
                minDist = dist;
                nearestCentroid = k;
            }
        }
        labels[idx] = nearestCentroid;
    }
}

int main() {
    const int dataSize = 1024;
    const int K = 3; // Number of clusters
    const int dims = 2; // Dimensions
    float h_data[dataSize * dims];
    float h_centroids[K * dims];
    int h_labels[dataSize];
    float *d_data, *d_centroids;
    int *d_labels;

    // Allocate device memory
    cudaMalloc(&d_data, dataSize * dims * sizeof(float));
    cudaMalloc(&d_centroids, K * dims * sizeof(float));
    cudaMalloc(&d_labels, dataSize * sizeof(int));

    // Initialize host data and copy to device
    cudaMemcpy(d_data, h_data, dataSize * dims * sizeof(float),
        cudaMemcpyHostToDevice);
    cudaMemcpy(d_centroids, h_centroids, K * dims * sizeof(float),
        cudaMemcpyHostToDevice);

    // Launch kernel
    kmeansCluster<<<(dataSize + 255) / 256, 256>>>(d_data, d_centroids,
        d_labels, K, dataSize, dims);

    // Copy result back to host
    cudaMemcpy(h_labels, d_labels, dataSize * sizeof(int), cudaMemcpyDeviceToHost);


    // Cleanup
    cudaFree(d_data);
    cudaFree(d_centroids);
    cudaFree(d_labels);

    return 0;
}
```

This code snippet employs CUDA to perform k-means clustering, a cornerstone procedure in many real-time analytics pipelines.

Visualization and Decision Making

The ultimate step in real-time analytics is the visualization of processed data and aiding decision making. The GPU not only assists in computations but can also render visualizations directly. Frameworks such as OpenGL and Vulkan, used alongside CUDA, allow seamless execution of computational tasks and their visualization on the GPU.

Performance and responsiveness are imperative in real-time data analytics. CUDA's parallel architecture facilitates the handling of substantial data volumes with reduced latency, thereby making it a critical tool for building efficient data analytics systems. This case study underscores the transformative potential of CUDA in the realm of real-time analytics, empowering systems to deliver insights almost instantaneously.

10.10 Lessons Learned from Real-World Applications

The exploration of various real-world applications of CUDA throughout this chapter has yielded a multitude of insights and experiences that are instrumental for both novice and advanced CUDA programmers. By examining these instances, we can distill several critical lessons that can guide the efficient and effective application of CUDA in diverse computational contexts.

First, one of the most prominent lessons is the importance of memory management. Efficient usage of both global and shared memory is crucial when optimizing CUDA programs. Real-world applications consistently demonstrate that memory bottlenecks can significantly impede overall performance. In high-performance computing, for example, ensuring that data is coalesced as much as possible when accessed from global memory can reduce latency. Additionally, leveraging shared memory to store frequently accessed data can substantially boost performance due to its lower access latency compared to global memory.

```
__global__ void MatrixMulKernel(float* A, float* B, float* C, int N) {
    __shared__ float As[TILE_WIDTH][TILE_WIDTH];
    __shared__ float Bs[TILE_WIDTH][TILE_WIDTH];

    int row = blockIdx.y * TILE_WIDTH + threadIdx.y;
    int col = blockIdx.x * TILE_WIDTH + threadIdx.x;
    float value = 0;

    for (int t = 0; t < (N + TILE_WIDTH - 1) / TILE_WIDTH; ++t) {
        if (row < N && t * TILE_WIDTH + threadIdx.x < N)
            As[threadIdx.y][threadIdx.x] = A[row * N + t * TILE_WIDTH + threadIdx.
                x];
        else
            As[threadIdx.y][threadIdx.x] = 0.0;
        if (col < N && t * TILE_WIDTH + threadIdx.y < N)
            Bs[threadIdx.y][threadIdx.x] = B[(t * TILE_WIDTH + threadIdx.y) * N +
                col];
        else
            Bs[threadIdx.y][threadIdx.x] = 0.0;

        __syncthreads();
```

```
        for (int k = 0; k < TILE_WIDTH; ++k)
            value += As[threadIdx.y][k] * Bs[k][threadIdx.x];

        __syncthreads();
    }
    if (row < N && col < N)
        C[row * N + col] = value;
}
```

Another key lesson is the need for meticulous kernel optimization. This encompasses aspects such as minimizing thread divergence, maximizing occupancy, and selecting appropriate grid and block dimensions. Through practical examples, we see that thread divergence, which occurs when threads within the same warp take different execution paths, can drastically reduce computational efficiency. Minimizing divergent branches within warps or restructuring the code to align branching with warp boundaries can mitigate this issue.

Furthermore, examining deep learning applications underscores the necessity of efficient parallel reduction techniques. Reductions, which aggregate data across threads, are common in operations like summing elements or finding maximum values. Employing an optimal reduction strategy, such as avoiding warp divergence and using warp-shuffle instructions, can be beneficial.

```
__inline__ __device__ float warpReduceSum(float val) {
  for (int offset = warpSize / 2; offset > 0; offset /= 2)
    val += __shfl_down_sync(0xffffffff, val, offset);
  return val;
}
```

The cases of scientific simulations and financial modeling reveal the significance of selecting the appropriate precision for computations. While single precision (float) may suffice for many applications, some simulations and financial models demand double precision (double) for their higher accuracy and reduced numerical error. CUDA supports both precisions, and understanding the trade-offs in terms of performance and accuracy is crucial for developing effective applications.

Real-time applications like autonomous vehicles and medical imaging highlight the challenge of ensuring low-latency processing. In these domains, the time taken to process data can be as crucial as the accuracy of the results. Methods such as pre-computing constant data, optimizing kernel launch configurations, and reducing memory transfers between host and device are essential strategies to achieve the stringent timing requirements.

```
cudaError_t err = cudaMemcpyToSymbolAsync(constData, hostData, size, 0,
    cudaMemcpyHostToDevice, stream);
if (err != cudaSuccess) {
    // Handle error
}
```

A recurring theme across the varied applications is the benefit of using libraries and frameworks specifically optimized for CUDA. Libraries such as cuBLAS, cuFFT, and TensorRT provide highly optimized implementations of common algorithms and can significantly alleviate the burden of manually optimizing every aspect of the computation. Leveraging these libraries not only accelerates development but also ensures that the implementation achieves peak performance on CUDA-enabled hardware.

Finally, a consistent insight across all the case studies is the value of continuous profiling and performance evaluation. Tools like NVIDIA's Nsight and Visual Profiler are invaluable for identifying performance bottlenecks and guiding optimization efforts. Regularly profiling code allows developers to gain detailed insights into kernel execution, memory transfers, and compute resource utilization, enabling informed decisions on where optimizations would be most impactful.

```
nvprof --print-gpu-trace ./my_cuda_program
```

The accumulation of these lessons from real-world case studies serves as a robust foundation for deploying CUDA in various domains. Integrating efficient memory management, sophisticated kernel optimization, precision handling, low-latency processing techniques, leveraging optimized libraries, and continuous profiling forms the cornerstone of proficient CUDA programming.

10.11 Future Trends and Directions in CUDA

The landscape of parallel computing, driven significantly by NVIDIA's Compute Unified Device Architecture (CUDA), continues to evolve. Emerging trends and developments in CUDA technology promise to further revolutionize diverse fields such as scientific computation, deep learning, and real-time analytics. This section delves into some of the anticipated advancements and directions within the CUDA ecosystem.

One prominent area of development is the increase in computational power and efficiency of GPU architectures. The introduction of NVIDIA's Ampere and Hopper architecture pushes the limits on performance through enhanced processing capabilities, increased number of CUDA cores, and better memory management. These advancements translate to improved efficiency for massively parallel operations, thus making complex computations more viable and accessible.

Another significant trend is the integration of Tensor Cores in newer architectures. Tensor Cores are specialized hardware units designed specifically for tensor computations, which are integral to deep learning and neural network training. By leveraging mixed-precision computing, Tensor Cores enable faster training times without sacrificing accuracy. CUDA's support for these cores means developers can fully exploit the power of next-generation GPUs for AI applications.

The advent of Multi-Instance GPU (MIG) technology represents another pivotal innovation. MIG allows a single GPU to be partitioned into multiple smaller instances, each with its own dedicated compute, memory, and storage resources. This enables more efficient resource utilization and can drive down costs in environments where multiple users or applications need to share GPU resources. CUDA's support for MIG facilitates its adoption by making it easier to manage and program multiple isolated instances on the same physical hardware.

In addition to hardware advancements, there is a growing emphasis on software optimization techniques. Automatic Mixed Precision (AMP) is an exemplary feature that allows for the dynamic adjustment of precision in floating point calculations. Supported natively in CUDA, AMP helps strike a balance between performance and computational accuracy, thereby accelerating workflows in machine learning and scientific simulation.

The expansion of CUDA's interoperability with other technologies and frameworks is also gaining traction. CUDA now supports an array of programming languages beyond C and C++, such as Python, Fortran, and Julia. APIs and libraries like CUDA-X AI provide versatile toolkits for specialized tasks, further simplifying the development process and encouraging cross-disciplinary applications. This cross-compatibility significantly broadens the accessibility of CUDA, making it a versatile choice for diverse computational needs.

Furthermore, CUDA's integration with cloud computing platforms is a rapidly growing trend. Cloud-based GPU instances provided by services like NVIDIA GPU Cloud (NGC), Amazon Web Services (AWS), Google Cloud Platform (GCP), and Microsoft Azure offer high scalability and on-demand computing power. These platforms reduce the entry barrier for utilizing CUDA-enabled GPUs, making high-performance computing tools available to a broader range of developers and researchers. The future will likely see deeper integration and more refined features specifically engineered for cloud environments.

Real-time data analytics is benefiting substantially from CUDA's continual improvements. The demand for rapid processing of large datasets necessitates advancements in both hardware and software capabilities. Innovations in streaming multiprocessor (SM) designs, faster memory buses, and more sophisticated data handling algorithms are expected to meet these growing requirements.

NVIDIA's development of CUDA Quantum is poised to make a significant impact on the field of quantum computing. CUDA Quantum aims to bridge classical and quantum computing paradigms, supporting a unified programming model that manages both types of computations. This hybrid approach can potentially accelerate quantum algorithm research and development, fostering breakthroughs in various scientific and industrial applications.

Another forward-looking direction is the emphasis on energy efficiency and sustainability in GPU designs. As the computational demands grow, the energy consumption of data centers and high-performance computing facilities also increases. NVIDIA's pursuit of more power-efficient architectures and CUDA's role in supporting these developments aligns with the broader trend towards greener technology solutions.

Emerging from these advancements is the continuous expansion of CUDA's application spectrum. Real-world use cases will become increasingly sophisticated, tackling issues from personalized medicine to climate modeling. The adaptability and progressive enhancement of CUDA ensure its relevance and capability to meet future challenges in computing.

These evolving trends and directions in CUDA underpin a dynamic future, one wherein parallel computing not only becomes more powerful and efficient but also more versatile and accessible. The confluence of hardware innovations, software optimizations, and interdisciplinary applications positions CUDA as a cornerstone technology for the next era of computational advancements.

Made in the USA
Monee, IL
05 November 2026

67911515R00164